In an educational era characterised by oversi... ...plex
problems, Ala...ter Scott Douglas provid... ...ook
into how school... ...'d
in the creation of education...
theory framework and ethnog... ...esti-
gate the social processes throug... ...v to teach
their academic discipline in rela... ...itions of their
community. Within this setting, D... ...dies how apprentice
and novice teachers are socialised int... ...sion through their engagement in departmental discussions and ...ent response to instruction.

Policy makers and teacher educators would be wise to read this research
and learn that learning to teach is a multidimensional, difficult process
whose effects cannot be easily reduced to student test scores or other
superficial measures of how teaching affects learning.

*Peter Smagorinsky,*
*Distinguished Research Professor of English Education,*
*University of Georgia, USA*

This book makes a significant contribution to the growing literature
examining teacher education. In doing so, it asks new and important
questions about the nature of the practicum in particular and the aims
of initial teacher education in general. The clearly written account of
'Market Town High School' and 'Downtown University', and the work
they engage in together to prepare new teachers, should be compulsory
reading for everyone who cares about teacher education and the role of
the teaching practicum.

The description of the culture of school departments is not only applicable to secondary schooling contexts but to primary and early years
settings too. Indeed, any setting where novice teachers enter into
groups of teachers organised around historically accumulated cultural
norms and expectations. In adopting a cultural-historical approach to
analysis of the work of preparing teachers, Douglas takes us beyond
dominant assumptions about how individuals learn to teach – that
learning to teach is something that primarily goes on inside individual
minds – to an understanding of learning to teach as a collaborative form
of workplace learning.

*Joce Nuttall,*
*Associate Professor, Acting Associate Dean Research,*
*of Education,*
*...lic University*

At a time when teacher education systems around the world are placing increased importance on student teachers' learning in schools, this book offers very valuable analyses of how, why, where and when opportunities for learning can be developed. In particular, drawing on cultural-historical activity theory and ethnographic research, the book offers insights into the ways in which schools – and the micro communities within them – can work with higher education institutions to structure in-depth learning opportunities for the benefit of both student teachers and their teacher colleagues. This highly recommended book also gives insightful analysis of the debates which characterise the field of teacher education and the research which contributes to its international development.

*Jean Murray*
*Professor of Education*
*University of East London, UK*

Alaster Scott Douglas has produced an important book, which explores initial teacher education (ITE) at the level of the secondary school subject department. This is timely, given the recent direction of ITE policy in England, pushing increasing responsibility for ITE into schools. Scott Douglas spent a year in one school following 15 student teachers across four departments. Much of what he says about his time has the convincing feel of authenticity and therefore the reader is able to read beyond the data reported here to think about the implications for ITE more generally.

Scott Douglas argues that ITE must do more than equip student teachers with the skills to fit in with established practice in the placement department; it must help them prepare to teach in any school. The final chapter strikes the positive note that ITE could play a part in opening up department cultures to be more reflective and thus more able to embrace and explore the diversity of perspectives on teaching and learning. Scott Douglas is optimistic that such a shift would be beneficial to teachers because this form of critical discussion is the basis of continual self-improvement as well as being important for ITE. The book underlines the urgency of engaging with this issue.

*Lee Jerome,*
*Queen's University, Belfast, Northern Ireland,*
*British Journal of Educational Studies*

Scott Douglas's text points to some of the complexities and nuances of teacher training. With such radical changes to Initial Teacher Training (ITT) in recent years, this book provides a useful framework for considering the key learning opportunities for trainee teachers. This is a valuable, well-researched yet practical text for anyone involved in teacher education. Many of the observations Scott Douglas makes would provide a useful audit for evaluating ITT provision: whether university or school based. However, this text also highlights some key messages for all educators. For instance, Scott Douglas's analysis of 'the research school' is relevant across the system. *Student Teachers in School Practice* should be seen as an important book within educational discourse today.

*Tom Middlehurst,*
*Head of Research,*
*SSAT (The Schools Network)*

This book explores the different responses of subject departments to participating in student teachers on teaching practice. The book comes alive when Scott Douglas introduces us to the trainees and teachers in the subject departments at the school where he conducted his research. There is a richness and authenticity to the data.

For those that manage student teachers or who have them working in their schools, it offers some very important points. Scott Douglas was a school teacher and he uses his experience as a teacher and school manager to good effect. He was evidently accepted readily to the school and university alike; this is played out in the discussion of the tensions between the school, university and the student teachers. His conclusions are important ones as the business of teacher training is becoming less reliant on a university-based route and new school-based pathways continue to grow. For those who work with student teachers in schools it offers a new perspective and for those in leadership positions, it reminds us about the micro-politics and the cultural significance of the way we work both in the classroom and the staffroom.

*Susan Tranter,*
*Executive Headteacher,*
*Education Today*

This book is a welcome and timely addition to a burgeoning literature on teacher education. Not only refreshing but bold, Douglas comments how so many texts err on the descriptive side, rather than as this book does so well, analyse the thinking behind the actions of student teachers, school staff and university tutors in the realities of school teaching practice. A strength of the book is the richness of the data generated which offers the reader unique insights into how subject departments, operating as micro-communities within school co-join with the Higher Education Institution to construct learning opportunities for the student teachers. Snippets of dialogue with school mentors and university tutors are beautifully presented in the book and capture the very real experiences of the student teachers. On many occasions I found myself almost there listening to the conversations with the students and joining in the staffroom discussions. The detail and richness of the contextually grounded data relating to the cultural, historic and social circumstances of the school provide freshness to data that I found compelling.

The book has important messages for teacher educators and policy makers. It offers important insights into subject departments in secondary schools. It has, I feel, important ideas for future and currently undeveloped research into the nature of student learning in primary schools too. It has made a new and extremely valuable contribution to knowledge around school–university partnerships and finally, whilst located in England, contributes directly to a global dimension of teacher education. In a time of immense change in education, Douglas contributes a refreshing and insightful book that causes us to reflect deeply on the nature of learning and re-examine the opportunities in schools that promote it with student teachers. I can recommend this book very highly and assuredly it will be top of the reading list of teacher education and education studies students in my university.

*Jonathan Doherty,*
*Leeds Trinity University, UK,*
*Journal of Vocational Education & Training*

*Policy and Practice in the Classroom*

Series Editors: **Richard Race**, School of Education, University of Roehampton, UK; **Barbara Read**, School of Education, University of Glasgow, UK; **Alaster Scott Douglas**, School of Education, University of Roehampton, UK

This series will publish monographs exploring issues to do with education policy and practice in relation to classroom settings, with each book examining the implications of its research findings for educational policy and practice. Themes explored include teaching and learning; youth identities; inclusive education; education policy-making; de-schooling; student teachers; the primary classroom; and science teachers.

*Titles in the series include:*

Alaster Scott Douglas
STUDENT TEACHERS IN SCHOOL PRACTICE
An Analysis of Learning Opportunities

Michael Singh and Bobby Harreveld
DESCHOOLING L'EARNING
Young Adults and the New Spirit of Capitalism

**Policy and Practice in the Classroom**
**Series Standing Order ISBN  978–1–137–26856–3 Hardback**
**978–1–137–26857–0 Paperback**
(*outside North America only*)

You can receive future titles in this series as they are published by placing a standing order. Please contact your bookseller or, in case of difficulty, write to us at the address below with your name and address, the title of the series and the ISBN quoted above.

Customer Services Department, Macmillan Distribution Ltd, Houndmills, Basingstoke, Hampshire RG21 6XS, England

# Student Teachers in School Practice

## An Analysis of Learning Opportunities

Alaster Scott Douglas
*Assistant Director of Education and Professional Practice, School of Education, University of Roehampton, UK*

First published 2014
Published in paperback 2015 by
PALGRAVE MACMILLAN

Palgrave Macmillan in the UK is an imprint of Macmillan Publishers Limited, registered in England, company number 785998, of Houndmills, Basingstoke, Hampshire RG21 6XS.

Palgrave Macmillan in the US is a division of St Martin's Press LLC, 175 Fifth Avenue, New York, NY 10010.

Palgrave is the global academic imprint of the above companies and has companies and representatives throughout the world.

Palgrave® and Macmillan® are registered trademarks in the United States, the United Kingdom, Europe and other countries.

ISBN 978–1–137–26867–9   hardback
ISBN 978–1–137–52464–5   paperback

This book is printed on paper suitable for recycling and made from fully managed and sustained forest sources. Logging, pulping and manufacturing processes are expected to conform to the environmental regulations of the country of origin.

A catalogue record for this book is available from the British Library.

A catalog record for this book is available from the Library of Congress.

Typeset by MPS Limited, Chennai, India.

# Contents

# List of Figures and Tables

## Figures

## Table

# Acknowledgements

I would like to acknowledge and thank those people who have worked with me throughout my school career; in schools in Newbury (St Bartholomew's School), in Melksham (The George Ward School), in Bristol (The Cotham School) and in London (Lea Valley High School). In each setting I have been challenged and supported by dedicated and inspiring colleagues and friends. Subsequently, my teaching in higher education enables me to research alongside highly stimulating professionals whose work and encouragement I hold in high esteem. I am particularly indebted to Viv Ellis (Brunel University), John Furlong and Anne Edwards (University of Oxford) for their support and guidance in my research and to my co-editors of this book series 'Policy and Practice in the Classroom', Richard Race (University of Roehampton) and Barbara Read (University of Glasgow) for their considered feedback and suggestions during the various stages of writing this book. Finally, I would like to express my appreciation to all the teachers, student teachers and teacher educators in my research schools for their generosity of time and spirit and for their willingness to take part in the research projects.

# Foreword

Learning to teach happens in schools, but what is learnt depends largely on the demands made on student teachers while they are there. This common-sense statement is underpinned by the account of learning offered by the late Vygotsky, which goes like this. People can be said to be learning when their existing relationships in and with the practices they inhabit change. That is, they reposition themselves within practices through their own attempts at making sense of the meanings and demands in the practices (Childs, Edwards and McNicholl 2014; Edwards 2014).

Much therefore depends on the meanings and expectations that are highlighted for student teachers in school discourses. Alaster Scott Douglas' book takes us inside the black box of the school practicum to reveal the knowledge in play and the associated demands while student teachers are supported as beginning practitioners. The primary focus is their interactions with their school-based teacher-mentors and their university curriculum specialist tutors, in four departments in the same secondary school in England.

It is a timely book; there is global recognition that initial teacher education needs to include a significant amount of time spent in schools. Yet we know all too little about the expectations placed on student teachers by their training programmes, the demands that shape them as beginning professionals while in school and the role that school department cultures can play. The book offers us a set of detailed case studies as a snapshot of one year in an initial teacher education programme which continues to evolve.

What can we take from the richly grained snapshots offered here? First, that initial teacher education partnerships, whether university or school-led, benefit from being built on relationships of trust which focus on developing the thinking practitioner. Second, initial teacher education programmes have much to gain from building strong research-based connections between school subject departments and curriculum teams in university departments of education. Finally, that we have been helped in coming to these important conclusions by the systemic analysis that has been employed in the study at the core of the book.

Let us therefore start with how Alaster approached the study. Taking Engeström's idea of an activity system as a framing device, he has presented each subject department's engagement with initial teacher education as an activity and has organised the vast amount of data he gathered using that framing. Consequently, he has been able to interrogate the data to show how tools, such as handbooks, were used and to identify the motives revealed when participants discussed initial teacher education. By analysing each department separately and examining the different meaning systems into which the student teachers were inducted, Alaster also reminds universities just how important it is for partnerships to be more than efficient arrangements for placing students in good schools.

The cultural historical roots of activity theory, of course, offer far more than sets of triangles for organising case studies, as Engeström's own work attests. As I read about the school departments I wanted to know more about the evolution of each department's relationship with the University. It is a cultural historical commonplace that we inhabit the practices shaped by those who have passed this way before us. At the same time we shape those practices as we reconfigure our relationships with them. It was beyond the scope of this study to examine either of these features, but there is more to the Vygotskian legacy. Alaster acknowledges this, noting the wider potential of these resources in his brief, but interesting, account of an intervention study he undertook some time after completing the work discussed here.

But what are the lessons for teacher education? The omission of 'initial' in the previous sentence is deliberate. First, trusting professional relationships are crucial, but they need to be based on more than knowing and liking each other. As teacher educators we need to understand what matters for those we are collaborating with (Edwards, 2010, 2012), what motives we each bring to our joint work on shaping the learning trajectories of student teachers. We know that student teachers over decades have reported being 'torn in two' when this mutual understanding between school and higher education is not there. In Alaster's study we see, for example, what happened when a teacher-mentor did not recognise what matters for the university tutor and used the handbook as a tool to protect the student teacher from the demands being made by the tutor.

This level of detail alerts us to the pressure on student teachers as they move between the demands of university practices and those of schools, even when university practices, as they are here, are geared towards supporting their development as thoughtful and knowledgeable professionals. This observation takes us to the second lesson and Alaster's concluding argument, that there is much to be gained from stronger connections at an institutional level between school subject departments and university tutor teams. There were examples of strong links in the study, but these were personal rather than institutional.

Here I go beyond Alaster's focus on the activity of initial teacher education, to reflect on how much the wider interests of departments and teams might be served by closer collaborations. At Oxford we have taken these ideas forward in the Education Deanery, also rooted in Vygotskian ideas on learning and teaching (Childs *et al.* 2014; Edwards 2014). The idea is that not only will student teachers find their transitions between university and school to be smoother, departments and tutor teams will gain from the knowledge that circulates in a much wider array of collaborations.

I do recommend this book. I have focused on its implications for how we design teacher education programmes, but it is also an important reference text, capturing many of the debates that have influenced the field and the research that has informed them. School-based teacher education is necessary; Alaster's study tells us we must continue our efforts to ensure that student teachers are given the opportunity to shape themselves as thoughtful and informed professionals while in school.

*Anne Edwards*
*Oxford University Department of Education*

## References

Childs, A., Edwards, A. and McNicholl, J. (2014) 'Developing a Multi-Layered System of Distributed Expertise: What Does Cultural Historical Theory Bring to Understandings of Workplace Learning in School University Partnerships?' in: O. McNamara *et al.* (eds) *Teacher Learning in the Workplace: Widening Perspectives on Practice and Policy* (Dordrecht: Springer).

Edwards, A. (2010) *Being an Expert Professional Practitioner: The Relational Turn in Expertise* (Dordrecht: Springer).

Edwards, A. (2012) 'The Role of Common Knowledge in Achieving Collaboration Across Practices', *Learning, Culture and Social Interaction*, 1 (1), 22–32.

Edwards, A. (2014) 'Learning from Experience in Teaching: A Cultural Historical Critique' in: V. Ellis and J. Orchard (eds) *Learning Teaching from Experience: Multiple Perspectives, International Contexts* (London: Bloomsbury).

# Preface to the Paperback Edition

In writing a new preface for this book for its paperback edition, I have looked at the most recent literature on teacher education policy since the book first published in January 2014. Articles in journals of teacher education indicate that the momentum for school-based pre-service teacher training is still dominant in UK government discourse with upcoming reviews on teacher education likely to promote the craft of teaching by looking 'favourably on practice-based forms of Initial Teacher Training' (Marshall, 2014, p. 268). Such an approach to teacher education is also recognised in research literature in the US where there is 'an increasing number of efforts to develop what is often referred to as "practice-based" teacher education, or professional training that attempts to focus novices' learning more directly on the work of teaching rather than on traditional academic or theoretical topics' (Forzani, 2014, p. 357). A tendency to focus on the practical aspects of learning (by extending the time student teachers spend in schools and putting greater emphasis on this experience, for example) has been noted in other countries too (Gilroy, 2014) which is why this book has been described by a number of reviewers as 'timely'.

Wanting to publish a paperback version of this book was driven by a desire for the text to be easily available to readers beyond those who have access to the hardback editions ordered for university libraries. The reviews of the book have thus far gratifyingly highlighted the value of the text for everyone involved in teacher education; for student teachers, school mentors, school leaders, university lecturers and policy makers as well as for other scholars involved in teacher education research. It is with this wide readership in mind that this paperback edition has been published.

I believe the content of the book is relevant to everyone involved in teacher education. Spurred on by reviews in both academic journals and the professional literature, I also hope the book 'causes us to reflect deeply on the nature of learning and re-examine the opportunities in schools that promote it' (Doherty, 2014, p. 431). I believe that the text offers ways of understanding the practices of teacher education that can be best developed to suit the needs of the participants, schools and universities in which teacher education occurs. Ideally, the chapters help to set an agenda for the development of the practices and conceptual base of teacher education.  In order to use that agenda to direct professional development, readers will need to consider their own ideas on teacher education and their own practices.  I suggest questions such as those below may help start this process:

1. Is conversation around teacher education mainly planning or evaluation in focus?
2. Is conversation mainly centred on giving advice or are new questions asked?
3. What kinds of questions are asked?  Do they open up ideas for discussion?
4. Are all participants seen as potential learners?
5. How is constructive criticism managed?  Are contestable ideas acknowledged and welcomed as part of discussion?
6. What topics are raised beyond task implementation?  Is teacher education viewed as a complex activity?
7. Are a number of sources sought and valued in relation to teacher education?
8. Are new forms of practice created by questioning current practice?

The different analysis and findings chapters in the book offer detailed considerations in relation to how the teacher education process may be realised.  Student teachers, school mentors and university tutors can consider the case study departments in the research in relation to their own experiences in school practices.  The case study chapters are designed to enrich an appreciation of how teacher education activity may occur in school settings:

> The book comes alive when Douglas introduces us to the trainees and teachers in the subject departments at the school where he conducted his research. There is a richness and authenticity to the data. (Tranter, 2014, p. 31)

I hope that the text is read in a way that recognises the contributions of those participants in teacher education activity who see themselves as learners when shaping an understanding of teacher education.  Both research studies in the book are offered as vehicles for stimulating thinking about our own practices in teacher education.  I am aware that evidence presented is from small-scale studies but I see this as a starting point for readers' own speculations.  This has been commented on in the book's reviews:

> Much of what Douglas says about his time in schools has the convincing feel of authenticity and therefore the reader is able to read beyond the data reported here to think about the implications for Initial Teacher Education more generally. (Jerome, 2014, p. 1)

One strength of the subject department case studies is that there are substantial differences between them despite the participants all working within one teacher education school–university partnership. However, it is not my intention to suggest that these examples describe the only ways that subject departments can work with student teachers. Rather, the cases help to develop themes that seem to represent aspects of the teacher education process; the cultural histories, social practices and specific learning opportunities of teacher education activity. I hope the ideas forwarded help readers define and test their views on what makes effective teacher education.

The book advocates the potential for teacher education to support teachers' and schools' improvement strategies. It considers the changing shifts of emphasis in the ways that universities conduct their relationship with schools:

> The final chapters strike the positive note that Initial Teacher Education could play a part in opening up department cultures to be more reflective and thus more able to embrace and explore the diversity of perspectives on teaching and learning. (Jerome, 2014, p. 2)

Attempting to bridge the gap between the often divided audiences reading academic and professional literature, the book is aimed at both sets of readers. For example, it is structured in such a way as to appeal to students as well as to other interested parties. One reviewer comments:

> This book offers an excellent framework for someone writing their PhD thesis as it follows the conventions of introduction, literature review, methodology, data presentation and conclusions. The literature review and methodology sections will be of particular interest to those studying teacher development and as a handbook for research. (Tranter, 2014, p. 31)

But the text also tries to appeal to 'those in leadership positions, as it reminds us about the micro politics and the cultural significance of the way we work both in the classroom and the staffroom' (ibid.). For school mentors and university tutors in particular, the book has also been recommended for 'slow[ing] down the treadmill and provid[ing] the reader with much needed space to reflect on the complexities of learning within the evolving picture of change in teacher education and new models of school-university partnerships' (Doherty, 2014, p. 429). I believe that constant reflection is vital if effective learning opportunities in teacher education are to be sustained. Other reviewers focus on opportunities for policy makers and note the value of the book in providing 'a useful audit for evaluating Initial Teacher Training provision' (Middlehurst, 2014).

Whatever the reason for reading the book, its primary aim is to analyse how, why, where and when opportunities for learning occur in teacher education in schools. I sincerely hope this aim is realised for everyone who may find the book interesting and applicable to their professional practice.

*Alaster Scott Douglas, London, January 2015*

## References

Doherty, J. (2014) 'Student Teachers in School Practice: An Analysis of Learning Opportunities', *Journal of Vocational Education and Training*, 66(3), 429–31.

Forzani, F. M. (2014) 'Understanding "Core Practices" and "Practice-Based" Teacher Education: Learning from the Past', *Journal of Teacher Education*, 65(4), 357–68.

Gilroy, P. (2014) 'International Teacher Education: Changing Times, Changing Practices', *Journal of Education for Teaching: International Research and Pedagogy*, 40(5), 445–6.

Jerome, L. (2014) 'Student Teachers in School Practice: An Analysis of Learning Opportunities', *British Journal of Educational Studies*, DOI: 10.1080/00071005.2014.970794

Marshall, T. (2014) 'New Teachers Need Access to Powerful Educational Knowledge', *British Journal of Educational Studies*, 62(3), 265–79.

Middlehurst, T. (2014) 'Student Teachers in School Practice: An Analysis of Learning Opportunities', *The Schools Network* (SSAT).

Tranter, S. (2014) 'Student Teachers in School Practice: An Analysis of Learning Opportunities', *Education Today*, 64(2), 31.

# 1
# Introduction

This book considers the learning opportunities for student teachers when they are on school teaching practice. These opportunities are discussed in relation to the changes in student teacher education in the UK and globally. In England, there are increasingly centralised requirements for teacher education partnerships between schools and providers of student teacher education. The changes in teacher education have placed and continue to place schools in a more prominent and influential role with regard to student teacher learning. Research in teacher education highlights the importance of schools in the student teacher learning process and the difficulties inherent in enabling learning opportunities for practitioners and student teachers in the classroom (Edwards *et al.*, 2002). Believing in the need for research evidence to inform practice (Douglas, 2012), the book derives from extensive observations of and interviews with practitioners involved in teacher education. My general approach to the text comes from the need to increase understanding of not only the definition of student teacher learning but how key ideas within the concept are applied to learning opportunities in schools and school subject departments. The book develops and analyses the substantive issue of learning opportunities for student teachers in their teaching practice as well as explores the benefits of a rich ethnographic research process.

Making comparisons in teacher education internationally is difficult as there is little 'consensus on the skills and qualities required to be a teacher' (Sayer, 2009, p. 159). How these skills and qualities can be learnt therefore is very much open to debate:

> There are few certainties in [student] teacher education. Perhaps one of them is that student teachers need to have experience of teaching in a school. (McNally *et al.*, 1997, p. 485)

1

McNally *et al.*'s study which investigates the support received by student teachers in their school practice concludes by identifying 'a need for greater conceptual and semantic clarity in understanding and describing the school experience' (*ibid.* 497). Traditionally, school practice has been seen as an expectation 'to provide a place for student teachers to practise teaching [and] to try out the practices provided by the university' (Zeichner, 2010, p. 90). Often referred to as field experiences or school practicum, calls have grown in the research literature for a greater integration of the different aspects of teacher education courses by tackling the divide between course content taught in the higher education institution and the practical experience of working in schools (Grossman *et al.*, 2009, Cochran-Smith *et al.*, 2012). Research in school practice has been recognised as playing a determinant role in student teacher education (Caires *et al.*, 2012) as well as in early teacher development (Britzman, 2003, Evelein, Korthagen and Brekelmans, 2008). A review of 54 research articles published between 1990 and 2010 on how school teaching practice contributes to student teacher development in relation to urban contexts highlights the need for research to focus on the situated and mediated nature of student teachers' learning in the field, and criticises previous research as having 'a lack of focus on what pre-service teachers actually learn from such experiences and how' (Anderson and Stillman, 2012, p. 2). It is the importance of the school settings and the learning opportunities they afford student teachers which are the focus of this book. The influence of the higher education institution is seen in the visits of the university tutors to the schools.

## My background in education

For twelve years I worked as a teacher and senior manager in four secondary schools. In the year 2000 I became a high school deputy head teacher. After eight years of teaching in the classroom my new leadership role involved working with teaching staff from all subject departments. During my four years in senior school management I had responsibilities for staff development and teaching and learning. I developed an awareness of how school subject department environments differ with regard to their ways of working. As a member of the senior team my weekly timetable comprised regular 'on call' lessons. With the benefit of a two-way radio I could be instantly summoned to classrooms in order to respond to requests of teaching staff. This often involved intervening in lessons where a senior teacher's presence was considered necessary or appropriate. Such incidents usually arose from situations where pupils refused to follow instructions. After behaving unacceptably pupils sometimes absented themselves from the classroom and on occasions from the school, disappearing over the school fence into the neighbouring housing estate. Although mainly focusing on the negative aspects of classroom teaching my 'on call' sessions illustrated for me the differences in classroom learning environments. Variations were evident in behaviour management strategies and in pupil and staff expectations when engaged in teaching and learning. Such variations often reflected the differences in the subject department environments in the school.

Prior to my senior management role I gained an appreciation of the importance of subject department learning environments in relation to my responsibilities in teacher education. In the 1990s I co-ordinated teacher education activities with student teachers. Three universities had agreements with the school in relation to student teachers' school practice. The student teachers visited the school at various stages in their training. The universities ran different teacher education courses, and I became familiar with the specific requirements of the teacher education partnerships between the universities and the school. At this time the nature of partnership between schools and higher education institutions in England was realised relatively independently of government directives, which primarily dictated the amount of time to be spent in schools and the number of school practices. My work in student teacher education started to coincide with major reforms to secondary student teacher training announced by the Department of Education (DfE, 1992). These led to a large shift in policy with student teacher education courses in England and Wales becoming school-based by 1994 (Whitty, 2002). Consequently, my career in schools and working with student teachers grew alongside fairly substantial changes made to teacher education.

## Partnership in teacher education

The different interpretations of partnership in student teacher education possibly indicated the different understandings of the nature of teaching and of the relative expertise of teachers and university staff in discussing matters of pedagogy within student teacher education courses. Attempts centrally to make teacher education more consistent post-1992 meant that the broad structure of teacher education courses (the most popular in England being the one-year full-time Postgraduate Certificate of Education, PGCE) shared overall characteristics in different education institutions, and were seen as having distinctive features. Partnership arrangements suggested that some joint responsibility was given to the school and the university for planning and managing courses. This included the assessment of student teachers. The regulations (Teaching Agency, 2012) stipulate that 24 weeks out of the 36-week Postgraduate Certificate of Education course are to be based in schools for student teachers. A minimum of two schools are used. The structure of the school experience requires a specifically designated school-supervising teacher (often known as a mentor) who arranges and co-ordinates the teaching practice in the subject department with the higher education institution.

In this way:

> The partnership (is) characterised by an intention that university teacher educators and mentors work together to enable students as they progress through the programme to analyse and reflect upon their school experience. (Taylor, 2008, p. 70)

The view here is premised on an idea that there is a shared understanding of how student teachers learn to teach. However, the way teacher education partnerships have been seen to operate differently suggests that this idea is unfounded (Furlong, 2000). Although government policy appears to encourage a consistent approach to student teacher education, the similar features of the student teacher education courses belie the contested purpose of student teacher education work. Indeed, I had noted variations between course objectives in my earlier co-ordinating role with three university teacher education courses.

'Worldwide, many teacher education programs state that they have changed toward a more practice-based curriculum' (Lunenberg and Korthagen, 2009, p. 229). Alongside this have been calls for a greater amount of time that student teachers should spend in schools (see, for example, Ure, 2010, for developments in Australia). A continuing shift to school-based learning in teacher education courses and in many other routes into teaching in England (15% of all new recruits to teaching enter through either an employment-based system or a school-centred programme (House of Commons Report, 2010)) promotes the capabilities of schools to work with unqualified teachers. Innovations with regard to different types of higher education input and subsequently different ways that schools should work with student teachers have continued with numerous policy initiatives (Whitty, 2002, p. 73). Government papers further emphasise the role of the school in teacher education in England (DfE, 2010a and b, 2011). New partnerships between schools and universities give greater onus to schools to approach universities for the education needs required for newly recruited student teachers. This has meant that funding for teacher education is being opened up, with new opportunities for the responsibility of training increasingly located within the school rather than the higher education institution. A move away from higher education input in student teacher education has also been noted in the USA where 'increasingly, school districts are taking over the task of preparing teachers for their schools' (Grossman, 2008, p. 11).

## Teacher education policy

How student teacher education is shaped is often strongly influenced by ideological positions about the nature of schooling and teaching. Governments around the world frequently aim to remove the influence of certain interests in favour of their own (Menter *et al.*, 2006). Research into teacher education policy in the USA indicates that 'policy (and policy proposals) [are] unavoidably political, and that policy making involves contentious debate as well as complicated political maneuvering and strategies' (Cochran Smith *et al.*, 2013, p. 6). Driving teacher education policy in many countries 'has been the growing significance of globalization' (Furlong, 2013, p. 28) and the consequent belief in neoliberal policies. In England, national politics greatly influences teacher education policy, which has been dependent on different governments' interpretations of neoliberalism. In Asia too, the impact of the policy and practices in teacher education are seen to be shaped by 'global forces underpinned by an overriding economically-driven ideology' (Tang, 2011, p. 113). In many European and North American settings teacher education policy has also been affected more by the need to recruit teachers than by longer term planning and thinking (Menter *et al.*, 2006, p. 2). Most schools in England have preferred working with higher education in a partnership model of training (Barker, 1996) with only a few wanting complete responsibility. A concern of teacher education when considered as a problem of policy is that the contexts and cultures of schools and how these 'support or constrain teachers' abilities to use knowledge and resources' are not the focus (Cochran-Smith, 2006, p. 139). Instead, this is replaced with discussions on training and testing 'to ensure that all teachers have basic subject matter knowledge and the technical skills to bring pupils' test scores to minimum thresholds' (*ibid.* 140). Such an apparently rational and commonsense approach ignores the complexity of the many problems related to teacher education and fails to take account of the settings where learning happens.

The central research study in this book focuses on school settings and presents four secondary school subject departments working with student teachers during their school practice. This research was a year-long ethnographic study and explored teacher education work with fifteen student teachers in the subject departments of Geography, History, Modern Foreign Languages (MFL) and Science. The departments are in one secondary school (for 11- to 18-year-old pupils) in the south of England. The research focused on a one-year Postgraduate Certificate of Education programme at a university in England. The course has consistently been rated as highly successful in the national inspection grade system and course evaluation outcomes. The school in which the student teachers were placed was well regarded for the way its staff worked with the university, and had many connections with the work of the university's teacher education course, with which it had been involved for over fifteen years. Two questions guided my research: first, what were the opportunities for student teacher learning as constructed in the different departments in one school? And second, if not the same, to what extent and why were these learning opportunities constructed differently?

## The methodological focus

### Ethnographic research

In wanting to appreciate student teachers' learning opportunities in school departments, I believed it was necessary to spend a considerable amount of time in these departments observing and talking to the staff and student teachers working there. During the school year I made 80 visits to the research school in order to appreciate the learning opportunities afforded. Working in an ethnographic way seemed appropriate for such a study. A distinctive feature of ethnography revolves around an appreciation of the 'need to understand the particular cultural worlds in which people live' (Goldbart and Hustler, 2000, p. 16). In this research, transcripts of interviews were considered alongside observation field notes and documentation when analysing the learning opportunities for student teachers in the school subject departments. Data were generated separately and at different times with my perspective as an interviewer, observer and document analyser deciding on data selection and reduction.

The research comes from a sociocultural perspective in that it regards the participants as people in context (Cole, 1996). In this research the context is the school and the subject department in which the student teachers are working. These contexts are distinct from one another in the way participants interact 'within a network of individual and collective histories and cultural expectations' (Kozleski, 2011, p. 253). It is in the interaction of the cultural histories that teachers and student teachers bring with them to the department coupled with the institutional cultures of schooling that the department cultures are constructed. The resulting *negotiated* cultures of the departments, through their patterns and rituals, afford and constrain learning for the participants.

Research on school subject departments (discussed in Chapter 2) highlights the complexity of their make-up as learning environments. Student teachers' school practice in secondary high schools is centred on teaching in specialist subject areas with subject teachers and the support of a subject specialist mentor and university tutor. The variety of opinions evident on all matters of education and differences in possible working styles suggest that there may be considerable variation in how departments operate. Factors such as beliefs about the school subject and opinions on teaching and learning may influence the work. Such factors inform the first research question which considered the learning opportunities for student teachers. The second research question asked *why* student teacher learning opportunities were different and sought to explore the reasons behind why teacher education activity differed in school subject departments. A theoretical and analytic framework was needed to address such complexity in order to help me consider the learning opportunities for student teachers.

## The theoretical framework

The use of Cultural Historical Activity Theory (CHAT) has dramatically increased in educational research over the last two decades (Nussbaumer, 2012). The theory is an approach to analysing contexts for learning, where the culture of the context is revealed in how people think and act. It draws on Vygotsky's concept of mediation, in which human action is seen to be mediated by what he called tools. Tools mediate the interaction of individuals with their environment (Vygotsky, 1986). By analysing tools (their choice and use) it is possible to get an understanding of what is considered important in an activity, as tools indicate how one interprets and tackles a task, for example, in the way a school mentor might use a lesson planning framework as a tool in a conversation with a student teacher. The CHAT concepts (*object, subject, tool and activity system*) which are discussed in Chapter 3 describe the cultural historical psychology that guides this research on the complex settings of school departments. They show how it is possible to 'ground analysis in the culturally organised activities of everyday life' (Cole, 1996, p. 5). A CHAT methodology focuses on questioning why the school learning environment is like it is and how practices have evolved over time and in relation to other practices. It therefore analyses the social situation of (student teacher) development, which in this research is seen in the major influence of the school subject departments.

I draw on Engeström's (1999a) concept of the activity system in order to study how teacher teams in student teacher education operate as cultural systems which afford particular ways for student teachers to be learners. The analytic focus is on the participants (subjects) in the system, the relationships between them and the purposes and values in the work practices. The subjects, their interactions and the cultural system are in 'a constant mutually shaping dialectic' (Edwards, 2011), and it is this dialectical relationship between mind and culture that makes CHAT distinctive as an analytic framework. In considering how the use of tools differs between school mentors working with student teachers in a teacher education programme, the aim is to get insight into how the school department practices create opportunities for learning and how these opportunities both shape and are shaped by the participants in the activity. An emphasis on descriptive analysis in some of the research literature on teacher education and subject departments rarely gets to the heart of where the contestation lies with regard to teaching and learning or how and why it is realised in school departments.

It is particularly important when considering school subject departments as places where learning opportunities arise for student teachers that the school teaching practice enables student teachers to feel prepared to move on from their training and work in other school department situations. Student teachers should not feel that they have been inducted into the established practices of their training school. Considering activity systems in CHAT instead of focusing solely on workplace practices has the advantage of the analysis of learning being at the systemic level. Looking at opportunities for systemic learning changes the focus of the research to the social context, and shifts attention from the individual to the setting. This better fits with the area of inquiry in this research: the student teacher education activity in the school subject departments.

When considering the generalisation of the findings in the research the reader may feel that they come to know the described cases of the four subject departments when they parallel their actual experience. This has been called 'naturalistic generalisation' (Stake, 2000, p. 442).

Researchers cannot predict what readers know or how they might think about the cases being researched (as in school subject departments), so they therefore need to find ways to 'protect' and establish as valid the ideas they report. Adopting 'abstract dimensions for comparing cases' (Spiro *et al.*, 1978, cited in Stake, 2000, p. 443) as, for example using CHAT concepts in the findings, may help to protect these ideas. The case studies of the four subject departments (Chapters 5, 6, 7 and 8) can be seen as prototypes and as such are not representative or viewed as samples to be generalised to a greater population. They have been co-created by the researcher in the field (Langemeyer and Nissen, 2005). My role as the interviewer, observer and document analyser in the generation of data inevitably shaped the research with choices made about who to interview and what to observe (see Chapter 4). It was therefore important to constantly question myself through a reflexive approach and acknowledge that what was researched reflected my own conceptualisation of teacher education influenced by past experiences and my work in the field.

## The book in outline

In Chapter 2 I outline research which has specifically looked at school subject departments as learning environments. This literature paves the way for the exploration of school subject departments in relation to the central ethnographic research in the book. The chapter then considers professional learning and how this has been theorised in the workplace learning literature taking into account the implications and effects of the multi-voiced nature of complex activity. The discussion is further developed by considering settings for joint activity where learners such as student teachers work in partnership across two institutions: a school and a university.

Chapter 3 addresses some foundational and epistemological questions and gives a direction for the book as a whole. A sociocultural pedagogy is explained, which aims at assisting learners' participation in school communities where knowledge is used and constructed, therefore highlighting the importance of school practice in teacher preparation. Benefits from school-based learning are seen to arise not only from increasing participation in teaching practices but also in the critical examination of those practices by participants. I elaborate on the theoretical framework of CHAT for considering student teacher learning opportunities in their teacher education practice. This is built from the arguments forwarded on workplace learning and complex activities. The chapter shows how this framework for understanding informs the research design and the generation of data. CHAT concepts are explained and these describe the cultural historical psychology that guides the research on the complex settings of school departments.

In Chapter 4, I outline the research questions and introduce the research school, Market Town High School, as the main fieldwork site and the research university, Downtown University. I also explain how the higher education institution worked with the research school and the nature of the student teacher education course. The ethnographic case study design of the central research study and how to integrate ethnographically generated data with a CHAT analytic framework is discussed. I explain how and why the data were generated and analysed. The discussion also supports the reasoning behind the structure of the subject department case studies which are presented in the next four chapters.

Chapters 5, 6, 7 and 8 present the four department case studies. Each follows the same format structured in three sections: cultural history, social practices and specific student teacher learning opportunities. The sections analyse descriptively the concepts that make up a mediational model of activity as described by Engeström (2001): the rules, community and the division of labour of the student teacher education activity systems. The case studies contextualise the student teacher education work in the departments and are preparatory for showing how tools mediate the participants' work on the objects of the student teacher education activity system. These extended case studies start to address what the subject department staff consider to be the object of student teacher education activity and how this affords or constrains the learning opportunities for the student teachers. The case studies begin to answer the first research question which asks what the learning opportunities are for student teachers as constructed by different departments in one school.

Chapter 9 focuses on how the tools of student teacher education mediate student teachers' learning. This and the subsequent chapter start to answer the second research question: to what extent and why are the student teachers' learning opportunities constructed differently in the subject departments? In seeking to explain the different ways in which the student teacher education tools are picked up and used within the school department student teacher education activity systems, the chapter explores why they appear to serve rather different functions and why the negotiations and social exchanges around the tools in the course of mentoring and student teacher education activity have a different character and lead to such different kinds of learning.

Chapter 10 takes the ideas from the previous chapter forward and offers an analysis of the underlying processes behind the student teacher education tools by focusing on the objects in the school department student teacher education activity systems, where these are viewed as the 'true carriers of motives' (Engeström and Blackler, 2005, p. 309) and are seen as providing direction for the work. Each subject department is considered in relation to its student teacher education activity object and how far this is affected by tensions in the motives of those involved in student teacher education. The differing and sometimes contradictory approaches to student teacher education highlight the importance of the activity systems' objects acting as the motivating forces in the activities.

Chapter 11 starts by considering research that has noted how student teachers' ideas on pedagogy are affected by conflicting motives. It acknowledges a lack of consensus in the literature with regard to the possibilities of discussing contestation openly. The chapter considers student teacher education models in international contexts and research initiatives that have been seen to strengthen student teacher education through research partnerships. A further qualitative study is introduced, which integrates an interventionist research model (Developmental Work Research, Engeström, 2007) into a student teacher education school/university partnership, and considers the role of the school leader in this. Possibilities for student teachers, teachers and teacher educators to work together in a research process that is integral to a student teacher education partnership are forwarded, with the aim of ensuring that critical enquiry and learning are kept at the forefront of student teacher education activity.

Finally, Chapter 12 considers how the book's discussion might contribute to our understanding of student teacher education and to the role of the school practice in particular in changing policy contexts. I also suggest implications for student teacher education in terms of how student teacher education programmes might better reflect an understanding of student teacher learning opportunities as being amongst participants in an activity system rather than predominantly within themselves. The professional and political implications of this understanding are profound, for if it is seen that student teacher learning is dependent upon a dynamic system that is capable of being worked on, as well as working on its participants, then teaching must be seen as a collective enterprise and a relational practice embedded in specific social, cultural and historical conditions.

This book is an important account of how the mechanisms of student teacher education partnership between a school and a university can be appropriated and employed in ways that reflect the discourses of the school and different subject departments. The analysis and the discussion in the book aim to significantly contribute to understandings of how student teachers learn and consider how learning opportunities can be developed and promoted in student teacher and teacher education.

# 2
# Researching Workplace Learning

## Introduction

'In England, as in the USA, the subject department acts as a basic social unit within secondary schools' (Hennessy *et al.*, 2005, p. 155). Research into school subject departments in schools is scarce (Visscher and Witziers, 2004), and the majority of research that exists is fairly old. Consequently, little has been written about how secondary school subject departments support the learning opportunities of student teachers. What becomes clear from much of the research literature is that school departments and their subcultures play significant roles in the lives of most secondary school teachers and consequently for student teachers when learning in them (Goodson and Ball, 1984; Grossman *et al.*, 2000; Hodkinson and Hodkinson, 1997; Paechter, 1995; Wildy and Wallace, 2004; Childs *et al.*, 2013). The importance of subject departments in the organisation of secondary schools has led some researchers to come to the conclusion that to affect change in the school environment one needs to work with departments (Harris, 2001; Siskin, 1994, 1997; Visscher and Witziers, 2004). This is also the case when considering the learning opportunities for student teachers (Ball, 1987; Butcher, 2000; Childs and McNicholl, 2007; Hodkinson and Hodkinson, 2005; Lacey, 1977).

Leach and Moon (1999, p. 95) have explored the 'personal constructs' of teachers: 'a complex amalgam of past knowledge, experiences of learning, a personal view of what constitutes "good" teaching and belief in the purposes of the subject'. Their research suggests that student teachers are likely to be influenced by a variety of beliefs and teaching styles not only with regard to teaching and learning but also with regard to student teacher education. Edwards and Protheroe (2003) reported in research on two Postgraduate Certificate of Education courses that the main concern for the experience of student teachers was learning about curriculum delivery rather than understanding children's learning and debating contestable pedagogical issues. Departments and teachers may be involved in student teacher education for a number of different reasons. For example, there may be a desire to create better teachers, to enable student teachers to pass their course, to recruit new staff, to benefit the department by working closely with a university and/or to enhance career development by providing teachers with mentoring opportunities. Reasons are likely to vary across department staff and may therefore influence the nature of the student teacher education work. Hence, teacher responses to new teaching styles initiated by student teachers (as in the introduction of new technologies) will be mediated by teachers' beliefs about subject matter and pedagogy as well as by the norms and organisation of their department.

## Department unity and contestation

Data generated from my earlier research when interviewing university-based teacher educators responsible for the curricula on a student teacher education course indicated that there were differences in the notions of teaching and learning both within and between school subject departments (Douglas, 2005). This is borne out in other research on teacher and student teacher learning (for example, Britzman, 2003; Busher and Blease, 2000; Cook *et al.*, 2002; Donnelly, 2000; Goodson and Mangan, 1995; John, 2005; Siskin, 1991). It is therefore important to highlight the possible tensions and contradictions in the learning opportunities for student teachers working within subject departments. The relative isolation of departments as independent units (Siskin, 1991; de Lima, 2003) with geographically separate classroom teaching areas and departmental work routines (meetings, assessment considerations, policy decisions and teaching practices for example) suggests that comparing and contrasting them as situations for student teacher learning is important, as such comparisons are not readily appreciated in the school context. As noted in the introduction, my work in schools has made me aware of the different departmental cultures that exist within secondary schools. I see culture as something that 'comes into being wherever people engage in joint activity over a period of time' (Cole, 1996, p. 301). Subject department environments shape but are also shaped by individuals whose beliefs, behaviours and customs are shared amongst members of a group. Hargreaves' work (1994) articulates particular features of different kinds of teacher culture from individualistic to collaborative. He particularly criticises a culture of contrived collegiality as one that creates inflexibility and inefficiency as teachers simply 'meet and work to implement the curricula and instructional strategies developed by others' (Hargreaves and Dawe, 1990, p. 227).

The potential strength of department cultures and their individual characteristics makes a comparison of the learning opportunities for student teachers across departments particularly interesting, as it is likely that these learning opportunities will be different. Research into subject departments has acknowledged this diversity, as in Esland's descriptions (1971) of departments as 'epistemic communities'. He emphasises the separateness of subject areas reinforced by the fact that teaching and learning concepts are shared among the teachers in the separate subject communities because of their joint participation and understanding of their subject through the use of textbooks, examination specifications and journals for example. The National Curriculum in the United Kingdom (DES, 1989) gave 'renewed emphasis to separate, traditional subjects' (Jephcote and Davies, 2007, p. 208) and dissuaded integrated project work by further defining subject areas, thereby establishing clear subject boundaries and maintaining the organisational structure of schools.

However, the nature of subject knowledge and how it is viewed is considered to be more complex than is implied in the concept of an 'epistemic community', with the identification of varied opinions about subjects and how they should be taught. Ball (1987) points out how the differences between (and within) school departments represent sub-cultures from both a technical point of view (the conception of subject content and structure) and assumptions about the broader purposes of education and how children learn. Such contestation is clearly illustrated in Wildy and Wallace (2004), which illustrates the differences of opinion possible on subject matter and educational aims by two teachers working in the same science department. A contrast in approach to the subject ('he values science for its own sake ... she values science for what it can do for students', p. 107) leads to disagreement on what the purpose of their teaching is about. Their differing conceptions of science (delivering a set of universal truths as opposed to a personal sense-making process that involves experimentation and inquiry) are in conflict, and such a deadlock makes it 'hard to imagine a process by which they would arrive at a shared vision' (*ibid*, 110). It is possible that student teachers during their school experiences will encounter such opposing views too. It is therefore crucial to consider how they are supported and enabled to work with such diversity and whether it is seen as a learning opportunity by the school department.

In Lacey and Ball's research (1984), the importance of an outward display of department unity is stressed in order to achieve departmental demands (resources and initiatives for example). However, some discontinuity can be contained and managed so that departments still appear unified. Lacey's previous description (1977) of 'latent cultures' (those that teachers hold because of their strategic compliance in their practice) implies that departments enforce united agreement among staff. Yet Goodson and Mangan (1995) believe that subcultures are sites of greater contestation with room to express individual educational philosophies and pedagogical styles. However unified a department may appear, it is important for student teachers that they have the opportunity to discuss alternative viewpoints. This avoids a feeling that there is either only one view or that opinion on teaching and learning should be a private matter. The latter would more likely lead to strategic compliance. If tensions are openly acknowledged in the school department, then these can be productive and useful for student teachers in that they may encourage them to consider their own opinions on subject matter and educational aims. In turn, this may help them in their future learning when moving to new schools (Grossman *et al.*, 1999).

## Subject subcultures

The strength of subject subcultures is widely noted in research. Subject subcultures may represent views on 'the nature of the subject, the way it should be taught, the role of the teacher and what is expected of the student' (Paechter, 1995, p. 75). Departments in Siskin's research (1991) exhibit distinctive cultures arising from a separate knowledge base with a distinct language, different environments that explore different kinds of learning, different policies, practices and varying responses to the same external policies. This inevitably has an effect on student teachers, as Lacey noted in his classic book *The Socialisation of Teachers*:

> The subject subculture appears to be a pervasive phenomenon affecting a student teacher's behaviour in school and university as well as their choice of friends and their attitudes towards education. (1977, p. 63)

Departments provide a special sense of identity for staff and some teachers see their careers tied closely to the development of subjects (Lacey and Ball, 1984). Consequently, the potential for influencing how student teachers learn is considerable, as they often work very closely with teachers who share their same subject interests. Research on school subject departments acknowledges a strong sense of department identity

(Havnes, 2009), and this is often most evident when a subject's status is threatened by an opening up of the curriculum to include new subjects (see Harris and Haydn (2012) in relation to school history in the UK). Territorial wrangling is evident in Paechter's study (1995) on the implementation of a new subject of Design and Technology into the curriculum where she notes how subject subcultures are focused on a common understanding of teaching and learning, and a shared language. With a conflict in status, and power play between the Home Economics and Communication and Design Technology departments in creating the new subject of Design and Technology, differences in understanding teaching and learning are highlighted in her research. As a consequence, many staff retreat into the subcultures of their originating departments. Similarly, a subject's subculture is influential in research that looks at the introduction of new technologies into the curriculum. Whether seeing computers as mediating tools or as hardware getting in the way of teaching, existing department subcultures have been seen to limit transformation of practice (Hennessy *et al.*, 2005; John, 2005).

Stodolsky and Grossman (1995) differentiate between subjects by considering how well defined or dynamic they are. The many connections (the learning of vocabulary and grammar for example) across courses and year groups in Modern Foreign Languages (MFL) make it a more defined subject than say Science, which may be considered as a subject that changes 'continually generating new knowledge' (McLaughlin and Talbert, 2001, p. 57). In sequential subjects where learning is considered to be cumulative as in Mathematics and MFL, teachers report more co-ordination with colleagues and more emphasis on the coverage of content than in less sequential subjects. Compulsory subjects like Science are often larger departments with more accountability in the form of pupil external testing. Optional subjects may attract pupils who are more motivated as they have chosen the course, as in History and Geography (Stodolsky and Grossman, 1995).

In connection with the variation of opinion on school subjects, it is important that student teachers are aware of the possible micro-politics in schools (Hoyle, 1982; Ball, 1987; Hodkinson and Hodkinson, 1997) where these are seen as 'those strategies by which individuals and groups in organisational contexts seek to use their resources of power and influence to further their interests' (Hoyle, 1982, p. 88). Material interests (status, resources and career) influence the pay, promotion and conditions of teachers (Goodson and Ball, 1984). Specialist subject communities make a difference to this, with the more academic subjects gaining higher status in terms of examinable knowledge, thereby attracting greater resource allocation. Goodson and Ball (1984) outline possible conflicts between departments and the status hierarchies that exist in schools. This is illustrated in Hodkinson and Hodkinson's research (1997), which emphasises the importance of introducing student teachers to the micro-politics of schools and the possible marginalised position of subject departments (in this case Physical Education). They note a lack of discussion of the ways in which wider contexts and relationships affect the workings of student teacher education partnership schemes, and illustrate this by explaining a school situation with a Physical Education student teacher, his university tutor, his school subject mentor and the school student teacher education co-ordinator. Each has different positions in relation to school experience in a partnership scheme, and the article considers the differences they have in relation to resources of 'power' and interests. The point is that their perceptions are located within different sub-cultural and micro-political groupings, and it is this micro-political dimension that is generally lacking in student teacher education literature, even though it is well represented in the study of schools. Micro-politics is often invisible and only surfaces where conflict is apparent; the student teacher in question fitted in well with the marginalised position of the Physical Education department but experienced problems working with the student teacher education co-ordinator.

## School department leadership and management

The above discussion considers how subject departments can be seen as relatively autonomous units with differing levels of unity and contestation within them, which may influence the working situation for both teachers and student teachers. How departments operate, their organisational and leadership and management style will also affect both teachers' and student teachers' work (Aubrey-Hopkins and James, 2002; Little, 2002). Research suggests that the form a culture takes within a department is greatly affected by the degree of collaboration. This is clearly evidenced in James' and Goodhew's (2011) analysis of a Design and Technology subject department over a thirteen-month period. The role of the manager/subject leader in developing collaborative working practices and the importance of this being done proactively with a consideration of previous leadership practices in the department is stressed. This has also been acknowledged in previous studies that consider departments as learning communities (Busher and Blease, 2000; Donnelly, 2000; Eraut *et al.*, 2000; Jarvis, 2008). A variety of working practices in the same subject departments in different schools (as well as in different subject departments in the same school) highlight how it is more than just subject subcultures (and schools) that influence the working conditions in departments (Donnelly, 2000; McLaughlin and Talbert, 2001; Hodkinson and Hodkinson, 2005). In Donnelly's research (2000, p. 261) on secondary school science teachers, teachers referred to the managerial style of the department as 'significantly influencing their professional working environment, and the experience of teaching'. However, this finding was very closely linked to other variables that influenced teachers' work identified in department settings (the use of schemes of work, the emphasis on the science discipline and the characteristics of pupils) making the science teachers' working experiences very varied across schools, as numerous permutations of the effect of these variables were evident. In conclusion, Donnelly can all but acknowledge that 'departments are very distinctive working environments' (*ibid.* 271).

Styles of leadership are examined by Busher and Blease (2000) who studied eight secondary school science departments for the way they work with their science technicians. Effective leadership is characterised as balancing formal organisational structures (roles, responsibilities and accountability) against people-oriented values (a respect for staff as individuals and openly acknowledging shared values of the purpose of teaching science). This style succeeds in making staff in the majority of the departments feel included and be part of a close community. Similarly, a study with teachers of Maths, Humanities and Technology (Helsby, 1996) suggests that department cultures and how they are managed are influential in shaping teachers' sense of professionalism, and this can have a significant impact on teacher learning. This can act as a potential form of professional development if collaboration is encouraged. Alternatively, it can result in teachers becoming less collaborative in the department's work:

> A culture of individualism was experienced by the staff where a system of top-down decision-making meant that curriculum development was seen as a management task and classroom teaching as an individual concern. Thus in both the History and Geography departments, schemes of work were drawn up unilaterally. (Helsby, 1996, p 143)

Strong collegial interaction in departments can potentially provide a strong learning community (Talbert and McLaughlin, 1994), and the 'role played by subject leaders at establishing, promoting and nourishing teacher leadership' can be crucial (Ghamrawi, 2010, p. 318). However, the kind of collaborative working practices described may be seen to be in tension with developments in school management in England. 'There is now a huge enthusiasm on behalf of the government to intervene in the detail of educational processes with advice on all aspects of teaching' (Furlong, 2005, p. 125). Some subject departments are now overlaid by a strong national system. Ball, when speaking about school reform in the UK at the beginning of the 1990s, noted the change in the political climate and the possible effects this may have on the working lives of teachers: 'market ideology is clearly embedded in a broader commitment to possessive and competitive individualism' (Ball, 1990, p. 10). Subsequent research suggests that subject leaders are now 'given a limited amount of authority within highly defined levels of outcomes and focus mainly on managerial/administrative aspects of their result-oriented departments' (Friedman, 2011, p. 289; Kerry, 2005), and 'lacking essential power [subject leaders are] mostly forced to work in situations that [are] not always susceptible of direction or control' (Jarvis, 2012, p. 490).

School department performances are more visible, seen both collectively and individually by the data produced from examination results. Departments and individual teachers can be compared with other departments and teachers both within and outside of a school. Consequently, the added pressures of meeting targets and middle manager objectives can impact on the work. With increased use and interrogation of performance data, uncomfortable relationships may exist between the collective and the individual in subject departments when 'values derived from a result-orientation school culture [are] tightly exercised' (Friedman, 2011, p. 300). Whether the work in the department is viewed as being important and worthwhile in its own right or whether it is geared towards performance targets in order to compete with other school departments by attracting the most able students (see Davies *et al.*, 2009) may also be evident to the student teachers, and indicate underlying beliefs in teachers' practice.

### Departments as places for teacher and student teacher learning

The importance of consultation on pedagogy, reflective dialogue and feedback in creating professional communities rather than 'mechanical units' is emphasised in Visscher and Witzier's research (2004) on 39 Mathematics departments in Dutch schools. Their data suggests that departments, although cohesive, focus on regulating teacher behaviour with teaching goals, lesson content and pupil testing. Such a department is likely to be a poor learning environment for a student teacher if it does not focus any activities specifically on developing the teaching and learning within it.

The norms of schools can create a situation where teacher learning may only be considered either outside the workplace, at brief unplanned encounters in between lessons (Mawhinney, 2010), or during irregular in-service training (Grossman *et al.*, 2000). This creates difficulty in developing a community for teacher learning. A stronger collective enquiry generates knowledge *of* practice, whilst a teacher's individual learning in a weaker department draws upon knowledge *for* practice, often derived from theory from outside the setting (McLaughlin and Talbert, 2001). In order to counter this there is a need for departments to be concerned with teacher as well as student learning, and this could be considered a benefit for schools involved with student teacher education. Teachers working directly with student teachers may gain opportunities to consider and further develop understanding of their own practice. This is seen in research that looks at the effect of subject departments hosting student teachers (McIntyre *et al.*, 1994; Shaw, 1992; Stanulis, 1995; Williams, 1994). These studies also indicate greater discussion, collaboration and sharing of practice within departments. Nevertheless, other research highlights a resistance to change and professional learning within schools, and notes that student teacher education is often simply accommodated in school systems rather than able to change them (Edwards and Collison, 1996).

Departmental cultures were seen to exert a major influence on teacher learning in a study that has strong parallels with the research central to this book (Hodkinson and Hodkinson, 2005; Hodkinson, 2009). The research consists of longitudinal case studies that look at the learning opportunities in four secondary school subject departments (but for qualified teachers in two secondary schools). The different cultures in the departments strongly influence the learning of the teachers, with a collaborative culture leading to 'richer and more effective learning' (2005, p. 122). The research recommends that departments engender 'expansive learning environments':

> A radically different approach to enhancing teacher learning is required. It needs to focus on maximising the learning potential within the participatory practices of teachers, and recognising that different teachers will respond differently to the same circumstances ... thus this approach should be based on maximising opportunities to learn, incentives to learn, and support for learning. (*Ibid.* 123)

Such a culture of learning could provide an ideal place for student teachers. The factors identified as being part of expansive learning environments (as opposed to restrictive ones); collaboration, support, extending learning opportunities and a focus on teacher learning would ensure that student teachers could benefit from this way of working in the department.

In summary, to engender teacher and student teacher learning, there is a need for learning environments where the potential of school practices to support student teacher learning is maximised and where through collaboration, the development of student teachers' knowledge can be supported by working with experienced teachers. This is recommended as one of the strategies to adopt for science teachers teaching outside of their subject specialism (Childs and McNicholl, 2007). Teachers teaching outside their own science discipline are cast 'into the role of learners, creating a need to collaborate and learn from each other' (Childs *et al.*, 2013, p. 43). These teachers identify colleagues who have the relevant specialist subject and teaching knowledge as the most significant form of help when they seek advice and wish to develop expertise in the discipline. Such developments and ways of working are important for creating opportunities for student teachers to learn in subject departments too.

## A definition of learning

Hodkinson and Hodkinson (2005) draw on Sfard (1998) in their discussion on learning theories when they refer to differing ideas between two learning metaphors, one of 'acquisition' and one of 'participation'. With much of the teacher development literature favouring the former (particularly with regard to centralised government policy approaches) and workplace learning literature concentrating on the latter, they argue for a combination of the two perspectives in their research on teacher learning in schools. An acquisition metaphor considers learning as the gaining of knowledge and skills that have been identified as absent in the learner. These can be directly addressed through making 'commodified content' available (Hodkinson and Hodkinson, 2005, p. 111). It is then possible to measure the successful acquisition of such content (for example in the learning of computer skills). However, this process assumes that appropriate content is already known and that it is readily available. It does not take into account the varying processes by which for example teachers and student teachers learn, the unexpected and fortuitous learning opportunities that occur in day-to-day work and the encountering of new situations where prior learning content is not available. This could be in relation to student teachers working with a particular class in collaboration with the class teacher and experimenting with innovative teaching styles.

The participation metaphor of learning acknowledges the more 'non-formal' processes of learning (Eraut, 2000): those that occur outside instruction (considered as 'formal learning'):

> Learning is a process of *transformation of participation itself* (emphasis in the original) ... how people develop is a function of their transforming roles and understanding in the activities in which they participate. (Rogoff, 1994, p. 209)

In the central research study discussed in this book, learning is viewed as a sociocultural process with the focus on where and how the learning is taking place as much as on the individual. Other major theories of learning (behavioural, cognitive) focus on the individual and conceptualise learning as 'the response of humans to an external environment, as a question of responding to external stimuli, progression through a series of predetermined conceptual stages, or as the processing of information' (Griffiths and Guile, 2003, p. 57). However, it is necessary to acknowledge the importance and applicability of both the acquisition and participation metaphors as forms of the learning process (Edwards, 2005b; Hodkinson and Hodkinson, 2005). Subsequently, 'common ground is emerging between those who espouse an acquisition metaphor of learning and those who use a participation metaphor' (Edwards, 2001, p. 169). In my research I consider both aspects of learning as being under a sociocultural umbrella.

Learning opportunities from student teachers working in school departments are most likely to fit more readily into the participation learning metaphor. Whereas, student teacher learning at the university, although unlikely just to be based on an acquisition learning metaphor, will possibly cover some aspects of teaching that may fit more readily into a notion of acquisition (for example, lectures and seminars on the National Curriculum and on forms of assessment, as well as student teacher audits on, for example, Information and Communication Technology skills and curriculum knowledge). Although requirements that 'providers of student teacher education check and then fill in gaps in student teachers' subject knowledge' (Ellis, 2007, p. 146) are no longer compulsory in the teaching standards in England, research suggests that audits are still being used (as was the case in my research). Nevertheless, a focus on the acquisition of knowledge need not necessarily imply that once knowledge is stored it is automatically retrieved and then applied when in the work situation. The relation between knowledge and its use is more complex than this, and cannot be described by just using acquisition and participation metaphors.

In explaining what learning is when considering the many meanings of learning by participating, Edwards states:

> Learning reflects a concern with within-person changes, which modify the way in which we interpret and may act on our worlds. Learning is therefore a change in state, which alters how we act on the world and in turn change it by our actions ... [this] allows us to connect knowledge and emotion so that we see that both come into play in our responses. However, because those responses in turn impact on the world, we are both shaped by and shape our worlds. Finally, the model of mind underpinning this view of learning does not emphasise efficient knowledge storage as the be-all and end-all of learning. Rather, the mind looks out on the world, interpreting it and acting on it. (Edwards, 2005b, p. 50)

Here knowledge (possibly acquired from more formal instruction) is recognised and will act on part of a changing process as it 'connects' with emotion, and helps to interpret the specific situation. This influences responses, which in turn are also affected by the situation. For example, a student teacher may wish to use a new kind of individual pupil testing introduced to them at the university in order to gain feedback on pupil progress, but may decide to forego such assessment on a Friday afternoon (but still use it at other times) in favour of a teaching strategy that better fits in with the school department's ethos of not testing pupils at the end of the week. The student teacher may recognise that pupils are more likely to invest in their usual way of working because the teaching decision of complying with the department style appears to endorse accepted routines. However, if this 'within-person change' is not acknowledged in the participation metaphor of learning, the learning is being viewed in a more traditional apprenticeship sense, where learners simply take on and copy existing practices in order to comply with the accepted way of working. This does not allow for knowledge creation, but endorses a static form of learning where the existing practices remain unchanged. In the example above, a student teacher who introduces new ideas on testing (albeit not on a Friday afternoon) could open up new opportunities for considering pupils' progress, and is learning how to do this within the specific department context.

## Types of participation

The discussion on subject department research emphasises the importance a lot of research gives to department culture in providing rich development opportunities for both teachers and student teachers. This sees learning as a social and cultural process, and many of the examples described in the collaborative activities of learning departments acknowledge that learning can be integral to workplace practices. Research that specifically looks at work-based learning explores how learning is part of everyday practices (Eraut *et al.*, 2000, 2002, 2004; Eraut, 2005; Lave and Wenger, 1991; Wenger, 1998; Wenger *et al.*, 2002; Billett, 2002, 2003). This is differentiated from formal learning (that gained from instruction), which is acknowledged but treated separately from learning 'on the job'.

Edwards (2005b, p. 51) distinguishes 'two broad strands of ideas which are both given the participation label', those that look outwards to how cultural conditions interact with the way people think and act, that is how people adapt to different social situations, and those that consider how the social situation is incorporated into the self. The former give a greater emphasis to the individual and, although concerned with cognition, give greater focus to how the learner fits into the learning environment. For example, when looking at how professionals learn in his research, Eraut (2005) does not focus on their inner processes (how the mind connects knowledge with the world) but explores the working conditions that enable learning to happen (the kind of work, the support learners receive and the confidence with which they approach tasks). The emphasis is on individuals and their interaction with the context of the working environment. Patterns of working are compared across professions. In the Early Career Learning at Work Project (Eraut, 2005), explanations and examples of how learning opportunities differ in accountancy, engineering and nursing are elucidated. The research is strongly empirically driven in that the theoretical basis for the investigations is often taken from previous research. For example, findings on mid-career learning (Eraut *et al.*, 2002) are extended to a learning model looking at contextual factors as well as learning factors (Eraut *et al.*, 2004). The LiNEA study considers how new professionals learn to belong to a particular profession and how they are supported in doing this within an apprenticeship type model. The onus is not on creating new knowledge but of learning how to participate in established professional practices.

The theory of communities of practice (Wenger, 1998) can also be seen as 'an account of learning as socialisation into existing beliefs, values and practices'. Lave and Wenger (1991) consider the kind of social engagements that provide the context for learning to take place in their book on situated learning and legitimate peripheral participation. They locate professional learning in the increased access of learners to participating roles in expert performances, but this does not sufficiently address how new knowledge is produced (Edwards, 2005b, p. 57). Engeström *et al.* (1999, p. 12) criticise this 'one-way movement from the periphery', as it neglects to give sufficient attention to movement in other directions: the 'questioning of authority, criticism, innovation, initiation of change'. However, Wenger (1998) does acknowledge that communities are not considered to be static in their ways of working, as 'old timers' and 'newcomers' may disagree and generate competing viewpoints on the practice and its development. Newcomers are in an awkward situation as they need to engage in the existing practice and become full members of the community, but they also have an interest in the development of the community. Therefore, granting 'legitimate participation' to newcomers with their own viewpoints introduces tensions of 'continuity-displacement contradictions' (Lave and Wenger, 1991, p. 115). These may be weakened and controlled by differences in the power structure of relationships, although not necessarily eradicated. Such dynamics of continuity and discontinuity 'propel the practice forward' (Wenger, 1998, p. 101). Wenger *et al.* (2002) have also noted the benefits of newcomers entering into a community. As well as bringing new ideas, their lack of awareness and experience could be useful in getting the more experienced to evaluate their own position.

The kinds of analyses outlined above consider how learners adapt to social situations. They tend to separate how social situations interact with how the learner thinks. Student teachers who are based in subject departments for a relatively short amount of time may regard the departments differently to more established teachers, as they know that their work there is primarily preparing them for succeeding in teaching in other departments when they leave the relatively short school teaching practice. Possible tensions of continuity-displacement may be seen when regarding work in the department with student teachers' ideas on current research and their pedagogical interests. Nevertheless, the community of practice theory does not attempt to analyse what is being learnt in such situations, but concentrates on what is being done, that is how the culture supports the learning. The pressures student teachers exert on wanting to be full rather than peripheral participants in teaching from an early stage have also been noted (Maynard, 2001; Edwards and Protheroe, 2003). Here the desire to 'go it alone' and teach full classes is often seen to outweigh the benefits of a more gradual induction into the work. This way of working also stands in contrast to the Legitimate Peripheral Participation model.

The central research study in this book is interested in school departments as places where new learning can take place. 'If learners are to understand the limitations of practice, they require opportunities to recontextualise their theoretical and practical knowledge and skill in new contexts, in order to create new knowledge and practice' (Griffiths and Guile, 2003, p. 68). The social situations of the departments are important in that they afford and constrain learning opportunities. Vygotsky recognised that all means of cultural behaviour were social and explained this in relation to cultural development, which appears on two planes:

> Each function in cultural development ... appears on the stage twice, in two planes. First as a social, then as a psychological function. First between people as an interpsychological category. (Vygotsky, 1960, p. 197)

It is possible to arrange social situations as learning environments so as to optimise development. Vygotsky believed that successful teaching could create possibilities for development through the kind of active participation that characterises collaboration. It should be 'socially negotiated and entail transfer of control to the learner' (Daniels, 2001, p. 61). In his empirical work, Vygotsky recognised that 'forms of discourse encountered in the social situation of formal schooling provided a framework for the development of conceptual thinking' (Wertsch *et al.*, 1993, p. 344). Consequently, his understanding of the social situation of development was that of 'a series of relations between a learner and social reality' (Vygotsky, 1978, p. 199). This concept is further explored in relation to school subject departments in Chapter 4.

When expert practices are less prescribed, such as the many decisions that are made when teaching in complex classroom environments, teachers have numerous opportunities to reshape their work situation. They therefore need to be continually aware of the purposes and values of their work. Focusing on the social situation for the development of student teachers' learning, it is important to consider whether the school department encourages questions about the purpose of the school situation, rather than simply analysing how learning is enabled by others in the workplace and by the workplace itself. Arguably, this is less of an issue in other professions.

## Is learning by participation enough?

Maynard's (2001, p. 39) consideration of learning as participation questions whether the participation metaphor is sufficient in representing the 'complex relationship' between the newcomer and the school community. The perceived importance of the student teacher 'fitting in' with the social situation and succeeding in their teaching course assessments means that they don't question practice or necessarily think for themselves, but instead superficially adopt other teachers' behaviour and pedagogical strategies. Although giving the appearance of learning, the research exposes student teachers' partial understanding of pedagogical concepts with them unaware of 'the rich and complex meanings' (*ibid.* 46) that teachers often ascribe to these concepts. In school the adoption of partial knowledge may still give the impression of learning at a more sophisticated level.

Data in research on how student teachers' beliefs are mediated through a series of different contexts (from university to first school experience and then to induction year in first post), and the effect that this has on classroom practice also analyses partial understandings of concepts (Smagorinsky *et al.*, 2004; Smagorinsky *et al.*, 2003; Cook *et al.*, 2002). As in Maynard's work, these are compared to Vygotsky's idea of pseudoconcepts: those that appear like a concept use the same terminology but in practice are inconsistently applied and the ideas behind them incorrectly articulated. In Smagorinsky *et al.*'s research (2003) this is illustrated by the incompatible ways a student teacher understands constructivism. Rather than identifying the problem as being the student teacher's, the study questions the variations in how the concept was defined by the teachers in the school department and in the university to explain the confusion: 'the conflicting means of mediation in the environment in which the (student teacher) learned to teach ... an inconsistency between what was espoused and what was practiced' (*ibid.* 1417). Viewing student teaching through the lens of sociocultural learning theory highlights the tensions that arise when student teaching activity spans the boundaries between the university and the school (Roth and Lee, 2007). This brings into focus the complexity of student teacher learning which is mediated by context and culture across activity settings, and stresses the importance of a 'deep understanding of the contexts and cultures within which learners learn' (Anderson and Stillman, 2012, p. 3).

Seeing student teachers who are learning how to engage in the social practices of the school department in which they are placed recognises the situated nature of learning. How this is related to the learning of general principles, from, for example, staff room and mentor conversations or visiting university tutors, can be related to Vygotsky's idea of spontaneous and scientific concepts:

> Spontaneous concepts are learned through cultural practice and because they are tied to learning in specific contexts, allow for limited generalisation in new situations; scientific concepts are learned through formal instruction and, because they are grounded in general principles, can more readily be applied to new situations. (Smagorinsky *et al.*, 2003, p. 1399)

The challenge for school departments which offer opportunities for engagement in their social practices is to enable learners to see relationships between spontaneous and scientific concepts and to take from them experience, mature concepts that will enable them to interpret and work in other school department settings.

## Concluding comments

Arguments for different types of higher education contribution (and consequently different ways that schools should work with student teachers) have been outlined in the English teacher education research for many years (Barker, 1996; Pring, 1996; Blake *et al.*, 1995; Ellis *et al.*, 2010). Those advancing a more technicist view often refer to initial teacher training rather than education and have conceptualised learning to teach as a matter of simply acquiring competence 'on the job' (Furlong and Smith, 1996). This viewpoint is disputed from a range of perspectives, including those that privilege teachers' tacit or 'craft' knowledge (for example, Hagger and McIntyre, 2006). Forms of distributed expertise found in the school context have been increasingly identified as key to student teacher learning (Edwards *et al.*, 2002). Benefits from school-based learning are therefore seen to arise not only from increasing participation in teaching practices but in the critical examination of those practices by participants (Ellis, 2010).

Overly concentrating on prescribed teaching standards limits the opportunities for student teachers to learn, as 'a standards-based technicised approach is unlikely to be responsive either to social contexts or to individual needs' (Menter, 2009, p. 226). A participatory approach to student teacher education leads to questions about why good teachers work in the way that they do. This does not view learning simply as a way of understanding 'what works', but recognises the need to understand why particular strategies work in specific classroom situations. In this school-based approach, one of the mentor teachers' aims is to help student teachers understand the local setting and its practices. Therefore, experienced teachers help student teachers interpret and respond to events by sharing their expertise and local knowledge 'and the reasoning behind their actions' (Skinner, 2010, p. 281). Such a sociocultural pedagogy aims at assisting learners' participation in school communities where knowledge is used and constructed (Edwards *et al.*, 2002; Ellis *et al.*, 2010), and therefore highlights the importance of school practice in teacher preparation. The next chapter elaborates on the idea of a sociocultural pedagogy and outlines the cultural historical activity theory framework for considering student teacher learning opportunities in their school practice.

# 3
# Cultural and Historical Activity Theory: Identifying the Object of Student Teacher Education Activity

## Introduction

Part of what is missing in a lot of the research literature discussed in the last chapter is the need for a detailed understanding of how the phenomena described (for example, the concepts of strategic compliance and department subcultures) are realised in practice. An emphasis on descriptive analysis in some of the literature on school departments does not get to the heart of where contestation is, or how and why it is realised. The focus of analysis in Activity Theory firstly considers the social situation (rather than the individual). 'Activity Theory is increasingly viewed as a potentially fertile paradigm for research in education' (Bakhurst, 2009, p. 197). Activity theorists view activities at work as the basis of learning, and investigate learning processes with reference to the theory. Developments in 'workplace research have been working to re-emphasise individual learning but without losing the social and cultural perspective' (Hodkinson and Hodkinson, 2005, p. 114). Billett (2002) refers to learning at work as a reciprocal process of co-participation. It is about what the workplace affords and how the individual engages with this. In a study on customer service, manufacturing and packaging work environments, Billett (2002) identifies reasons for worker motivation as well as affordances for learning in the work practices, and considers the likely consequences for learning. In researching the vocational curriculum and pedagogy (2003), Billett concentrates on individuals' experiences of learning and proposes the importance of learners gaining a variety of occupational experiences and then transferring understanding from these to other practical experiences. This is promoted in place of concentrating on 'canonical knowledge' (*ibid.* 15) and then transferring this into practice.

Rather than seeking to just develop the capacity to adapt knowledge to operate across the diverse instances of the occupation, through broad or generic competencies, it might be more effective to base expectations of transfer on the variations of practice and experiences within those practices. (Billett, 2003, p. 14)

The idea of transfer (how patterns of behaviour build up in one setting and are then deployed in a new setting as the individual moves between them) is a problem identified by Edwards (2005b) in her discussion on participation learning as it focuses on the individual adapting to different social situations (or workplace activities). Billett (2003) acknowledges the difficulty of considering how learners encounter new situations never previously experienced or how more extreme cases of practice can be catered for in the learner's vocational training. Yet, if the learning analysis focuses on how the environment is incorporated into the individual, the difficulties with the problem of transfer are reduced.

Considering activity systems (Engeström, 1999a) instead of individual workplace practices has the advantage of the analysis of learning being at the systemic level (exploring how tools are used and objects interpreted and expanded in particular activity systems). Looking at opportunities for systemic learning changes the focus of the research to the social context, and shifts attention from the individual to the setting. This better fits with the area of inquiry in researching school subject departments and the student teacher education activity in them. When considering opportunities for learning in school subject departments, this activity theory perspective allows for an analysis of the consequences of different approaches to school-based activities in student teacher education, for example, how mentor meetings, university tutor visits and lesson observations create learning opportunities for student teachers.

## Cultural and historical activity theory

In recent years Cultural and Historical Activity Theory (CHAT) 'has evolved into an influential analytic framework for research into professional learning and work practices' (Warmington, 2011, p. 145). In educational settings there have been many research projects using CHAT to analyse pupil behaviour and teaching in the classroom (O'Brien *et al.*, 2012). For example, focusing on curriculum subjects, CHAT has been used as a theoretical framework to explore the relevance of Chemistry for pupils (Joke, 2004), how pupils relate to History (Hedegaard, 1999) and the use of information technology in Economics (Lim and Barnes, 2005). The CHAT theoretical framework has also been adopted when researching school settings and the relationships between teachers and pupils involved in formative assessment practices (Crossouard, 2009). In my research, CHAT explores learning opportunities for student teachers by addressing the core questions of what and how teachers are learning. Because of its emphasis on settings (social contexts and practices which are the product of cultural history) CHAT looks at how teachers' and student teachers' beliefs are affected, and accounts for changes in their thinking, that is how social systems affect decisions and behaviour. CHAT helps to further illuminate the social situation of student teacher learning in schools by analysing learning processes and by understanding these processes as culturally and historically nested. My using a CHAT framework requires an elaboration of the key concepts involved (mediation, object motive, tools, activity system, the interaction of activity systems and expansive learning). These important concepts are explained below, as seen together they describe the cultural historical psychology that guides my research on the complex settings of school departments. They show how it is possible to 'ground analysis in the culturally organised activities of everyday life' (Cole, 1996, p. 5).

## Mediation

Artefacts and tools mediate the interaction of individuals with their environment (Vygotsky, 1986). These mediators serve as the means by which individuals act upon and are acted upon by the social situation. Vygotsky associated human consciousness with tools in that he believed that one's contact with the world was indirect or mediated by them (Wertsch, 2007). A triangular notion of mediation of subject, tool and object (see Figure 3.1) models how the tool enables the action of subject(s) on the object in activity. Having tools that are central to how one acts and how one is acted upon emphasises the importance of context in that development takes place through the use of these tools and is therefore directly affected by the tools that are available in the social situation. The importance of tool mediation in the development of human consciousness was elaborated by Vygotsky (1986) although he did not use a triangle as below to represent this action.

By analysing tools (their choice and use) one can get an understanding of what is considered important in an activity, as tools indicate how one interprets and tackles a task. Put another way, Cole (1996, p. 108) explains that:

Human *psychological* processes emerge through culturally mediated, historically developing, *practical activity* [emphasis in the original].

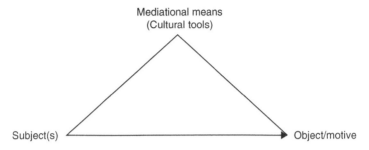

*Figure 3.1* A representation of mediated action and object motive

In considering how the use of tools (for example, course handbooks and lesson plans) differs between subject departments in my research, an aim is to get further insights into how departments' existing practices create learning opportunities for student teachers. There are commonalities of practice between the departments as they are all taking part in the same student teacher education course. However, material tools (for example, course handbooks and student teacher reports) and non-physical tools (for example, speech and the use of language) can take on varying significance and use by the different department participants.

## Object motive

The essence of an activity is that it has an object (the problem space or societally significant goal that is being worked on by the participants in the activity), which in the student teacher education activity could be student teacher learning. This object defines the activity and provides a direction:

> An activity's object is its real motive ... some need always stands behind it. Thus, the concept of activity is necessarily connected with the concept of a motive. (Leont'ev, 1981, p. 59)

The research explores the object of an identified activity (school-based student teacher education, which is one of many school department activities) in order to help reveal aspects of social practice and support interpretations of the ethnographically generated data. In the context of this research, the motive for the activity of school-based student teacher education, as mentioned in Chapter 2, could be seen in a number of different ways. Motives could be about improving student teacher learning, but they could also be about teacher recruitment, creating new department affiliations with higher education institutions and creating better teachers. In other words, a number of activity systems could be in play within the same social setting each with different and potentially conflicting objects. A key contribution of Engeström's third generation of activity theory is the attention he pays to multiple activity systems in play and the potential of contradictions within and between them to become spaces for learning and development (Engeström, 2000).

Some research (Nardi, 2005; Kaptelinen, 2005) questions how far motives can be separated from objects, and therefore whether it is possible to have a number of different motives working towards the same object. Leont'ev (1978) describes the object as the true motive of the activity with other motives fitting into a hierarchy of importance. The possibility of multiple motives working on the same object is important for this research, as this could suggest that identifying different motives (providing they are linked and not in direct opposition) may not necessarily mean that subjects are working on different activities. However, if they are working towards different objects, then the activity is not being understood in the same way. For example, one teacher's motive for being involved in student teacher education may be to develop new ways of teaching and learning in the classroom with a wish to extend their pedagogical knowledge, whilst another may primarily want to 'give something back' to the profession and may greatly enjoy working with new teachers. Whatever their main motives, voicing how they see the object of the activity would help to develop their understanding of it. Participants rarely talk in terms of how the object of an activity is constructed. However, for the researcher, understanding how participants see the object may be possible by analysing how tools are used in the activity (Stetsenko, 2005; Kaptelinin, 2005).

## Tools

Tools are understood as anything that mediates subjects' action upon objects (Russell, 2004). Wertsch (1998) writes extensively on tools and mediated action. He advocates sociocultural analysis as a way of making clear the relationships between human action on the one hand and the cultural, institutional and historical context in which the action occurs on the other. In order to clarify Vygotsky's (1987) earlier discussions on mediation, Wertsch (2007, p 191) notes how mediation emerges in a variety of ways. For example, explicit mediation is where a tool is purposely and obviously introduced in order to develop an activity. This is distinguished from implicit mediation (which 'typically involves spoken language'), where a tool appears more ephemeral, as it is part of everyday communication and may be used unintentionally to mediate actions on tasks.

Tools can be categorised into different types. Within student teacher education, conceptual tools are those that can apply to a number of situations concerning teaching and learning, for example, frameworks like the communicative theory of teaching in Modern Foreign Languages. Practical tools are those that are immediately applicable, for example, resources (lesson plans, observation sheets, reports and handbooks). Engeström finds it useful to categorise tools by the processes involved in their use. He describes four kinds of artefacts or tools and distinguishes between 'what' (naming and prescriptive), 'how' (processual), 'why' (diagnostic and explanatory) and 'where to' (speculative or potentialising) artefacts (Daniels, 2001, p. 91). Tools are not fixed as such but obtain one of these categories depending upon how they are used at a particular time. However, such categorisations can be misleading, as to a certain extent all tools contain a 'where to' element and could be used in such a way to discuss future considerations. For example, a 'how' tool in student teacher education may be a course handbook, which is designed to guide the ways the work on the object can be carried out. But this can also be seen as a 'where to' tool and used to envision the future state or potential development of the object.

Cole (1996) uses Wartofsky's (1979) understanding of different types of artefacts (his preferred name for tools) to suggest that there are three types – primary, secondary and tertiary. Primary tools are ones that are used directly in order to transform an object such as a pen or hammer. Secondary artefacts build on these in that they combine the material with the abstract in order to represent the primary tools, for example, diagrams and words on a page, as in the compilation of a course handbook used to guide the work in student teacher education activity. This tool may become tertiary when used in an entirely abstract way, for example, when handbooks represent an ideology for understanding the object of the student teacher education activity, and consequently their mediating work on the object alters how one looks at the work, and encourages changes in practice. When analysing the use of tools, Wartofsky's (1979) categories encourage the researcher to focus on the kinds of tools that are being used and how they are being appropriated.

The process of adopting a tool when working on an object is referred to as 'appropriation' (Leont'ev, 1981; Wertsch, 1998). This can be seen as a developmental process occurring when using the tool in a social situation. The level at which the tool is appropriated often depends upon how closely the subject's values, experiences and goals are aligned with those of more experienced subjects in the environment (Cole, 1996). Appropriation is particularly important, as through this process, subjects 'reconstruct the knowledge they are internalising, thus transforming both their conception of the knowledge and in turn, that knowledge as it is construed and used by others' (Grossman *et al.*, 1999, p. 15). A mentor, teacher or tutor may appropriate a tool but use it in a different way from its original purpose. Their levels of appropriation may lack complexity. If used superficially, student teachers may not appropriate the tool in a complex way, as the conceptual and theoretical basis on which the tool was initially conceived is not apparent to them in its use. For example, a school mentor may use a student teacher education course handbook as a checklist for ensuring that student teachers are complying with the prescribed tasks in the student teacher education course instead of using it in the way it was designed, as a tool to guide opportunities for student teacher learning by opening out diversity of opinions. The tool is therefore being used instrumentally and acts as a rule in the activity, and does not work on its intended object. A lack of theoretical resources and historical understanding of the tool's purpose may be apparent if this is the case.

In the process of transformation, tools leave traces of their past use which might determine how they are used in the future. Such traces may be expressed as rules, which guide how the tool is used (Boag-Munroe, 2006, p. 82). Engeström (2000) defines rules as being either explicit or implicit rules, regulations, norms and conventions that constrain actions and interactions within the activity system. They can also open possibilities for action. Rules in a student teacher education partnership may be designed to enable tools and artefacts to work on the object of student teacher learning. These tools (course handbooks, subject profiles and descriptors, schemes of work, student teacher reports, discourse and focused conversations for example) would be used in mentor meetings, university tutor visits and lesson observations. In themselves the rules may lead to learning opportunities, but do not necessarily guarantee this if they and the tools simply ensure that tasks are carried out instrumentally. In such situations, they remain as rules and may not work on the object at all. When analysing the significance and use of tools, and how they are inherently situated culturally, institutionally and historically, one can consider a number of claims that characterise them in the context of the department's cultural history. Are the tools used because of historical precedence? Are the tools employed because they are a fixed and unquestioned part of the context?

In order to give an account of culturally mediated thinking it is necessary to specify not only the tools and artefacts through which behaviour is mediated but also the circumstances in which the thinking occurs (Cole, 1996, p. 131). It is therefore necessary to consider the social structures of the situation in the subject department that affords and constrains the negotiations around the tool's meaning, as well as considering how the tools are being appropriated. In conducting research of this kind, Kaptelinin and Miettinen recommend concentrating on this and on the evolution of cultural tools:

> The only way to get an insight into the nature of an object-related activity is to understand the material production of tools, the social exchanges among people, and the individual subjective processes that participate in regulating the production of tools and social exchanges. (Kaptelinin and Miettinen, 2005, p. 3)

By considering how cultural tools are involved in activity enables one to see beyond the individual when trying to understand what shapes human activity. This enables one to view how tools are used at a systemic level. As Engeström *et al.* (1999, p. 8) point out:

> Any local activity resorts to some historically formed mediating artefacts, cultural resources that are common to the society at large.

Specific tools produced for student teacher education may be appropriated differently in different activity systems. In the school department they may be sidelined as mediating artefacts on student teacher learning in favour of more informal feedback and discussion based on contextual information from the school practice. Consequently, the use of language and discourse could become the main tool for mediating learning.

### Activity systems

Whilst advocating the study of tools as central to how people work, learning in CHAT is considered at the level of the system. Engeström (1987) enlarges the activity from a model of subject – tool – object to include community, rules and division of labour. This expansion of Figure 3.1 'aims to represent the social/collective elements in an activity system while emphasising the importance of analysing their interactions with each other' (Warmington *et al.*, 2004, p. 5). This provides 'a unit of analysis in the concept of object-oriented, collective, and culturally mediated human activity, or activity system' (Engeström *et al.*, 1999, p. 9). This (illustrated in Figure 3.2) creates Engeström's second generation of activity theory. Particularly appropriate to this research, it emphasises the importance of the study of the collective within a system of activity, with the analysis focusing on contextual and historical elements. This is relevant to school subject departments participating in student teacher education because there are a number of teachers in each department supporting student teachers, and all will have had different experiences in relation to the student teacher education work in the department and in relation to their own training as teachers.

The activity system is created from the perspective of the subjects working in it, those working in school-based student teacher education in the subject departments in the research school. This includes the school mentors, the teachers working with the student teachers, the university tutors (but only in so far as their visits to the school are concerned) and other staff in the school with responsibility for student teacher education (for example, a senior manager who co-ordinates the programme). By using tools, participants will act on the object in order to produce an outcome. So a teacher mentor might use a planning framework as a tool in a conversation with a student teacher. Figure 3.3 illustrates an activity system for school-based student teacher education and helps to put student teacher learning in the research school into a context:

> Human activity is endlessly multifaceted, mobile, and rich in variations of content and form ... the theory of activity should reflect that richness and mobility. Such a multivoiced theory should not regard internal contradictions and debates as signs of weakness; rather they are an essential feature of the theory. (Engeström, 1999a, p. 20)

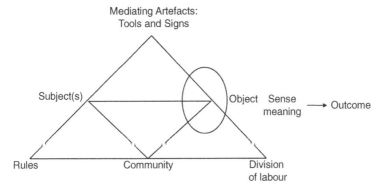

*Figure 3.2* The structure of a human activity system (Engeström, 1987, p. 78)

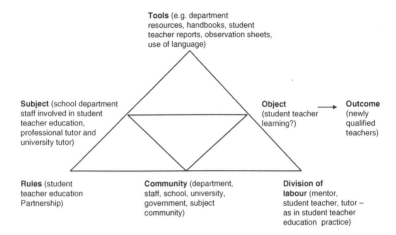

*Figure 3.3*  An activity system for school-based student teacher education

Figure 3.3 highlights the multivoiced influences on the student teacher learning process. This helps explore how and where the process of student teacher learning differs in the subject departments, and considers the numerous influences and contradictions on the departments (for example, the subject communities, central subject specific initiatives and the organisation of the student teacher education programme).

### Interaction between activity systems

Participants in the student teacher education activity systems are working in more than one activity system, as their work is complex and requires them to be involved in a number of different activities. For example, a teacher may also be working as a tutor, year team or department leader. Hence, their interpretations of the student teacher education activity system object could be seen differently as a result of working in other activity systems:

> Given our capacity to inhabit multiple activity systems ... what matters most is our ability to recognise and engage in these relationships in order to enhance our interpretations of the objects of our actions and resources that might support those actions. (Edwards and D'Arcy, 2004, p. 150)

A focus on performance from a department leader (who may be working on the activity of improving pupil test results) may strongly affect a student teacher education activity system's object. For example, whilst a mentor may focus on the student teacher's learning, a department leader may see the student teacher as an extra pair of hands. Hence, the object of the student teacher education activity system may be understood differently (or even contested) by the system's participants, who are likely to bring many motives to the collective activity. This effect on the object by multiple activity systems is illustrated in Figure 3.4.

Therefore, Third Generation Activity Theory has joint activity as its unit of analysis, and addresses the structure of the social world with a focus on possible contradictions in the interaction of multiple activity systems' objects. Engeström (in Warmington *et al.*, 2004, p. 5) sees evolution as the 'transitions and reorganisations within and between activity systems'. Tensions may arise from different activity system perspectives, but these may not necessarily represent problems and may help to develop the activities in innovative ways.

Engeström (1995, p. 333) acknowledges diversity in activity systems when he considers polycontextuality and boundary crossing. For successful collaboration, it is necessary to connect separate systems. Student teacher education activity systems in a university and a school are from 'familiar domains' and should therefore more likely succeed in 'collective concept formation'. Tools used in student teacher education that operate in both the university and the school (course handbooks, observation sheets and reports) could be considered as 'different types of shared external representations of a problem', for example, the problem of student teacher learning, and 'the realisation of their potential

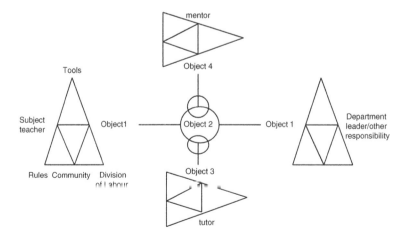

*Figure 3.4* Third Generation Activity Theory – School Teachers

depends upon the way they are used' (Engeström, 1995, p. 322). This research aims to capture important interactive processes and mediating tools involved in boundary meeting and in crossing activity systems. These processes and tools are constructed and employed by departments and individuals in ways that may vary and develop.

## Expansive learning

Activity can constantly change, and this is shown in the idea of the expansive cycle (Engeström and Cole, 1997). The expansive cycle is the result of a process of what Vygotsky (1978) termed 'internalisation' and 'externalisation': a learner absorbing what is around them, interpreting it (internalisation) and, consequently, acting in and on their social worlds in newly informed ways (externalisation). Expansive learning is important to activity theory work:

> The theory of expansive learning ... is a method of grasping the essence of an object by tracing and reproducing theoretically the logic of its development, of its historical formation through the emergence and resolution of its inner contradictions. A new theoretical idea or concept is initially produced in the form of an abstract, simple explanatory relationship, a *germ cell* [emphasis in the original]. In an expansive learning cycle, the initial simple idea is transformed into a complex object, into a new form of practice. (Engeström, 2008, p. 129)

Beginning with the 'germ cell' of people questioning established practices, expansive learning is possible when work is collaborative and new forms of practice are developed. 'The object and motive of the activity are reconceptualised to embrace a wider horizon of possibilities than in the previous mode of the activity' (Edwards, 2010a, p. 160). This way of working is feasible with CHAT, which can be used with an interventionist methodology (see Chapter 11) where researchers work directly with participants in the activity system in order to develop new tools and transform the objects they are working on (Engeström, 1999a; Cole, 1996). The learning comes from individuals questioning practice, which leads to analysis (that is, looking at how practice has evolved in the social situation) with the possible outcome of recommending solutions to any tensions raised. Subsequent new ideas or models of practice may be considered and then implemented in order to create a new form of practice. Engeström divided this process into learning actions, and these form an expansive learning cycle.

## Critiques of CHAT

Criticisms of CHAT have questioned how appropriately the activity system model accounts for aspects of power (Avis, 2009; Langemayer, 2006), especially with regard to the division of labour and the different roles which subjects play within the activity. Warmington's study (2011, p. 144) on professional learning of staff working in multi-professional children's services notes an 'insufficient distinction in activity theory between divisions on the horizontal plane (that is, between different professional groupings and agencies) and the vertical plane (that is, relationships between staff and their managers)'. Consequently, wider social tensions around the management and control of labour may be little acknowledged in activity systems that are primarily depicted as having self-regulatory subjects working on an activity's object. Similarly, an activity theory approach although offering 'radical possibilities' is criticised by Avis (2009, p. 151) for neglecting 'the wider social context in which activity systems are located'. This view is echoed by Piem (2009) who highlights the 'radical localism' that he says is the end-point of the historical trajectory of CHAT despite it addressing issues from a more historically ambitious starting point (O'Brien *et al.*, 2012, p. 257).

The theoretical validity of activity theory has been questioned by Bakhurst (2009) who considers CHAT as a method or a model for analysing activity systems rather than a coherently developed theoretical position. He considers how the theoretical position around the concept of activity has changed since it was first explored in Russian philosophy and psychology with the work of Vygotsky, Leont'ev and Luria (see Bakhurst (2009) for a discussion on the development of activity theory). Similarly, Roth (2013) notes problems which have arisen from the difficulties of translating from the original Russian writing of Leont'ev and the consequent loss of meaning and underused aspects of cultural historical activity theory. Nevertheless, Bakhurst (2009, p. 206) accepts that even with minimum predictive power, the activity theory model 'seems to work particularly well for the sorts of activity systems that activity theorists typically study: health care, work settings, some education contexts'. Acknowledging that my research does not focus on the wider social context beyond the school departments, CHAT is nevertheless an appropriate theory for exploring and helping to develop an understanding of how the school subject departments are working in relation to the opportunities they are affording student teachers. Therefore, even though the use of the theory is restricted to a departmental focus, CHAT provides a 'framework that has considerable potential for researchers who are interested in how conditions for learning are created' (Edwards, 2005b, p. 55).

## The use of CHAT in the research

The central research study in this book studies the work settings in education contexts and follows the steps at the start of the expansive learning cycle (identifying tensions and analysing how practice has evolved in the social situation). But this study does not then work for change, as in Engeström's Developmental Work Research method (2006) as in the research reported in Chapter 11. Even though the research does not change the system (as would be Engeström's intention) a consideration of the potential and the possibilities for expansive learning (when regarding the analysis done in the school departments) is possible. This happens by hypothesising on the capacity of departments to change their practices in student teacher education in order to help student teachers manage their relationship with the social situation of development. In other words, to consider a recommendation from a government report on student teacher preparation, the research questions student teachers' agency and how far they have control of their learning: 'many find themselves in situations where they appear to be "done to" rather than actively and proactively "doing"' (Ashby *et al.*, 2008, p. 76).

As subject departments in secondary schools are complex organisational settings for student teachers' learning, it is helpful to augment the focus on mediation with attention to the collective practices of the departments by drawing on CHAT. CHAT is helpful because it enables a setting where people are working together on a shared task or object to be examined in order to see if it is a system that is conducive to learning (Edwards, 2005a). The object of inquiry is the student teacher education work in each subject department and not the departments and the variety of activities that occur there. For analytic purposes I present the activity of student teacher education in each department as an activity system, which reduces the focus of the research to the student teacher education work. Modelling the activity of student teacher education as a system allows for comparisons across departments, for example, in exploring what tools are used and how they are employed. It also enables a consideration of how different activity systems interact with one another.

CHAT allows researchers to consider the practices identified in an activity system in a broad context, taking into account how and why these have developed in the past. Therefore, insights into why department staff work the way they do in student teacher education activities may be gleaned from questioning how their practices have developed over time and in relation to other practices in the department. It is important to achieve a sense of the evolution of student teacher education activity in order to reflect on present practice and the construction of the current social situation of teacher development experienced by the student teachers. In using Engeström's activity system models to assist the cross-department analysis, I recognise that I am talking about student teacher education as an activity where its object is negotiated, unfolding and often indeterminable. Nevertheless, the activity system heuristic is helpful because it allows an exploration of whether people share their understandings of objects and outcomes of systems by considering their use of tools.

## Concluding comments

The research focuses on student teacher learning opportunities in subject departments and questions why they may be different. CHAT concepts are used to analyse the units of analysis, which are the tools being used to mediate the work on the object of the department's student teacher education activity system. How tools are used when working with student teachers reveals what the participants see as the objects of the student teacher education activity systems. How the student teachers perceive their capacity for freedom of movement (their agency) within the activity system in which they are participating will affect their learning. This will likely be dependent on the participants they are working with and how they are enabled in that work. Taylor (1985, pp. 3–16) considers one's power of self-evaluation as 'an essential feature of the mode of agency' and describes how being a person 'is to exist in a space defined by distinctions of worth'. He acknowledges that even though such feelings of worth come from one's own self-understanding, they may also 'have been given authoritatively by the culture more than they have been elaborated in the deliberation of the person concerned'. In student teacher education the student teacher will look to the expertise in the school department to assist them in interpreting their actions and the environment they are in. This necessitates a form of relational agency (Edwards, 2005a, p. 171) so as to 'align one's thought and actions with those of others in order to interpret problems of practice and to respond to those interpretations'. Such support should not encourage dependency or compliance but encourage a mutual and collaborative engagement with the world.

The effects of interacting activity systems are also considered with regard to the impact they have on how the student teacher education activity system object is construed. CHAT is a useful theoretical perspective for the research as it focuses on interrogating practices, and pays attention to motives inherent in an activity's object. These motives reflect professional values and opinions on teaching and learning, and the purpose of education. This is an important part of student teacher learning if it is recognised that student teacher education needs to prepare student teachers as responsive learners rather than simply inducting them into long-established practices (Edwards, 2010b).

# 4
# The Methodological Implications of Working Ethnographically

In Chapter 2 I outlined the possible factors that make school subject departments different as places to learn and highlighted the importance of the department setting for student teachers in their school practice. In Chapter 3 I explained how this research views learning as a social and cultural process, and why CHAT is an appropriate theory for the research. This chapter describes the design for the study accepting that in social science research the theoretical perspective should inform the research design. The chapter illustrates how seeing subject departments as case studies and also as social situations for the development of student teacher learning enables research of school subject departments, in relation to their student teacher education activity systems, over an extended period of time.

## Research questions

As outlined in the last chapter, CHAT focuses on how tools mediate work on an object of activity. Vygotsky (1986) saw language as a key psychological tool and this was regarded as being in a dialectic relationship with the development of thinking. Thinking is not just represented in spoken language and speech, but is worked on through, and in speech in a kind of constant movement that works backwards and forwards between the two. Similarly, participants that use tools to mediate work on an object are affected when the object works back on them. In the same way, when a teacher uses a tool to mediate work on a student teacher's learning, the learning works back on the teacher and affects future learning opportunities. It is therefore appropriate to talk in terms of learning opportunities as constructed and reconstructed, as in the first research question:

1. What are the opportunities for student teacher learning as constructed and reconstructed in different departments in one school?

One aim was to highlight possible tensions in learning opportunities for student teachers working within subject departments and this was inherent in the first research question. The second research question sought to explore why departments worked differently, and identify the reasons for this:

2. If not the same, to what extent and why are these learning opportunities constructed differently?

Initial responses to these questions started to describe the similarities and differences noted in the ways the departments worked with student teachers, and gave suggestions as to why this was so. These questions were viewed as central to the research. However, because I was using CHAT concepts to further analyse the data, specific questions were also asked within this intellectual framework as a means of exploring these issues. These were asked of each school department in order to guide the subsequent data generation and analysis for the study:

- How are student teacher education tools used and appropriated by participants in the department student teacher education activity systems?
- How do participants understand the objects and outcomes of the department student teacher education activity systems?
- How do the department student teacher education activity systems interact with other activity systems?

These questions enabled an analysis and comparison of the student teacher education activity systems in the departments and the social practices that occurred in relation to the student teacher education activity. They also questioned the evolution of student teacher education practices in the different departments together with participants' histories in relation to student teacher education. Tensions and contradictions noted in the student teacher education activity systems fed into further exploration and analyses of the student teacher education activity.

## The research school: Market Town High School

The selection of Market Town High School as a place to conduct the central research study in this book was made for a number of reasons, one of them being the recommendations of academic staff at Downtown University. The university staff were well positioned for suggesting research schools for a study of this kind, in that they had worked with a lot of schools over a number of years in the student teacher education course, and had additionally participated in student teacher education research with different schools in the past. Additionally, Market Town High School was well regarded for the way its staff worked with the university, and had many connections with the work of the university's student teacher education course, with which it had been involved for over fifteen years. The school worked with a number of Higher Education Institutions with regard to student teacher education, and received recognition and funding for its teacher development activities. Therefore, the research site was chosen based on issues of appropriateness and of opportunity (Silverman, 2011).

Situated in a small market town in England, Market Town High School was seen as a large successful 11- to 18-year-old mixed comprehensive school based on two school sites, one lower school for pupils in the first three years and approximately two miles away an upper school site for the older pupils. The most recent government inspection took place during the spring term of the research year and the report noted that there were over 2000 pupils on roll. The school was commended for its wide range of very effective partnerships with schools, colleges and other agencies. In the research year, Downtown University had 15 student teachers at the school, six for the first school practice and nine for the second. The departments were faculty based with Geography and History part of the Humanities faculty and Modern Foreign Languages (MFL) and Science faculties comprising departments in French, German and Spanish and Chemistry, Biology and Physics, respectively. For ease of reference in the research, the four areas that the student teachers worked (Geography, History, MFL and Science) are referred to as subject departments. The split site nature of the school added some complication to the organisation with department team rooms and general school staff rooms located on each site, with the majority of staff, but no pupils, commuting between sites for some lessons. Because of this, all lessons had a minimum 20-minute break between them in order to allow for commuting time.

## Downtown University and the student teacher education course

As outlined in the introduction, when explaining how student teacher education has become more school-based in its design, there are a number of features that now characterise all one-year full-time Postgraduate Certificate of Education courses. In England, schools share responsibility with the partner university for a variety of aspects, from the interviewing of prospective student teachers and planning student teacher education activities in school to training and assessing the student teachers during their school practice. The provision of Downtown University's Postgraduate Certificate of Education course was seen as very successful as indicated by numerous reports, including high grades in government inspections, and positive internal course evaluation outcomes. The number of student teachers gaining employment subsequent to course completion was high, and many schools showed a willingness to participate in the student teacher education partnership.

At Downtown University the first school practice was over an eight-month period with student teachers spending two days a week in the school for the first six weeks, increasing to three for the following four weeks in the autumn term. The remainder of the teaching practice they worked in school full time before changing to a much shorter second teaching practice in another school lasting approximately six weeks in the summer term. Each student teacher worked with a mentor who had reduced teaching time in order to work with the student teachers. The university also assigned a professional tutor (as well as specialist curriculum tutors who visited the school subject departments on average four times a year) in order to work with the student teacher co-ordinator in the school on the development and delivery of a general programme concentrating on whole school issues that were not covered in subject department settings. These arrangements although well established within this student teacher education course are now typical of arrangements in courses generally in England.

## Research design

It is worth recognising how a researcher's selection and use of a research design and research methods reflects their beliefs about the nature of data and how this can be generated. Locating research in relation to paradigms is important in order to enable a greater awareness of the inclinations of researchers and the relevance of key concepts such as validity and reliability (Newby, 2010). When discussing the nature of qualitative research, Stake (1995) comments on the distinction between research that aims to give explanations and research that promotes understanding. The latter has a sociological and/or psychological emphasis connected with the idea of future change coming as a result of new understandings, which is the desired outcome of this research. This is less likely in research based on explanations.

## Case study as a research focus

Differences in emphasis in qualitative research noted above can be related to differences in case studies, where some seek to identify cause-and-effect relationships whilst others seek the 'understanding of human experience' (Stake, 2000, p. 438). Simons (2009, p. 20) compares well-known case study theorists' definitions of case study design and highlights variations in the kinds of methods used (qualitative and quantitative), whether they are defined by the phenomena being studied, and their usefulness for generalising 'truths about the human condition'. Simons extends her definition by including the research purpose and focus of case studies:

> Case study is an in-depth exploration from multiple perspectives of the complexity and uniqueness of a particular project, policy, institution, programme or system in a 'real life' context. It is research-based, inclusive of different methods and is evidence-led. The primary purpose is to generate in-depth understanding of a specific topic (as in a thesis), programme, policy, institution or system to generate knowledge and/or inform policy development, professional practice and civil or community action. (Simons, 2009, p. 21)

In terms of this study, its design is a collective case study 'where several cases are studied to form a collective understanding of the issue', that draws on an ethnographic case study approach, as it uses qualitative methods and 'is concerned to understand the case(s) in relation to a theory of culture' (Simons, 2009, pp. 21 and 23).

Case study is a research focus, a 'choice of what is to be studied' (Stake, 2000, p. 435) rather than strictly a methodological choice. Identifying the boundaries of cases is sometimes difficult, but considering them as 'bounded systems' with 'patterned behaviour' can be useful concepts when specifying them (*ibid.*, p. 436). A case study approach is often chosen because of its emphasis on looking in depth, and this provides 'rich data' (Geertz, 1973) for the researcher to analyse. A case study design enables a focus on the social construction of cases, with the nature of cases realised in social action:

> Case study seeks to engage with and report the complexity of social activity in order to represent the meanings that individual social actors bring to those settings and manufacture in them. Case study assumes that 'social reality' is created through social interaction, albeit situated in particular contexts and histories, and seeks to identify and describe before trying to analyse and theorize. (Stark and Torrance, 2005, p. 33)

The case studies in this research are the first part of the findings reported. The intention is to identify and describe the school subject departments and establish the social contexts for student teacher learning opportunities. One aim in providing the details in the case studies is to understand them as individual cases rather than to generalise them to a population of school subject departments at large (Hamilton and Corbett-Whittier, 2013; Thomas, 2011). The four school departments had important atypical features, relationships and situations, but they were mainly chosen as a purposive sample as they were the only departments at Market Town High School that took part in Downtown University's student teacher education course. I chose to research these four departments in particular because I felt I could learn the most from studying these cases rather than limiting the number of cases further or working with multiple student teacher education courses in the same school, or with one teacher education course in a number of schools.

## Case studies of school subject departments as social situations for the development of student teacher learning

In looking at how the learning opportunities in school departments could afford or constrain student teacher learning, learning was considered in terms of the changing relationship a learner had with, in Vygotsky's terms, their social situation of development: 'the social situation of development is ... a system of relations between the child of a certain age and social reality' (Vygotsky, 1978, p. 199). When considering child developmental psychology, Vygotsky emphasised the social situation and considered cognitive ability not as a natural entity but as a sociocultural construct that emerges from interactions with the social situation of development (Kozulin, 1998). This view of learning highlights a complex and dynamic relation between the individual (the student teacher) and the social context in which the individual works (in this case the school and the subject department). As the student teachers were exposed to the department situation, their own values and beliefs were considered in light of this, and consequently their way of working in the department was newly affected. In turn these values and beliefs may have also contributed to the department's way of working. Therefore, they were not only being influenced by the social situation of their learning, but they were also influencing it themselves. Transforming oneself in the process of transforming the social situation suggests that in order to understand one aspect (the learner) one has to understand the other (collectively, the social situation). Therefore, in terms of exploring the learning opportunities for student teachers in school-based student teacher education, it is necessary to understand the subject department they are learning in. For example, research on student teacher learning shows that there is frequently a difference between the values and practices in higher education institutions that run student teacher education courses and schools where teaching practices take place (Furlong, 2000; Grossman, *et al.*, 1999; Mutton and Butcher, 2008; Smagorinsky *et al.*, 2003, 2004). Consensus may not be apparent on the motive of student teacher education activity, so competing outcomes can exist. Tensions may arise when a student teacher is encouraged by the university to experiment in order to try out different teaching strategies, and yet is expected by the school to show competence as a teacher in order to successfully complete the teaching course and gain a professional qualification.

## Ethnography

All methodologies are theorised to some extent, and this research clearly uses a CHAT framework to analyse the research data. However, the methodological process in generating data entailed decisions as to how this should be done in order to benefit the research's purpose. Generating data through participant observation of school-based teacher education activity and interviewing all those involved about their understanding of and participation in all aspects of student teacher education allowed me to address the research questions about student teachers' learning opportunities in the school setting. Being in the school setting for 80 days enabled me to gain an understanding of how staff interpreted their working situations. Characteristics typical of ethnography are shared with many of those associated with a case study design, such as extended time engaged in fieldwork, the generation of descriptive and multiple sources of data, the development of relationships with respondents and detailed understandings of the research site (Madden, 2010; Stake, 1995).

*The process of analysis in ethnography*

Traditionally, the ethnographer creates a 'thick description' (Geertz, 1973) from making analytic notes on data and establishing categories and codes. Once developed these create the language of analysis. Sometimes concepts may be used from existing literature, but the challenge comes from fitting the specifics of analysis into an analytical whole. I approached the evidence using a specific theoretical perspective to understand student teachers' learning opportunities in the school departments. Initial coding in my research was primarily organisational in order to arrange the data into themes (Cresswell, 2012), for example, subject department team rooms, course handbooks and mentor meetings. My subsequent use of CHAT to view and then drive my data was significant in that it provided a stronger theoretical input than would be usual in traditional ethnography. My observations as a participant observer, the interviews I conducted and the documentation I studied were all arranged around the school student teacher education activities in four subject departments. This also meant that initial flexible planning became more strategic as the year progressed.

In the ethnographic process, foreshadowed problems are accepted to frame the initial focus, but producing and analysing materials from multiple sources and perspectives are considered important in order to prevent over-steering from private ideas and concepts: 'a commonly remarked advantage of ethnography and of case study work in particular is its relative openness compared to other methodological approaches' (Hargreaves, 1987, p. 24). Once formed, ethnographic propositions, descriptions or theories are explored and tested in terms of their general scope against further data in a process of 'progressive focusing' (Glaser and Strauss, 1967). Data generation continues until one no longer sees different things and reaches theoretical saturation (Ball, 1991):

> The aim is to arrive at an understanding of events that can be expressed in terms of a general statement about variations and patterns that have been noted within data and ... checked against individual empirical instances. (Beach, 2005, p. 9)

Therefore, data is produced primarily to help change, expand and/or develop an idea by guiding the production of field materials for analysis. The process of developing a theory comes from the emergent design, which is often considered to be the distinguishing feature of ethnography (Walford and Massey, 1998):

> The most difficult skill to learn is how to make everything come together – how it might integrate one's separate, if cumulative analyses. If the final product is an integrated theory, then integrating is the accurate term for this complex process. (Strauss, 1987, p. 170)

However, by using a CHAT analytic framework the design in this research was there from the start and was not emergent. The content and not the theory emerged in line with the theoretical concepts and enabled contrast and comparison work. The goal was not the concept itself, but I used and adapted established concepts to explain and describe the differences in the opportunities for student teacher learning, and gave reasons as to why they existed. The CHAT framework helped to structure the analysis, but it was also open to meanings and interpretation. I therefore took some research techniques from ethnography (Mills and Morton, 2013) and embedded these in a CHAT theoretical approach. Therefore, an interrelationship between theory and technique became my methodology.

### Data generation

The dataset comprises extensive field notes written *in situ*, transcripts of recordings of interviews and numerous documents. The data discussed in the findings is representative of the research as a whole, with each subject department hosting a number of student teachers during two school teaching practices in the student teacher education course (see Table 4.1).

Although not rule-driven, when addressing criteria for validity and reliability, it is necessary and useful to outline the research methods used (observations, interviews and document analysis) and the decisions made and conventions followed when working with them during data generation and analysis. This helps to make the process transparent whilst also gaining the reader's trust in the quality of the research. A number of tests applicable to social science research have been set out with regard to validity and reliability in order that researchers meet accepted criteria for 'truthful' accounts (see Yin (2003) for example). Although useful to a certain extent, these can 'gloss over the more problematic and philosophical issues in the nature of qualitative knowledge production' (Stark and Torrance, 2005, p. 40). Reflecting a common

*Table 4.1*   Nature of the fieldwork data

| Nature of data | S1 | S2 | Total |
|---|---|---|---|
| Market Town High School visits | 59 | 21 | 80 |
| School interviews | 24 | 31 | 55 |
| Lesson observations | | | |
| MFL | 11 | 2 | 13 |
| History | 9 | 2 | 11 |
| Geography | 9 | 2 | 11 |
| Science | 16 | 1 | 17 |
| Total | 45 | 7 | 52 |
| Mentor meetings (student teachers) | | | |
| MFL | 12(2) | 3(2) | 15(4) |
| History | 9(1) | 4(2) | 13(3) |
| Geography | 11(1) | 4(2) | 15(3) |
| Science | 15(2) | 4(3) | 19(5) |
| Total | 47(6) | 15(9) | 62(15) |
| Downtown University tutor interviews | 0 | 6 | 6 |

*Note*: S1 – first school practice.
S2 – second school practice.

view, Hammersley (1990) focuses on attempts by researchers to develop 'true' accounts:

> By validity, I mean truth, interpreted as the extent to which an account accurately represents the social phenomena to which it refers. (Hammersley, 1990, p. 57)

Seen as prototypes, the case studies are not intended to be viewed as a representative sample from which macro-level generalisation can be made. However, it is important to show concern for the 'truthfulness' in explanations of how methods for generating data were conducted, but in doing so one must accept the limitations of the definition of truth with regard to the validity of the data when operating within an inter-pretivist research paradigm, as a participant researcher clearly working with a given sociocultural theoretical framework.

*Observations*

In participant observation one aim is to explain the meanings of the experiences of the observed through the experience of the observer. By spending a long time in the field it is possible for the researcher's focus to narrow and broaden in searching for breadth and depth in order to portray a cultural landscape, which is rich enough in detail for others to comprehend and appreciate (Fetterman, 1998). The major strength of direct observation is exactly in its directness, and this method encourages access not only to behaviours of participants but to attitudes, opinions and feelings as well (Cohen *et al.*, 2011).

Initially observation was about familiarisation with the departments and staff, and when observing lessons, I was able to experience aspects of department organisation and its geographical layout. Observations of student teachers' lessons were particularly useful for giving context to the feedback sessions student teachers had with class teachers, the mentor and tutor. I divided my time equally between the four departments but still noted key points in the week when I would attend activities wherever they happened to be (for example, mentor meetings and tutor visits). It was a source of frustration, especially at the beginning of the fieldwork that I felt I was always missing out. I quickly learned to accept 'the inevitable tensions of knowledge as partial ... and the impossibility of telling everything' (Britzman 2003, p. 253). However, questions and strategic decisions were constantly at the forefront of the fieldwork. I took Troman's (2002, p. 112) advice that 'in the serendipitous relationship the researcher needs to sustain a level of awareness in order to make maximum advantage of situations'. To make others more comfortable, some weeks I would act as if shadowing a particular student teacher. This was possible in the first teaching practice as there were only six student teachers from Downtown University in the school. This also meant it perfectly natural that I was around the department workspace with the student teachers, often looking at documentation in order not to participate actively in department conversations.

Most observation data was generated during the first school practice, as a lot of time in the shorter second practice was spent interviewing the staff that had worked with the student teachers. Consequently, the second group of student teachers were observed once during the university tutor visit and during a number of their mentor meetings. The mentors worked in role throughout the two teaching practices, and therefore I was able to see them working with different student teachers. However, some university tutors changed for the second practice (in Geography and Science), and in MFL the first school practice tutor worked with just one of the student teachers, and another tutor (who was also a part-time teacher at the school) worked with the other student teacher in the second practice.

*Researcher position*

What is observed during research reflects how one conceptualises the world with the methodological framework for the research determining what is seen. In generating data, it is important to question oneself through a reflexive approach taking account of the role one plays as a research instrument with choices to make in what to observe and how (Mauthner and Doucet, 2003; Alvesson and Skoldberg, 2009). My previous role as a member of a senior leadership team in school meant that as a researcher, I felt that I was perhaps viewed in a more informal and less potentially threatening way. As a senior teacher, one always wants things from staff and therefore may be seen as a fairly demanding colleague in comparison with an interested researcher. I felt that my presence was not daunting, and the majority of staff appeared confident in their work and proud of what they were doing with student teachers and within student teacher education. Also, the student teachers themselves were very used to constructive criticism, and so my non-judgemental manner was welcomed. Again, I felt I was considered as a non-threatening friendly face who had also experienced student teacher school practices during my own training.

I decided from the start to play as much of a non-participant role as possible (Breakwell *et al.*, 2012). I aimed to emphasise that the teachers' participation was a help to me. I suspect that any criticism may have changed the dynamic considerably, which may not necessarily be detrimental to research, but for the purposes of this research, I didn't think it would help me get a better understanding of the learning opportunities for student teachers in the student teacher education activities in the school departments, especially as I was seeing the practice over a long period of time, and my aim was to analyse a current situation rather than to change it or even make that situation more clear to those participating in it. When in small meetings (mentor meetings, for example with just one mentor and one student teacher), I aimed for a sense of familiarity and trust in order to best combat reactivity. I sat alongside the participants and took notes constantly. My field notes were handwritten in small notebooks, transcribed by myself and imported into qualitative data computer software. Guided by my own prior knowledge and experience of student teacher education and schools, and trying to make 'as few assumptions as possible' (Walford, 2009, p. 274), I noted all details relevant to the focus of the research and recorded key utterances verbatim, underlining them in my notes.

*Interviews*

The interviews were designed to find out what participants thought about issues relating to student teacher education, and encouraged an articulation of their tacit perceptions, feelings and understandings. I focused on their understandings rather than checking any accuracy of accounts, and in doing this I hoped to explore the relationships between similar or different feelings or perceptions (O'Reilly, 2012). This resulted in making explicit those ideas that had hitherto been implicit. I believed that interviews were an effective way of exploring the conceptual position taken by participants with regard to their work in student teacher education. However, it is accepted that an interviewer will inevitably make a difference to how a participant acts, no matter how controlled, bland or pre-determined the interviewer's behaviour is (Punch, 2009). Answers will be framed in terms of reciprocal understanding as meanings emerge during the course of the interview. By its nature, an interview situation is unnatural, and it could be argued that to try to regulate it so that it is as close an approximation to a model of scientific research (even more unnatural) as possible is inappropriate for exploring people's understandings. Accepted therefore as 'a fallible source of information about the world and as providing data about participant's perspectives' (Hammersley, 2003, p. 119), the interview can provide data relevant to (and sometimes testing of) the adequacy of the research problems identified.

The data generated examined understandings relating to social, cultural and historical circumstances, and therefore the information was contextually grounded. Advocating a more unstructured and flexible interview strategy in order to create a guided conversation to elicit rich and detailed information for qualitative analysis, Mishler analyses interview data in terms of contextually grounded discourse:

> My intent is to shift attention away from investigators' 'problems', such as technical issues of reliability and validity, to respondents' problems, specifically, their efforts to conduct coherent and reasonable worlds of meaning, and to make sense of their experiences. (Mishler, 1991, p. 118)

In order to understand the meaning of the participants' responses as much as possible, I let them control the flow of topics with relatively few questions, and encouraged them to extend their responses. I did not want to lose the importance of contextual meaning when analysing the data, and initially tended towards more narrative accounts of the qualitative information, thereby treating the data as contextually grounded discourse. Because I wanted to assess subjective perceptions that were related to past experience and current social practices, I accepted Convery's (1999) warning that identities may be created rather than revealed through narrative. By using observation throughout an academic year, which involved observing all the interviewees, I could supplement the data from interviews, and observe student teacher education work in school, in order to gauge how far working practices sat alongside interview responses.

I interviewed every member of the department staff who worked with the student teachers in the school during the research year, with the student teacher education co-ordinator and mentors being interviewed twice (once in the first term and again at the end of the student teachers' second school practice). The aim of the first interviews were to consider their roles both in terms of their involvement in student teacher education and in relation to working with others involved in student teacher education both in the school and at the university. In the second interviews the focus was on reviewing the research year in order to gauge their opinions of the ways they had worked in student teacher education and how they felt this had been. I also interviewed the student teachers in the first school practice near the beginning of the experience and again at the end to explore their feelings of the whole process, and the second practice student teachers just once at the end of their six-week teaching experience. The staff who were less well known to me owing to fewer opportunities to meet with them, I interviewed later in the year after they had got to know me better, and started with those of more senior responsibility who were perhaps used to and therefore more at ease with talking about organisational and strategic decisions: the student teacher school co-ordinator and the head teacher, followed by the heads of department.

Clarification of the purpose of the interview and of the research overall was made before the main part of the interview began. It was especially emphasised that the study was about the process of student teacher education in school departments generally and not an evaluation of the student teacher education work at Market Town High School or a judgement of how well the student teachers had done in their student teacher education course in particular. With a limited time frame it was necessary to arrange interviews in such a way that it was possible to build up a knowledge base about student teacher education work in the school and policy decisions taken about student teacher education. This knowledge made possible more specific and detailed questioning and understanding, especially in relation to the history of student teacher education activity in the school, the ways of working in the departments and whole school procedures.

*Documentation*

Open access was arranged with the student teachers for me to view their files in school. These contained their planning, self-evaluations, and observation summaries, and their mentor and tutor reports. My reading of these was also negotiated with the mentors and tutors who agreed with all documents being available providing the student teachers were happy for this to happen. Such documents complemented observation data from lessons, observation discussions and meetings, and illustrated physically how tools were being used in the departments (Bowen, 2009). Therefore, specific student teacher education documentation was open to analysis as well as other department-based resources (schemes of work, minutes of meetings, bulletins and staff handbooks) and also documentation relating to the department's support of student teachers (guides issued by the university for example). Downtown University also provided me with open access to key documents for the student teachers and mentors (the student teacher education course handbook, curriculum course handbooks, reading lists and supplementary materials for mentors).

**Ethical considerations**

Having obtained informed consent from all people involved, I followed the British Educational Research Association's ethical guidelines (2011) for conducting the research and secured Downtown University's research ethics approval. Informed consent procedures were intended to minimise negative personal and social consequences, and served the purpose of allowing subjects to assess the risks of their participation in the study. I was concerned about protecting the identity of respondents. Each was providing information on their understandings, beliefs and attitudes towards their work and aspects of their professional identity. To offer confidentiality was consistent with the aim of empowering respondents in the sense that they retained control over the circumstances under which their personal views entered into the discourse. Their behaviour towards myself as a researcher (and as an experienced practitioner) may also have resembled their behaviour with others, but I had to be attentive to the fit between my interpretations and their understandings, and this served as a validity check on the findings.

Despite the fact I gave assurance to interviewees and participants that they will not be identified by name (pseudonyms are used for the school and university, and genders of some of the key respondents have been changed), with relatively few people involved, it would be difficult to analyse the data without very few knowledgeable readers at a local level being able to identify sources. Richness of data is particularly important for the study, and therefore totally anonymising respondents was not possible for those most involved in the research. However, there are relatively few people who would be able to confidently identify sources, and this was the main reason for offering some form of respondent validation from those in the university whose work was still involved in student teacher education. The university tutors were sent the relevant department case study and a subsequent findings chapter in order to correct any factual errors. I did not offer them any form of editorial veto, but explained that it was my interpretations that were to be used for the research study. I decided not to return data to the school, principally because the main staff involved in the findings (the four mentors) were no longer in these roles when my draft findings were available for dissemination. Consequently, I was careful to use data that appeared typical of the year as a whole rather than highlighting any issues that arose out of specific and atypical situations (Arthur *et al.*, 2012; Punch, 2009; Cohen *et al.*, 2011).

## Data analysis

The notion of triangulation is often considered a way of verifying meaning by using a variety of data to comment on an area of analysis. Multiple and differently sourced perceptions may seem to help assure the repeatability of an observation or interpretation accepting that neither observation nor interpretation is accurately repeatable in qualitative data. Although questionable as a means of checking validity in this sense, triangulation does help to identify different ways phenomena may be seen (Silverman, 2011). However, rather than repeating data it provides new data that comments on the research. Therefore, distinguishing between the different types of data is important in order for a reader to appreciate how this is being interpreted. For example, what one has seen in observation may be considered to triangulate with what has been said in interview. However, this does not necessarily add to the 'truth' of the situation, but simply offers another perspective on it. Obtaining multiple measures of the same phenomenon is therefore not possible in qualitative research as all data is necessarily newly generated and needs to be analysed in the context it was produced.

Noting how different meanings are identified is offered by Stake as a way of ensuring the best possible analysis:

> Local meanings are important; foreshadowed meanings are important; and readers' consequential meanings are important. The case researcher teases out meanings of these three kinds and, for whatever reason, works on one kind more than the other two. In each case, the work is reflective. (Stake, 2000, p. 445)

Local meanings in understanding how the school departments afford or constrain learning opportunities for student teachers is central to this research, with foreshadowed meanings (those suggested when preparing and planning the research in advance of the fieldwork) obtained from the analytic framework helpful in giving a way to view and analyse the data. The data should be constantly interpreted in a number of different ways, in order for meanings to be explored during analysis (Silverman, 2011). The researcher should remain ever reflective and constantly revise analysis in light of newly considered data and subsequent analysis, aware that readers' consequential meanings will be shaped by this.

*Procedures for data analysis*

In describing the design of the research, I began to explain how data was analysed in terms of how the case studies were organised. The way data generation has been described also gives suggestions as to how the analysis process was seen (a comparison of data from observations, interviews and document analysis for example). Data analysis was not a linear process but one that involved many different ways of viewing the data generated from the fieldwork. Initial familiarisation was partly influenced by an interactive approach outlined by Miles and Huberman (1994). Although having in mind the CHAT analytic framework, I purposely did not want to reduce data analysis opportunities by considering the data initially in these terms. Data reduction had already begun in how I generated data in the field, and subsequent initial coding into wide-ranging organisational categories reduced the data further. Computer software was used to label the transcribed field notes and interviews with categories that could then be extracted and arranged into data sets, which were then further reduced to bullet points in order to create synopses around the initial codes, for example the use of team rooms, the use of handbooks, mentor meetings, tutor visits, school student teacher education practices and student teacher responsibilities.

Displaying the data in different formats, as in a tabulated style with columns given for each of the four departments, was used in order to reduce the data sets further and aid a comparison across the departments. This also sliced up the data and offered other possibilities for considering the main categories, with some new categories emerging from doing this. For example, when exploring how mentor meetings compared across departments, ideas about how the mentors considered their own learning emerged. Interpretations of specific areas were developed in analytic memos with longer papers produced comparing and contrasting different student teacher education activities in different departments, for example looking at how tutor visits were structured. Consequently, general procedures adopted for analysing data for the case study analysis and for identifying the subsections within the organising concepts were by immersion in the data with the aim of generating areas for collation and comparison. As Miles and Huberman (1994) recognise, it was advantageous to continually move between reduction, display and drawing tentative conclusions in order to maintain a reflective stance. In order not to limit the scope of potential findings in the initial stages of analysis, I refrained from concentrating my focus on the CHAT concepts.

The CHAT concepts were latterly used as the focus of analysis with student teacher education tools becoming the units of analysis with their use helping to identify both participants' perceptions of the student teacher education activity systems' objects and the relationships between participants and student teachers in the student teacher education activities. I continued to explore the objects of the department student teacher education activity systems and considered how they were affected by interactions with other activity systems, and hypothesised the possibilities for expansive learning in the departments with regard to the learning opportunities of student teachers. This together with considering the nature of student teachers' relationships with their social situation of development enabled me to address the two overarching research questions.

## Concluding comments

In the school department case studies in the next four chapters, I analyse descriptively the concepts that make up the expanded mediational model as described by Engeström (1999a): the rules, community and division of labour in the student teacher education activity systems (see Figures 3.2 and 3.3 in Chapter 3). The case studies contextualise the student teacher education work in the departments and are preparatory for showing how tools mediate the participants' work on the object of the student teacher education activity system, which is analysed closely in Chapter 9. In Chapter 10 I reinterpret the concepts of rules, community and division of labour as cultural history and social practices, and show how these affected, structured and organised the participants' work on the various objects as identified in the different department student teacher education activity systems.

# 5

# The School History Department: Cultural, Historical and Social Practices in Student Teacher Education

### The subsections of the case studies: Organising concepts

To understand the social situation of development for the student teachers, it is important that the school department case studies are considered in terms of their cultural histories, the social practices within them and the specific opportunities that are created as a result of working in student teacher education. The social situation of development is a product of cultural history in which individual histories come together. The social contexts of learning to teach include the imagined outcomes, relationships among participants, underlying philosophies and the kind of activities that engage the different participants (Grossman *et al.*, 1999). The format of the case studies enables initial comparisons across departments. The generic divisions allow for the possibility of noting the variety of working practices within them. For example, the use of the subject team rooms was particularly central to the student teachers' experience in some departments, but this was not the case for the student teachers in others. In considering Stake's warning about allowing comparative comments to outweigh aspects of intrinsic importance (2000, p. 444), I have not worried about giving equal attention to all subsections for each case study. These subsections analyse descriptively the concepts that make up the expanded mediational model as described by Engeström (1999a), the rules, community and division of labour in the student teacher education activity systems (see Figures 3.2 and 3.3 in Chapter 3).

In each case study I try to be appreciative of all participants' efforts in their work in student teacher education, which as previously explained in Chapter 3 was just one of many activity systems the subjects were participating in. The first research question asked what the learning opportunities were for the student teachers, and these are described in the case studies, as is the context in which they were constructed. The case studies' organising concepts are sub-divided in order to address the social and collective elements of the student teacher education activity system with the first section focusing on the department's profile and staffing, its link with Downtown University and its approach to student teacher education with specific emphasis on the roles of the tutor and mentor. The second section looks at department routines, relationships and resources, and the third focuses on mentor meetings, tutor school visits and the department teachers' support of the student teachers.

## The school History department

The History department along with Geography and Religious Studies was part of the Humanities faculty. These departments were situated together on both school sites. There were five members of staff working with the student teachers during the research year with one student teacher in the first teaching practice (a second left the course very early on) and two student teachers in the second. History was taught as a compulsory subject in the lower school (11–13 year old pupils) and as an optional examination subject in the upper school (14–16 year old pupils) and taught as an option at Advanced level with the Post 16 students. (For a discussion of the teaching and studying of History, see Phillips (2008), Black and MacRaild (2007) and Hunt (2012)).

### Section 1 cultural history

*Department profile, staffing and links with Downtown University*

There had been a lot of staff changes in the History department in recent years, which appeared to add to curriculum negotiations when deciding on new schemes of work:

> In the last four years, four people have left. So new people have come in and we are aware there are differences. We had a recent discussion on whether we should introduce a new topic on Empire ... and there was a difference [of opinion]. One person wanted to talk about the British experience of Empire and pick out the major moments and the major people, whereas I'd say that most of the rest of the department were saying, well we want to kind of focus on the negative impact of Imperialism and the legacy in terms of developing countries. In the end, as a department we were not clear about why

we would want to teach it, so we're dropping it. (Interview with Head of History – 9 February)

This explanation of recent curriculum development was indicative of a department view that positively promoted debate as a means for teachers to work collaboratively. The department leader advocated open discussion and saw planning as a collaborative process ('the importance of a team is the sort of organic joint production. So, if we are going to plan a course, the department will get together' – 9 February). The senior manager responsible for the training school status alluded to this when she recognised the department's intellectual approach to many aspects of pedagogy and student teacher education:

History is a good example where there is an in depth feel of what is going on, and to me that's great. (Interview with Senior Manager – 27 June)

Two of the department's five specialist teachers were recent newly qualified teachers, and they had both been student teachers at Downtown University. All members of the History department seemed to be confident in expressing their views, and the department management (the Head and second in department, who was also the mentor) promoted an ethos of experimentation, sharing and debate:

The [student teacher] year is for experimenting because you can make mistakes. Things can go catastrophically wrong, but you go for it. If she [the student teacher] sees we are doing those kinds of things, then she may be more willing to go for it herself ... there is no lesson in our schemes of work which is just answer questions from the book. For me that is very sterile. (Interview with Head of History – 9 February)

The Head of Department welcomed the student teachers with enthusiasm, and she made a point of saying how she was anticipating learning from their experiences: 'I am looking forward to your imagination and the ideas you'll bring to the department, and to a great year' (Field notes – 27 September). Each year the head of department hosted a meal at her home to welcome the new student teachers, and this was referred to by all the History teachers interviewed, who thought it a generous and genuine way of aiming to engender strong working relationships.

The History teachers believed that they worked in a strong department where the staff experimented in their teaching and engaged pupils' interests. This was reflected in the relatively large numbers of pupils opting for History in examination classes, where the outcomes were celebrated: 'I think it is strong especially compared to other departments and I think our results hold that up as well' (Interview with History teacher – 17 May). The busy and committed way of working referred to by a number of school staff and by the university tutor meant that it was necessary for teachers and student teachers to actively seek out support from colleagues, which was available provided it was confidently broached:

> Teachers are enormously talented, extremely keen and determined, but sort of fragmented so there is not what I would say a sense of a unity and a driving forward in the same process. But on the other hand you know that some of the people you are working with are right at the top of their field and they are always there to go and talk to. From that point of view there is a lot of support when you need it, but you have got to be proactive to get it rather than it being a community feeling to the place. (Interview with History teacher – 17 May)

Both the mentor and Head of Department were worried when one of the student teachers in the first practice left the course very early on. They saw considerable benefit for the student teachers if they worked in a pair, as they accepted the fragmentary nature of the department owing to the split school sites, and the fact that a number of staff had pastoral responsibilities. They expected student teachers to provide mutual support with the possibility of collaborative experimentation, especially as the department was not always an easy environment for a newcomer to work in, owing to its busy and dispersed nature:

> We are such a big faculty and because of the split sites, they don't always feel welcome (I started off talking about me wanting them to feel welcome) but I am not sure they always do, but feel a little bit tentative and a little bit unsure of how they fit in. It's difficult to get around that sometimes … that's why for me it is really crucial that there are two of them. (Interview with Head of History – 9 February)

The department was open about the benefits of student teacher education as they saw them, and purposely rotated the role of the mentor in order for all teachers to make the most of this professional development opportunity. Teachers also openly voiced concerns about the challenges of the student teacher education process, for example the feedback between teachers and mentor on student teachers' progress, and the limited resources for preparing for the work. A wish to have the following year's mentor shadowing the work of the current more experienced mentor did not happen owing to a lack of funding. Ways for developing student teacher education within the department were sought, and the teachers showed confidence in acknowledging that this was not always successful.

The university History tutor was valued as someone who added a great deal to the learning opportunities in the department for the teachers as well as the student teachers. He was involved in some department meetings and asked the Head of Department to give a training session at Market Town High School for all the History student teachers in the teacher education course. This illustrated the strong links the school department had with Downtown University, and also emphasised the importance the Head of Department gave to training and her belief in learning. The frequent inclusion of the university tutor in department debates, and the high status given to subject and pedagogy development encouraged the student teachers to be seen as an ongoing and important aspect of all staff development (both in the input they brought to the department and in the ongoing relationship between student teacher education and the university). The head of department also acknowledged and praised the close links she had with the development of the student teacher education course over the years: 'I have worked quite closely with [university tutor] on various parts of it, and so I think it is superb – absolutely fantastic' (Interview with Head of History – 9 February).

*Working with student teachers; the school History mentor and the university history tutor*

The department had worked with student teachers regularly and the less experienced staff (both of whom were Downtown University student teachers two years ago but did not work in Market Town High School during their teaching practices) noted an established way of working:

> With [the head of department] and [the mentor] and [another experienced teacher] having done this now for 10 years or so, certainly one of the things I noticed when I first started was a kind of like – of course this is the way we do things – which is inevitable and maybe that is something with the [student teachers] as well. There

is a presumption that everyone will know what they are doing. (Interview with History teacher – 17 May)

Student teachers were spoken of as being beneficial to the department and the work that it did. The head of department talked about student teacher education as a two-way process that developed both novices and experienced staff, and saw the opportunity of taking on the mentor's role as one that kept staff motivated whilst also enhancing their management and negotiating skills. All department teachers worked with student teachers including newly qualified teachers, which was not the situation in the other three school departments, and it was accepted that this was a good thing for both the pupils and the teachers: 'It always gives me a bit of a wake up call in terms of trying new things and also seeing what is the current hot practice' (Interview with History teacher – 17 May).

This ethos of experimentation was prevalent across the department and always advocated and celebrated in meetings. Noticeably, a student teacher from Downtown University, but not one who worked in Market Town High School on teaching practice during her course, was successful in obtaining a permanent position in the department for the following year. The successful candidate was commended for her confidence, which was less strong in another student teacher who successfully completed her practice at the school but was not appointed when she applied for the permanent job.

It was the second year for the school History mentor working in her role, although she had been a mentor for just one year, eight years previously. She only took on the role again, as there were no other appropriate teachers in the department. Had she not already had experience of the role, she would not have offered to do it, as she spent little time in the department because of her pastoral responsibilities. However, the department having established a way of working with Downtown University and the student teachers on the student teacher education course meant that she was confident that being a mentor would not be too onerous:

I guess I am kind of assuming that because all of the department have either been mentors or have been [student teachers at Downtown University] recently, people are quite clued up on that (Interview with History mentor – 23 January)

Therefore, as well as the mentor 'knowing the system, other colleagues knew the system similarly so there was an official support there because people knew how we were meant to be working with [student teachers]' (23 January). Working in student teacher education had become an integral part of the department's history, and with half of the department's teachers having trained at Downtown University (and another due to join the team the following year) and with the head of department and mentor having close links with academic research and the work of the university tutor, an established way of working in student teacher education and a clear rationale for this had been developed and continuously revised.

The mentor greatly valued academic engagement and had many links with Downtown University for her own personal and professional development. She had worked extensively with the senior Downtown tutor, and she was admired for the 'wisdom' she had brought to mentor meetings at the university over the year (interview with tutor, 14 August). Her perception of the student teacher education course was therefore heavily influenced by its original principles or implicit rules such as debate without consensus, and the value in questioning all types of knowledge. She also recognised and valued how working with the university tutor had benefited the department in a number of ways:

> We have got a very good relationship with [Downtown tutor], and he feels part of our department now, and the input that he's had on some of the development work we have done has been really important. (Interview with History mentor – 23 January)

A pattern of student teachers from the university being employed in the department permanently reflected a strong belief in the value of the student teacher education partnership. Like the other members of staff, the mentor felt that this value extended into her own teaching and learning:

> The main reason I wanted to do the mentoring again, I felt that after ten years of teaching I needed to refresh some of those basics and go back to thinking about classroom management, transitions and so on. (Interview with History mentor – 23 January)

Rather than feeling solely that her own experience could directly help the student teachers in their teaching practice, she considered that her own learning would be enhanced by having to think afresh about pedagogy.

The university History tutor was the university's lead tutor for that subject and had worked on the student teacher education course for over twenty years. Consequently, he could outline significant changes that had happened over that time. He regarded the Market Town High School History department staff very highly and believed them to be 'extremely committed to teaching and learning, very prepared to develop and to think about new ideas' (14 August). His relationship with Market Town High School was unusually close and spanned a number of years:

> I think I am right in saying that it's the department that I have worked most with in a whole variety of different guises, so as a [university tutor], I have taught there myself, done research there myself, had a doctoral student there, had diploma students there and Best Practice Research scholarship student and so on. (Interview with History tutor – 14 August)

There were many instances of mutual admiration and gratitude for the developmental work of both the school and the university working together over the years.

### Section 2 social practices

*Department routines*

As the History department teachers divided their time between school sites and shared their team rooms with the other departments in the Humanities faculty, working space was very tight, as was also the situation in the Geography department. Staff but not the student teachers were allocated desks in the team rooms. The physical size of the team rooms was a daily hindrance and affected the workings of the departments greatly. Student teachers reported that they often felt 'in the way' especially when no space was allocated for them, and even more so when other staff were allocated desks (Field notes – 8 January). The improved staff room facilities on both school sites (more computers and a conference style desk in the lower school) had made working in the team rooms less congested and more pleasant, and some staff encouraged the student teachers to use the staff rooms, thereby making many of them mobile in their working habits.

This then became a balance between working with the department materials and resources close by and having access to other staff working in the team room (teaching staff rarely worked in the staff rooms unless they needed a computer) and working in the staff rooms, which were quiet and offered considerably more space, and the chance to sit with other student teachers. Without their own space or regular department contact the notion of them not being a 'proper teacher' (interview with History student teacher – 17 October) negated them from being members in the team room. The team room intimidated the History student teacher in the first teaching practice, and on a number of occasions she had to move from her seat as Humanities teachers arrived to 'claim their space':

> I don't go in the team room because it is scary. Full of scary people and [the other student teacher] and I went in the first week to look at resources and we put our bag in the wrong place and someone wasn't very happy ... so you are very aware, and the team room up here is quite tight, and you don't want to get in a proper teacher's way. So that is why I spend a lot of time in the staff room, but I suspect it would be better to be in the team room as then I could speak to them. (Interview with History student teacher – 17 October)

As the first student teacher was less integrated into the working practices of the department, it was noticeable that it was mainly the formal student teacher education structures that were used for gaining feedback and support (mentor meetings and staff observation summaries for example). The student teacher also relied more on the relatively formalised communication of phone calls and e-mails with staff out of school hours. The Head of History came into the staff room in order to talk to the History student teacher at her request for specific information about the new History specification and the department's self-evaluation policy for her school-based assignment. Although a relatively informal discussion on easy chairs in the staff room, it was apparent that it took place in the same area as all the History mentor meetings (and outside the team room with no other History staff present).

However, one member of the department felt very strongly that the student teacher should be in the team room, and made a point of saying this to the mentor so that it became a target for her first assessment:

> She barely went in and I tried very hard to coax her in because I felt she was missing out on that because what you also get from it more than anything else is that shared sense of the difficult people you deal with and when things go wrong. (Interview with History teacher – 17 May)

When asked if the History student teacher felt she was missing out on discussions on teaching and learning: 'they are not there for long and if I want to ask a specific question I'll go in' (Interview with History student teacher – 19 February). The student teacher in the first practice did not feel that the discussions were particularly relevant to her immediate teaching experience, and spoke about her teaching with staff outside the team room. However, the student teachers on the second school teaching practice, with less time to settle into the department needed to gain access quickly, and therefore utilised resources and staff more readily. They spent more time in the team rooms from the start, and because of their number and greater confidence were aware but less sensitive to feeling in the way and intruding. Relevant discussions occurred because they initiated them, and they also sought advice from one another when teaching out of their subject areas. The team rooms were therefore used more strategically. The History mentor commented that this led to some consternation from the Humanities staff, but maybe because of the much shorter second teaching practice, repercussions were not forthcoming.

*Relationships*

Nevertheless, meetings with the History teachers were always supportive and the student teachers valued how the teachers in the department worked with them:

> They are all really helpful, very different in their teaching styles, very supportive and it is really nice having people who have done the course, it's really nice because they understand that you don't understand what is going on. (Interview with History student teacher – 17 October)

Teachers recognised the first student teacher's lack of confidence and appreciated the importance of working on this, as her teaching was seen to be very promising: 'I spent a lot more time talking to [student teacher] than I have other [student teachers] and a lot of that was boosting self-esteem' (Interview with History teacher – 17 May). All staff adopted a personal approach when discussing lessons and although the meetings were set up in advance rather than in a more informal *ad hoc* manner, the teachers considered the school experience as something that involved the whole person, and therefore issues outside the classroom were also addressed and felt to be relevant to the discussions on teaching and learning:

> We did talk values – talk about that with a personal slant – her kids or my musical tastes, which her children shared, which she was not

happy with, and also state and private schooling. (Interview with History teacher – 17 May)

The university tutor was acutely aware of the tension this year when he realised that the first student teacher's children attended private schools, and that she also intended to apply for jobs in the private sector when she finished the course. There was a clear ethos in the History department and at Downtown University for preparing teachers for working in the state sector. The student teacher in question, after detailed telephone discussions with the tutor and conversations with the mentor, went on to secure a job in the state sector, and this was seen as a victory for the department, especially as all student teachers in the last three years had gone into the private sector, much to the chagrin of the mentor and the Head of Department (Interview with History mentor – 23 January).

*Resources*

Because all Humanities teachers taught across the departments in lower school, the resources and lesson materials for the lower years were prepared in such a way that non-specialist teachers could plan from pre-written schemes of work. The student teachers were encouraged to be aware of these, and it was expected that if they were teaching outside their own specialist teaching area, then they might rely more heavily upon the resources available in the faculty. However, when teaching their own subject area and when preparing lessons for the examination groups, a more individualised approach to planning was expected. The student teacher in her first practice expected to plan all History lessons herself. When asked about the resource situation:

> I don't think it is brilliant. It's good to have the schemes of work if you need them like for Religious Studies. [The head of department] always says that teachers are like magpies – they steal things and that's why it's useful. [History teacher] the other day, I said to her that I feel I am being boring on JFK, so she said 'try this, so they'll say something'. [Another History teacher] asked me something the other day: 'how did you do this with Malcolm X?' (Interview with History student teacher – 19 February)

Sharing resources was seen to be integral to how the department worked collaboratively when discussing teaching and learning strategies. Time-consuming in getting interesting and new artefacts together, there was an understanding that talking about and debating successful activities and lesson materials was expected:

> We have files up there in which we put our different ideas – the Nazi Germany course there is a file up there with all the different things that people do. So rather than have a set prescribed lesson plan or scheme of work people can just select, oh that looks like the kind of thing I would like to do. Because we are very aware that people teach in different ways and you have to provide things that enable people to do that ... I've borrowed a few things from [student teacher] already so for me that is when [student teacher education] becomes a useful two way street. (Interview with Head of History – 9 February)

This sharing of resources and teaching and learning strategies was formalised in the department meetings as the head of department explained:

> We have a light bulb slot, which is about the sharing of new ideas, and a lot of those ideas are trying to push ICT and increase the use of the whiteboard down at lower school, and using programmes on the laptops. (Interview with Head of History – 9 February)

Being included in all meetings, the student teachers were able to benefit from the light bulb agenda. However, other incidental chats about what the teachers were using in the classroom were more informal, and therefore were affected by the access the student teachers had to the teaching staff.

### Section 3 Specific student teacher education learning opportunities

*History mentor meetings*

There was one mentor and one student teacher in the department for the first school practice and two student teachers for the second. They rarely saw one another outside the mentor meetings, as owing to school pastoral commitments the mentor was based away from the department setting. This necessitated extensive e-mail contact and agenda items were kept until the one-to-one meetings Therefore, the meetings were focused on issues brought by all parties. Nevertheless, the formality was not business-like. On the contrary, the mentor was careful to discuss points at some length by considering a variety of perspectives and questioning the student teachers in order to open out the discussion, ensuring that for most pedagogical debates there were no easy answers.

The student teacher in the first practice referred to her learning as 'a never ending journey through a tunnel' (Field notes – 25 April) highlighting a continual exploration. The student teacher acknowledged how she was made to think ideas through carefully and how she was encouraged to take risks and challenge her own perceptions of what teaching involves:

> She [the mentor] does ask me to be specific about what went wrong in a lesson if I say that wasn't good. She doesn't like me just saying it was really rubbish. She wants me to tell her which bit was good, and why I think bits that didn't work should be analysed. It's a good hour I have with her. (Interview with History student teacher – 19 February)

If the evaluation of a lesson is seen as the main task of the activity in a session, then the mentor in asking the student teacher to expand upon the lesson is trying to reveal the student teacher's thinking and expose their concepts to scrutiny and development. It was evident that the mentor was also considering issues afresh in their discussions, and this enhanced a genuine sharing of ideas. When talking about resources, the mentor borrowed and valued new materials as much as did the student teacher: '[Mentor] looks at sheet – "this is really good, can I do a copy?" (Field notes – 10 January)'. Consequently, both seemed to operate as learners, and although a novice, the student teacher appreciated that her learning was not pre-determined but evolving. The mentor did not act as the expert and viewed learning as a complex process:

> I guess teaching isn't the kind of thing where you tell somebody this is what you do and then they go and do it, and it works. It is much more imprecise. (Interview with History mentor – 23 January)

The mentor welcomed differences of opinion and considered personal issues to be relevant. ('Have your children's teachers' attitudes to you changed since you started the course?' Field notes – 10 January.) This approach carried over to the student teacher's belief that her learning appeared continuous. Different styles of teaching were discussed and valued with the student teacher not expected to mimic them, but to see in them opportunities for expanding her understanding of teaching. As mentioned, this openness to alternatives, curiosity and capacity for learning was evident in the social practices of the department, and the student teacher was brought into these practices. This intellectual approach (extensive debate and discussion from a variety of sources including educational research literature) was demanding, and at times the student teacher felt daunted and was in awe of the mentor's expertise and intellect. Noticeably, the style of mentor meetings differed little from the student teacher's meetings with the university tutor when he visited the school. This seamlessness in the student teacher's experience reflected how the mentor saw herself as part of the broader activity of student teacher education and not simply as part of a department-based student teacher education activity.

*History tutor school visits*

The History department was aware of the different but complimentary roles of the tutor visits. They provided an opportunity to develop student teacher learning, but also acted as part of the assessment process as detailed in the Standards for the Award of Qualified Teacher Status. This was a delicate balance in that the visits corresponded with the assessment deadlines, and were frequently spoken of as 'assessment visits'. But in History the tutor visits were seen primarily as opportunities for detailed discussions about teaching and learning, and although anticipated by the student teachers with trepidation ('I just go to complete terror. It's so stupid because he is so lovely. But I am just completely, oh my goodness this is it. I will cry for days – I just find it so stressful.' Interview with student teacher – 19 February), the mentor and tutor went out of their way to play down the assessment focus of the visits. Owing to the first student teacher showing a lack of confidence (though not attainment) in her teaching, the tutor went to great lengths to put her at ease and he emphasised the developmental nature of the visits:

> The lesson is of no matter ... you have got to tell yourself you are a beginner but be inspired and don't measure yourself against them [other staff]. (Field notes – 28 November)

This insistence that the lessons observed by the tutor were not going to make a difference in the consideration of how successful the student teacher was progressing spilled over into the lessons themselves, where the tutor and mentor (when she was there, which was just for the third visit) acted as teaching assistants actively involved in the class (although not in the delivery or co-ordination of the lesson). The tutor then made his notes afterwards during the discussion with the student teacher and mentor. Interactions with the pupils took the onus off the student teacher, yet ensured the lesson was still hers. During the third visit, the mentor sent one of the pupils out of the classroom for not behaving appropriately, and this was later discussed in the feedback session. Any concern that the mentor took the action was not addressed, but instead they talked about the behaviour of the pupil, and whether the mentor's actions had been fair. This was indicative of the mentor and tutor always putting pupils' learning first in all situations, mutually recognising the roles each was playing but giving less regard to the relative 'status' of those present and the assessed nature of the visit (although one feels the tutor would not have taken this action, and the student teacher may have been loath to use such a sanction during her 'assessment'). However, it was the mentor's class and she acted in a way she felt benefited the lesson. Respect for the student teacher was already established and therefore her behaviour rather than appearing to undermine the student teacher as teacher was accepted as contributing to the learning in the lesson.

The History mentor asked the student teacher how she wanted to use the tutor for his visits, and suggested ways he could help in her lessons outside the observed ones (for example, interviewing one class in small groups to help with her assignment). Even though this did not happen, as the tutor sensed that the student teacher felt uneasy about using him outside the 'formal' nature of the visit, no other tutor was seen as such a resource. The tutor always commented on the pleasure of working with pupils and thanked the student teachers for enabling that to happen. He felt this a privilege and emphasised that this was one of the pleasures of his job. He commented on the atmosphere in the lessons and how the student teachers created this. A student teacher in the second teaching practice notes:

> Because of his experience he is able to get a very strong sense of a class's capabilities and a class atmosphere/mood, so that when he is giving feedback he will say that 'I noticed you were very quick to praise Billy. I thought that was strong, as when I talked to him I noticed that he was lacking in confidence'. He [the tutor] is good.
> (Interview with History student teacher– 12 June)

Such apparent pleasantries were a way of opening up for the student teachers the importance of their class relationship and the learning that positive atmospheres may engender. This underpinned a great deal of the subsequent discussion on the lessons and teaching in general.

During the visits the tutor frequently referred to student teachers in other schools and commented on what happened on his visits to them.

This helped to give the student teachers some perspective on their experiences especially for the student teacher in the first teaching practice who worked alone. It also helped to add to the idea that effective learning was not simply a case of cause and effect from 'good' teaching but a matter of thinking through the use of resources and how these worked for pupils:

> Student teacher: I find differentiation hard.
> Tutor: For differentiation [another student teacher] said to his class – 'if you want some extra challenge?' Brilliant for the hints on his worksheet, as he told them he underestimated them, so he was not giving them extra help but an extra challenge. (Field notes – 1 December)

Mentioning other student teachers on the course demonstrated an openness of relationships and also reinforced the idea of a learning community. This was done very rarely by the other tutors and never in a way that discussed other student teachers' work.

*Lesson observations, support and feedback from History department teachers*

Generally, class teachers were more engaged in how successful specific lessons were and how they could be developed within longer term planning objectives than the mentor who took more of an overview of the student teachers' learning and discussed what had been learnt over a period of time. Yet teachers did discuss lesson opportunities openly, and did not always engage in explicit suggestions as to what should be done in certain circumstances: 'Sometimes it is about saying I don't know what to do in that situation, but this is one way in which we could find out' (interview with teacher – 17 May).

Nevertheless, the student teacher in her first practice found that the reliance on formal written feedback and communal student teacher report writing created a feeling of evaluation. The mentor comments:

> I think there was an extent to where [student teacher] felt that she was being assessed all the time by everyone she was working with, and found it hard to see herself as an equal colleague as well, able to play a part in the team. I don't know how far being on her own affected that. (Interview with History mentor – 27 June)

The strong focus on debating aspects of pedagogy with an understanding that considering a variety of contestable issues and viewpoints from practitioners and researchers would enhance student teacher learning was occasionally intimidating for this student teacher who readily admitted to feeling inadequate and daunted at the prospect of being a successful teacher.

## Concluding comments

Innovation was encouraged in the student teacher education work in the History department. Concentrating on the student teachers' learning and on the learning of all participants allowed for new developments, as the teachers, mentor and student teachers interpreted what was happening and then worked together in newly informed ways as a result of their interpretations in a form of relational agency (Edwards, 2005a). The emphasis on experimentation and debate in department practices, modelled by the head of department and the mentor, promoted learning as a means of development (Engeström, 1999a). It was evident that the mentor was considering issues afresh in discussions with the student teachers and in her requests to borrow resource ideas. This enhanced a genuine sharing of opinion. Indeed, differences of opinion were considered vital for the development of the work in teaching and learning and in the department in general. Accepting that learning to teach is difficult and not straightforward acknowledged that an apprenticeship approach or one that relied upon learning through transfer was not viable. Encouraging the development of knowledge *for* practice (useful when working in a number of different classroom situations) was evident in the History department, and was given priority over knowledge *of* practice (that which is specific to the department context) (McLaughlin and Talbert, 2001). However, this was not the case in the MFL department, as illustrated in the next case study, where student teachers were strongly encouraged to take on staff advice for specific classes.

# 6
# The School Modern Foreign Languages Department: Cultural, Historical and Social Practices in Student Teacher Education

## The school MFL department

The MFL faculty comprised departments in French, German and Spanish. These departments were situated together on both school sites. There were six members of staff working with the student teachers during the research year with two student teachers in both the first and second teaching practices. A modern foreign language was taught as a compulsory subject in the lower school (11–13 year old pupils) and also as an examination subject in the upper school (14–16 year old pupils). Post 16 students could opt to take a modern foreign language course in French and/or German at Advanced level. (For a discussion of the teaching and studying of MFL, see Byram (2013), Field (2013), Johnson (2008) and Hinkel (2013).)

### Section 1 Cultural history
*Department profile, staffing and links with Downtown University*

The department was large for MFL with over ten teachers. There had been a relatively stable staffing structure in recent years, and this had created a confident and cohesive department ('it is a very stable department, prior to last year it had been the same for five years, we have the younger end of the department too so you get the enthusiasm … you do get the young input and new ideas' – interview with teacher, 7 June). However, because of the department's stability the Head of MFL felt that this made it even more important to host student teachers:

> This faculty in particular was quite stagnant for want of a better word for five years – nobody left. There are benefits to that and you

get continuity etcetera. But you need fresh ideas and you need new people around to challenge your ideas, and to throw things up in the air a bit. (Interview with Head of MFL – 1 February)

All but one of the teachers in the department was female. It was generally expressed as an advantage that a man taught in MFL in order to redress this female predominance ('They [the student teachers] don't work so closely with [male teacher], but he is a male teacher, which is gold dust these days' – interview with the Head of MFL, 1 February). It was also considered of benefit to the student teachers that a Newly Qualified Teacher (who followed Downtown University's course the previous year) worked in the department, and therefore had recently experienced being a student teacher. Having an ex-student teacher working in the department enabled opportunities for the current student teachers to see teaching practice recently deemed as successful by Downtown University, in that it met the descriptors required in order to gain qualified teacher status.

The MFL department had great confidence in its reputation within the school, and this was voiced in many of the teacher interviews:

I think we think we are really good. To some extent we know we are really good, and therefore we ought to share this good practice. A lot of good stuff goes on here. (Interview with MFL teacher – 7 June)

The student teachers were welcomed into this positive and confident environment. It was felt that they could gain a lot from being in the department. Many of the teachers were very experienced. Their experience was often seen as a reason why they may have useful 'tips' and ideas for lesson management and planning. This was valued, and as open criticism was not apparent, discussions tended to reflect personal viewpoints and preferred teaching strategies rather than offering an opportunity to challenge one another's opinions:

I don't think any of us are strongly for or against anything really. The good thing about working here is you are free to decide how we want to teach. We are not being told you must use 100% the target language, or we are not being told you mustn't teach grammar. Everyone is respected for having their own way of doing things and all are considered to be equally valid and worthwhile. So there is a sense that you are a professional, you know what you are doing. (Interview with MFL teacher – 19 June)

If advice was not followed, the concern for teachers came from feeling that their work and efforts with the student teachers were not fruitful but a waste of their time. In interview, the mentor explained that this was usually the source of frustrations from previous years when student teachers had not adopted teacher recommendations and had even repeated what was considered to be poor practice in front of other teachers. There appeared to be some tension between student teachers acting on advice and in them testing out personal ideas. This could have been due to resistance from some of the staff in allowing the student teachers to learn through their own experience, rather than them taking heed of the advice of the experienced teachers they were working with.

Links with the university were extensive, with some of the teachers either working there part time (one teacher was also a part-time university tutor), studying part time (one teacher was working on a PhD) or have previously studied there (a number of teachers had completed masters-level courses). There was a high regard and respect for academic study, and the student teacher education course was well considered:

> Because it is such an established system and we know [tutor], and [teacher in the MFL department] is involved with [Downtown University], and she has a real link with them, which is beneficial to us because we know what is going on and that helps [mentor] as well, and [mentor] has an established link with [Downtown University]. I think that makes life easier if you are within a system that you know and you understand and you know what to expect, otherwise it can become terribly onerous. (Interview with Head of MFL – 1 February)

A familiarity with the Downtown University department and a respect for the work it did made it seem less likely that teachers in the department would question the processes adopted for training teachers. Beyond the fairly heavy demands the course made on the student teachers, there was little evidence of it being criticised.

The student teachers were part of the faculty meetings. Although passive in their input, they were treated as full members of staff until the mentor mentioned to the team: 'give me your classes for the next batch of [student teachers]' (referring to the second school practice). One of the student teachers jokingly responded with 'we're not a batch!' (Field notes – 23 April). The earlier comment was indicative of a department view of student teachers (occasionally referred to as if a commodity), where there was a longstanding partnership with Downtown University, and many years of working in the student teacher education course, and therefore many years of working with different sets of student teachers.

*Working with student teachers; the school MFL mentor and the university MFL tutor*

Student teacher education was recognised as a valuable opportunity for the department to keep apace with new ideas (especially in information technology), but this was accompanied by a realistic acceptance of the demands of hosting student teachers:

> We have had [student teachers] in the past who have been very demanding and that makes life very difficult, as we don't have the time to give them moral support ... if there is a problem it causes a lot more work for a lot of people. Because of last year's experiences we really hoped that we were going to get two good ones this year, which we could run with, which is what happened. So I don't know if the message got back [to the university]. (Interview with MFL teacher – 7 June)

This suggests that 'good' student teachers required less work and time when being supported in school. Another teacher acknowledged the strength of the school department, but in spite of this also felt that 'sometimes the [student teachers] that we have had, have caused more heartache than they have been positive, but we do generally view them positively' (interview – 7th June). Consequently, student teacher learning seemed to be most appreciated when it met teachers' expectations. Aware of difficult situations with student teachers in the past, the new student teacher cohort was welcomed into the busy department environment but with sensitivity to the possible demanding and frustrating experiences that had occurred in student teacher education work previously. This anticipation resulted in a sense of relief when the student teachers this year were seen to be strong and a pleasure to work with.

As an experienced teacher and a school MFL mentor of five years, the MFL mentor initially co-mentored when she started the role with another MFL teacher who then worked part time as a tutor at the university and 'who had mentored for years':

> We took one [student teacher] each and she was very gracious to me as we had joint mentor sessions which she led and she was wonderful inviting me to contribute or saying *we* thought, or *we* decided when it would never occur to me in a million years to ask or think about

these things. The next year I was the mentor but went to her a lot to ask if this is what you do. (Interview with MFL mentor – 10 January)

Consequently, the role had been 'passed down' within the department and the way of working inherited. The ex-mentor still worked in the department and now had a part-time role as a Downtown University tutor. She indicated that she saw her new role as being closely related to student teacher assessment. Therefore, she kept more of a distance between herself and the student teachers in the department, in case they felt she was reporting back to their university tutor. The current mentor adopted a very protective approach when working with the student teachers. She dealt with issues on a personal as well as professional level. Rather than debating their opinions on education and their past experiences which have informed these, she concentrated on their experience as student teachers and the demands that came with following a student teacher education course. She was especially aware of the pressures of being seen and evaluated (albeit informally) on a day-to-day basis, and was keen to protect the student teachers from excessive criticism:

They are being attacked and pressured from everywhere – their essays have got to pass, they have got to read up, fill in all this paperwork, they go into classes and they are being observed – everything and anything depending on whose room they are in might be pulled up on, what is not, may be pulled up in the next. (Interview with MFL mentor – 10 January)

The mentor had a clear image of what she imagined a typical student teacher to be from her experience of working with student teachers. Her viewpoint was informed from her past experiences of working with Downtown University, and she frequently spoke in terms of what had been done in the past. The mentor saw her role as defending hard-working and competent student teachers and promoting their capabilities during the university tutor visits. She acted as their representative in the department and felt a responsibility to protect them and nurture their progress. She often used 'fighting' terminology and aimed to minimise the trials of following the course. She tried to shield them from further criticism by helping them fight against the demands of the course: 'so the big battle has been won – you can do your own thing now' (Field notes – 18 April). This was said at the penultimate mentor meeting in their first teaching practice after the tutor visits had taken place. She also talked about how student teachers had been reduced to tears every year: 'I don't like to see people crying on my shoulder. That happens almost every year without fail' (Interview with mentor – 10 January).

The university MFL tutor had worked in the role for just under a decade and was a tutor at another university prior to this for six years. She changed the 'substance' of the student teacher education course when starting in her current post:

> I think I did make quite a few changes in 1999 and subsequently [another tutor] has made some changes but I think they have all been in consultation with me and I've agreed that they should be made. I have made quite a lot of changes yes. (Interview with MFL tutor – 3 July)

The tutor explained how she wanted her visits to schools to be seen:

> I really resist the notion that I go in there as an evaluative person ... my view is that I go in there in order to support the [student teachers] in what they do by giving them another perspective from what their mentors or other members of staff in the school are doing. (Interview with MFL tutor – 3 July)

This ensured that alternatives to the school practice were discussed (at least when the tutor was present), and the student teachers acknowledged that they benefited from the questioning and challenging approach of the university tutor. In response to the question of how she wanted the student teachers to view the visit:

> I'd like them to view it in the completely opposite way than they seem to be at the moment, which is evaluative. I want them to feel they can show me their worst lessons. I want them to feel they can show me the messes they make or in fact the most difficult classes and I want them to be able to feel that they can talk to me. But I don't think that is happening anymore because of the number of visits is reduced ... it's very difficult for them to view me as someone coming in to give them some real advice, which I think is rather sad. (Interview with MFL tutor – 3 July)

The number of school visits had reduced in recent years, and the majority of tutors visited the schools four times. Some confusion was experienced in the MFL department as to why the tutor this year made an extra visit in order to observe one of the student teachers again. Each time the MFL tutor visited the department the mentor, teachers and student teachers felt the visits to be crucial with regard to them passing the course. The evaluative nature of the tutor's role was particularly emphasised by the mentor throughout the school practices: 'she [tutor] was pleased with the paperwork, but don't take your eyes off the ball. Marking – that'll be one thing she wants to see' (Field notes – 28 February).

## Section 2 Social practices

### Department routines

The MFL department had a very cramped Lower School Team Room, which was situated in the middle of their classrooms and was used a great deal by the staff working in the area. Here desks were allocated, including one for the student teachers. This necessitated the part-time administration assistant working in the corner of the room when she was there, making the room very busy. There was one computer. The Upper School Team Room was bigger as it was divided into two with the student teachers allocated space in the separate area with a computer. Both rooms were a long way from the main staff rooms and were central to the workings of the department. However, the cramped working conditions in lower school encouraged greater communication between teachers and student teachers, and with this greater opportunity to discuss teaching and learning. In MFL in particular where the student teachers had their own desk, the working environment was particularly sociable and inclusive. One MFL student teacher commented that 'the team room in Lower School is more personal, because it is just so much more cramped'. (Interview with MFL student teacher – 22 February)

MFL was the only faculty that allocated a desk to the student teachers and this was used a great deal by all of them throughout the year. All were very positive about being a part of the lower school department workspace. When asked if working in the team room was a conscious decision:

> I suppose it was a conscious decision as that is where all the resources are and where all the teachers are – they don't seem to go to the staff room a lot. So when I have been to the staff room it has really just been to have lunch on the odd occasion … I just feel more comfortable in the team room. (Interview with MFL student teacher – 19 June)

Noticeably, the MFL student teachers more than any others spent a larger proportion of time in their department's workspace and consequently gained access to teachers' talk on many aspects of pedagogy. For example, one discussion in the team room at break time was about the use of games in MFL, and one teacher commented on 'rationing' games: 'I don't do nearly as many now, as the trouble is the pupils get involved in the games and forget the point of the language' (Field notes – 24 January). Other staff then commented on how they got the best use of fun activities. MFL teachers freely gave lesson ideas:

> Something I did worked really well – that dialogue (points in book) level 4 – it worked really, really well. There are some funny clothes here – a bit smelly and some old fashioned. Get a boy to put a bikini on! (Field notes – 24 January)

And the student teachers greatly appreciated this communal approach to sharing resources:

> People will pull bags from under tables and say I've used this before. It worked really well, why don't you use it? It just feels more – community, just more of an entity. (Interview with MFL student teacher – 19 June)

*Relationships*

Team rooms were often sites for informal chats and prearranged meetings. Student teachers could ask questions of staff who happened to be in there, or they could arrange to jointly prepare lessons with easy access to the departments' resources ('it [the team room] is brilliant for sitting down with teachers and saying I am going to do this and that because planning segments can be quite difficult to organise' – MFL student teacher, 17 October). Spending most of their time in the team rooms the MFL student teachers experienced a range of uses: 'some [teachers] like to have their frees in the team room as a break and some like to use it as preparation' (Interview with MFL student teacher – 17 October). Other staff also acknowledged that the team room was a focal point for the faculty and was the place teachers came together: 'there is a chance to have a chat and to help each other and to spend those few extra minutes with the [student teachers] … and also to know there are going to be people around to support them if they need that extra bit of support' (interview with MFL teacher 19 June).

The camaraderie and atmosphere of the team room was important to many of the staff, and access to such a positive department ethos was emphasised by the MFL student teachers:

> It's a really energising environment to work in and if we are having a bit of a 'oh god I've got far too much work, how did you ever cope?'

we can ask the NQT [newly qualified teacher] who has been there for 6 months and it's really fresh in her mind the last year and things. Everyone is really supportive and also there is a real vein of humour that is really buoyant and keeps you up I suppose, when it can get quite difficult. (Interview with MFL student teacher – 23 February)

With the student teachers using the team rooms a great deal, immediate responses to situations often pre-empted further problems arising, and kept the department abreast of how the student teachers were experiencing their classes.

*Resources*

The student teachers in MFL spent a lot of time developing their own teaching resources, and planning and discussing them. The staff were very happy to share teaching materials and openly gave student teachers access to their files. However, these were very personally created, and the student teachers saw great benefit in developing their own files with some ideas from other teachers but with resource design derived from their own lesson planning. This was indicative of the 'individual' approach that many in the department had to their personal teaching materials. The student teachers felt that general department resources were difficult to locate or incomplete, and it was easier to make their own. The schemes of work, although recommended for the student teachers to look at on the intranet, were not followed closely. They were critically evaluated by the student teachers who did not see the teachers using them or feel there was an expectation for them to follow them either. It was the textbooks that governed the themes for the teaching (vocabulary and grammar). The limitations of the textbooks were widely acknowledged, and it was generally accepted that good teaching practice was best achieved by personally supplementing lessons with extra activities and games (with the occasional lesson solely using the textbook).

The lessons worked towards assessment tests and exam specifications rather than jointly constructed schemes of work. The tests were used to make sure the content in the lessons was appropriate for what the pupils needed to learn. The format and style of lessons was very much up to the individual teachers, and a variety of styles were accepted providing pupils succeeded in their tests. This suggests why a lot of the talk in the team rooms was about resources and ideas for lessons. The experienced staff had built up a considerable wealth of ideas (the mentor shared many of these in mentor meetings), and the student teachers arrived with new resources and homemade materials created from the work done at the university.

It was noticeable that the content of many discussions was relevant to all staff, as issues in language teaching across the curriculum and year groups were often generic and of interest to everyone. Whether it was talking in terms of themes (for example, school, clothing and houses) or grammar, to some extent this was relevant across all year groups and therefore all teachers were able to contribute to discussions. The impression was given that student teachers believed they were learning from experts, and there was a strong sense of imparting experience rather than learning together and working alongside one another. This was evident in the following response from the mentor:

> Researcher: Do you feel you have gained anything personally yourself this year by working with them [student teachers]?
> Mentor: It is always very satisfying when you send off two teachers that you think will be a credit to the profession. (Interview with MFL mentor – 27 June)

This does not suggest that working with student teachers was seen as a learning opportunity for the mentor but something she did to benefit the teaching profession and to engender a feeling of value and an affirmation of the way the department and staff worked. The department's work in supporting student teachers was valued for the link this created with the university, which was respected for its role in educational development. This value was reflected by the fact that a number of staff continued their own studies at the university, but this often appeared to be considered separately from the day-to-day practice of teaching in school, and consequently separately from discussions with student teachers.

### Section 3 Specific student teacher education learning opportunities

*MFL mentor meetings*

There were two student teachers and the mentor in the department for each school practice. Sharing a small working space in the department team room enabled an almost continuous dialogue with regard to general progress and incidental and informal chats. A more focused discussion on the practice took place in the mentor meetings where one priority was the detailed preparation for the university tutor visits. In interviews, the student teachers spoke of the mentor's caring approach to their experience of the course, and greatly appreciated the mentor's support and praise of their teaching efforts. The discussions in mentor meetings were characterised by talks on classroom management, resources and lesson planning, with the mentor questioning the student teachers on what they had observed and learned from their experience in the classroom. The mentor was forthright in her opinions and used anecdotes to illustrate practice, frequently taking on a dominant role in meetings. The student teachers, who always met as a pair, listened carefully and appeared content to take on the mentor's advice and contribute with anecdotes of their own. They appeared to particularly value the discussion of resources in the meetings and often spent an entire meeting sharing these and experiences of how they could be used effectively. The mentor's enthusiasm for her resources was genuine and infectious:

Mentor: Activities for introducing new vocab? Good old bingo, backwards bingo, last person to complete sheet is the winner. That gives more exposure to words but the downside is what are the people who are out doing? Downside – there is always one. Other versions of bingo – 'strip bingo' – you can only tear the end word off, so you get to say the words more often. Don't forget good basic games – banging on the wall, beat the teacher. (Field notes – 28 February)

Teaching and learning strategies were often considered at the ideas level, creating a view that they could be simply transferred to one's individual style of teaching. It was accepted that vocabulary was important in language learning, so discussions were based around 'ramming home vocab' and 'ways of drumming it in' for example (28 February). The mentor talked a great deal about resources and the implicit communication they gave in indicating how successful the student teachers were being in the classroom. This, she believed could be gleaned from observing the resources being used in the lessons. These would be evident in the team rooms and therefore were useful for gauging how effectively the student teachers were working with the classes:

It is blatantly apparent that when you go into the team room and see what is sitting in front of people that there is good practice. And the time that there wasn't, it was equally apparent. (Interview with MFL mentor – 10 January)

This indicates that resources in themselves were believed to be suggestive of the teaching and learning processes that were happening in the classrooms, and highlights the importance that teachers in the department appeared to place on activities and lesson ideas rather than on the conceptual premise on which they were based. Consequently, some student teachers found questions on the reasons behind using particular teaching strategies demanding when asked by the university tutor.

The mentor's self-deprecating humour and outspoken opinions were enjoyed by the student teachers:

> Mentor: I have never done a plenary in my life. The bell rang on Monday afternoon and I said to the class, 'what is that?' Because this clock is broken and I never wear a watch, I said 'what is that for?' 'End of the day Miss', and I had got 6 other activities I was hoping to do! (Field notes – 10 January)

There was no indication that the mentor was considering her learning anew. She did not expect the student teachers to emulate her style of teaching but did believe they needed to grasp the basics and then build their own style:

> I'm not saying I am right and they are wrong – you can only be true to a degree. You'll only be happy teaching if you are true to yourself rather than in a place that says you must be on page 20 by October. (Interview with MFL mentor – 10 January)

The student teachers did not criticise the school department or mentor's point of view at all during the mentor meetings, but in interview critically evaluated some aspects of the department, for example a perceived over emphasis on examination grades. It seemed that potential and contestable discussions did not occur in the mentor meetings due to a respect for the mentor and for what she and the department were doing in supporting the student teachers.

The style of mentoring reflected the social practices in the department in that the student teachers were made to feel part of a close-knit team. The relaxed nature of the interaction in the mentor meetings, the content of which was often initiated by the student teachers asking questions, tended to be unstructured with the mentor occasionally checking how much time was left. A communal feeling was established with each taking it in turns to buy food from the dining hall to accompany the hot drinks made in the team room. The mentor did not use the course handbook and structured the meetings around what the student teachers wanted to talk about, but 'still keeping an eye and making them keep an eye on the enormous amount of paperwork'

(Field notes, 10 January). The meetings prior to the university tutor's visits emphasised detailed lesson planning for the tutor's observations. The nature of the interaction changed as assessment considerations took over. The tension in the build-up to the visits was palpable with an emphasis on classroom performance and delivery. It was regarded as an opportunity to show what the student teachers could do and to impress the tutor. Consequently, the student teachers were encouraged to create lessons that particularly highlighted their teaching skills and put into practice the modelling and routines that the tutor had introduced at the university. The student teachers did not question the recommendations put to them for their lesson plans, and all student teachers were very happy with the support and advice they received from the mentor.

The mentor had worked with the tutor for many years and both regarded one another highly. The student teachers were aware of this, and may not have wanted to jeopardise such support by questioning and challenging school practices. The mentor saw her role as primarily supportive, and therefore she challenged the student teachers less, believing that the strongest student teacher 'needed no help whatsoever from me at any point, not anything. If I had not been here it would have made no difference' (interview with mentor – 27 June).

*MFL tutor school visits*

The tutor's wish to help the student teachers' learning during her visits, and the importance she attached to the body of recognised research in the teaching of second languages, was evident in how she discussed lesson observations. There was a greater emphasis on the technical side of teaching, and she thought this one of the distinctive aspects of the discussion that she could bring to feedback sessions in school:

> The whole issue about deconstructing a lesson and then reconstructing a lesson is very, very important. It is very difficult for [student teachers] to understand what is going on in a whole lesson. (Interview with MFL tutor – 3 July)

The lessons were looked at with particular emphasis on their structure and delivery with reference to established techniques in teaching languages. The classes were seen more as a whole, with pupil participation analysed in terms of access to the work and their success in doing it. This approach tended to offer advice that 'solved' problems or issues. A suggestion as to why this may be the case was offered by the MFL tutor:

> MFL and Maths have a big, big research literature and all that literature is starting with the learners ... there is something about language learning that you do need to understand things like transfer from L1, the first language, you do need to understand about over generalising from L2 and concepts and stuff like that. (Interview with MFL tutor – 3 July)

Consequently, the tutor worked in a more challenging way than the mentor, questioning specific aspects of lesson planning and analysing the student teachers' ideas about teaching. Their evident feeling of being assessed with the tutor judging their work (and this being at odds with the nurturing style of the mentor) meant that for some of the student teachers, this way of working felt threatening rather than supportive:

> [Tutor] always phrases things in a way that I always find very difficult to answer, and she always asks very open-ended questions, and I really don't know what she is aiming her question at. I find it more helpful when the teachers in the school say, you know this was the situation, do you think that this would have helped? (Interview with MFL student teacher – 22 February)

This appeared to reinforce the contrast between the teachers' informal advice-based notions of supporting student teachers and the theoretical underpinning of the university's course, which was promoted by the tutor.

Nevertheless, the student teachers were positive about the added insight and development opportunities that were created because of the MFL tutor visits:

> Perhaps what differ mostly are things on really recent topics and things that she's been doing research on like how much I speak compared to how much the pupils speak. (Interview with student teacher – 23 February)

The detail and change of focus ('she focuses perhaps more on the real learning, which is not to say the other teachers don't. But she really focuses on the whole communication side of things' interview with student teacher – 19 June) challenged their thinking and made them question what they were trying to do and how they were doing it. Open-ended conversations with the tutor could appear quite frustrating for some student teachers when they were used to getting advice and examples of what worked in lessons from the teaching staff.

*Lesson observations, support and feedback from MFL department teachers*

Unlike the staff in the History department, it was less apparent that the MFL teaching staff questioned student teachers' teaching and learning strategies, or saw their role as helping the student teachers reconcile conflicting advice within the department. They were concerned with providing information and insight into the specific context of teaching their classes, and most comments on observation sheets were with regard to practical management issues. Classroom presence and the confidence of the student teachers in taking the lessons were rated highly. Providing the student teachers were in control of their classes and organised, then their teaching styles were generally accepted as valid. The tendency to automatically take advice on board, because the teachers 'know what they are talking about' (interview with student teacher, 22 February), created some tension for the student teachers. In always second guessing criticism that came from lesson observations, the less confident student teacher worried that 'if anything does flop, you are going to be criticised for it':

> Everyone is so supportive, everyone is so nice and everyone always starts with positives and they are always really, really, really understanding but each teacher does have a certain style and it is hard to know how to reconcile that. By doing something that one teacher has advised me to do in another teacher's class, she will be a bit kind of like – oh I don't think you should do this so much – then it's hard to know how to develop your own style, so that it fits in with everyone else's styles. (Interview with MFL student teacher – 22 February)

The more confident student teacher questioned the situation rather than the strategy, and saw how one may affect the other, thereby making use of conflicting advice by considering it together with a context. This required that they worked this out for themselves, as the mentor when discussing teaching and learning strategies in the mentor meetings, instead of opening up learning situations for debate focused on the student teachers trying to identify and then justify their chosen style of teaching. This, she believed, would help them to make decisions in the classroom.

There was generally little evidence of argument and challenge in the department student teacher education activities. Contentious issues in student teacher education were seen in terms of the differences between Downtown University and Market Town High School practices:

> There are some things that [the student teachers] said there are things they couldn't do (I have to be careful what I say here), which are normal practice here but the reason why they couldn't do it was because it might have been frowned on as not being fantastic – for example, teaching for an assessment. [Student teacher] said that he couldn't be shown that he was teaching for an end of unit assessment because they were advised to have assessments as an ongoing process. (Interview with MFL teacher – 7 June)

These differences were acknowledged outside the university tutor visits and not debated in great depth. The mentor explained:

> [Tutor] wants an extreme version of [teaching style], and I can see why. Many leave here and don't believe in [tutor's] way so will never do it again. Many struggle to plan a lesson to teach so as to get her to tick the box, and don't understand why they are doing it in that way, so they never do it again. (Field notes – 25 April)

The focus of the department to help student teachers teach classes and to fulfil the teacher's role was sometimes in tension with the tutor's desire for student teachers to view pedagogy as learners with an informed notion of language teaching research.

## Concluding comments

An important reason for using the university's paperwork in the MFL department appeared to be for accountability. Strong collegial interaction seemed to provide a strong learning community (Hargreaves, 1994; Talbert and McLaughlin, 1994). However, the MFL teachers tended to view lesson plans, observation summaries and evaluation sheets as an administrative part of the department's student teacher education work, with their completion necessary for gaining the university tutor's approval. Therefore, the paperwork was not used in order to initiate discussions but was primarily seen as a representation of the teacher education course and was often viewed as belonging to the university. Student teachers were fairly passive when discussing the lessons with teachers, rarely elucidating on their decisions. This meant that they did not openly contribute to their own learning when evaluating pedagogical ideas. Student teachers were encouraged to take on advice for specific classes in a form of learning transfer (Billett, 2003) whilst contemplating their own way of working with pupils. This approach to evaluating learning meant detailed discussions on pedagogy arising out of particular contexts were not available to the student teachers, or considered beneficial for the teaching staff. This was similar to the student teacher education work in the Geography department, evident in the next case study, where the emphasis was on planning lessons rather than reflecting on work done in previous classes.

# 7

# The School Geography Department: Cultural, Historical and Social Practices in Student Teacher Education

## The school Geography department

The Geography department along with the departments of History and Religious Studies was part of the Humanities faculty. These departments were situated together on both school sites. There were four members of staff working in the Geography department with the student teachers during the research year with one student teacher in the first teaching practice and two student teachers in the second. Geography was taught as a compulsory subject in the lower school (11–13 year old pupils) and as an optional examination subject in the upper school (14–16 year old pupils) and taught as an option at Advanced level with the Post 16 students. (For a discussion of the teaching and studying of Geography, see Bonnett (2008), Gersmehl (2008) and Lambert and Balderstone (2012)).

### Section 1 Cultural history

*Department profile, staffing and links with Downtown University*

The Geography department was praised by the student teachers for its friendly attitude towards them, with two of the teachers regularly eating and talking with many of the student teachers from participating universities at lunchtimes in the staff room in the lower school. The lower school organisation in Geography was highly regarded and the mentor had responsibility for this. Some tensions in the department seemed to be exacerbated by the split site nature of the school. A recent history of disappointing examination results in the upper school (both in comparison with the rest of the school and particularly in comparison with History) had led to senior school management engaging the county adviser to help in the department. This appeared to put pressure on the head of department, who had worked at the school for fourteen years and who was responsible for the upper school site:

Lower school was really becoming very successful in terms of the resources and new ideas and so on. And upper school a little bit more *ad hoc* I suppose, not quite so organised, so there are quite clear differences in that sense. (Interview with Geography teacher – 11 May)

One teacher felt that the pupils in lower school were generally negative about the Humanities but Geography in particular:

There is always negative feedback when you are teaching Humanities, pretty much from all angles. I don't know where this starts, and I feel they are giving a similar response about Geography – really positive about History. (Interview with Geography teacher – 17 May)

The Geography mentor also acknowledged that History was a strong department in the school. The Head of Geography appeared concerned over the status of the subject as well as the department, and was concerned that much of what was traditionally seen as Geography was now being taken over by Science:

You're always being knocked in the press quite a lot because you are made to look a bit nerdy and boring, and Science has taken on a lot of environmental science, which was traditionally Geography ground. You know they have suddenly discovered global warming, which we have been teaching about for years/decades. So there are lots of things that are attacking the subject. (Interview with Head of Geography – 5 February)

In the research year there was some instability in the department with two staff leaving at the end of the year (one, the mentor, to be head of department in another local school and the other leaving teaching). Another teacher had gained an internal promotion to become head of lower school Geography and had also been given the mentor's role for the following year. Therefore, there was considerable imminent change, and some references were made to the differing loyalties of the Geography staff to the department with regard to the government inspection that had taken place in January. In conversations and interviews the Geography team were often referred to as being fairly disparate, and this was also evident in the fieldwork. Many considered the approach and style of teaching quite different throughout the department, and some commented that the aims of the group were varied:

> I would characterise the Geography department as having very different personalities and I think some elements of the department are working together as a team and I think others aren't. I think there are some who have got very much their own agenda, and it's not necessarily about collaborative working or having the best interests of the students at heart. (Interview with Geography teacher – 11 May)

When asked how the student teachers viewed the department, one teacher commented that 'I think that they feel we are all very different ... we all work in different ways and people approach things differently' (interview – 17 May). Another teacher acknowledged the different teaching styles as a good thing but felt that the team 'was not as cohesive as one would ideally like it, or talk about the work as much they should' (interview – 21 May). The mentor also commented that there was a varied level of discussion when it came to teaching and learning:

> Some people like to discuss it more than others. I think some people prefer to crack on and get it done, whereas others find a middle range and others just talk about it and that's it. (Interview with Geography mentor – 15 January)

There was little apparent discussion about teaching and learning among the department teachers, and consequently the student teachers appeared to rely mainly on the mentor's input when it came to completing handbook tasks, writing their assignments for the university and planning lessons.

The department had a long history of working with student teachers from Downtown University, and this seemed to continue more from a tradition of hosting rather than a desire to develop student teacher education and the teaching and learning in the department. The head of Geography accepted that student teacher education work was a good thing. In response to being asked why the department gets involved with student teachers, the reasons seemed passive:

> I suppose in this case because we always have. Even before my time student teachers were involved, but also we think it gives you freshness, somebody coming in from the university more recently

qualified, more recently graduated, keeps us all on our toes, keeps the subject alive and a bit dynamic. Sometimes you regret it; oh yes it is always a risk. (Interview with Head of Geography – 5 February)

The links to the university were further strengthened by a part-time teacher who also worked part-time for the university and was the tutor for the school during the first school practice. He had previously been the school mentor and had been helpful in training the current mentor. They were good friends and discussed student teacher education both in the formal occasions in school (tutor visits) and informally at other times as well. The mentor and another young member of staff had both trained at Downtown University. ('That is another benefit in that we get quite a lot of [student teachers from Downtown]. We don't restrict our recruiting to [Downtown] students but we have over the years taken quite a lot' (interview with Head of Geography – 5 February)). The Head of Department also did some work for the student teacher education course. However, he took a greater interest in the Geography subject matter than in the course structure:

> I don't know that much about the [university] course. I do a couple of bits on that course myself but it's more sort of subject specific teaching topics that I deal with, but the general course I don't really know much about. (Interview with Head of Geography – 5 February)

The department leader appeared to separate his subject knowledge from the university's process of working on the student teachers' teaching and learning, in that he saw a difference in his presence in the school compared to the tutor's. The part time teacher/tutor rather than being a resource in the department for the student teachers' benefit was purposely kept apart from the student teachers, seemingly so he could not be seen as compromising their reporting and assessment:

> He keeps like that [hands apart] as far as the [student teachers] are concerned. He keeps very separate … it works in that he is not doing upper school and he just does that little bit in lower school, and I think it is all quite separate. And it is a big enough place. (Interview with Head of Geography – 5 February)

This suggests that the tutor's role was seen as primarily being about assessment.

*Working with student teachers, the school Geography mentor and the*
*Geography university tutor*

Many staff noted the advantage of gaining some extra time whilst
student teachers taught their lessons, and the mentor spoke in terms of
the gratitude and satisfaction she felt once student teachers had qualified
and kept in contact with her. The head of department, when recalling
difficult situations that had occurred in the past, voiced the most qualified reservations. He felt it important that in his role he could play an
authoritative figure if required in order to make sure student teachers
were meeting expectations for the school practice:

> I can come in at a different level if necessary. If we have a problem or
> have issues, then there's somebody else in the department who can
> step in alongside the mentor in a more disconnected, dispassionate
> way – I have had to do that in the past, particularly when you get
> a weak student or a lazy student or someone who will take time off
> and lie to you. The mentor doesn't have to deal with that. (Interview
> with Head of Geography – 5 February)

This was not mentioned in the other three departments whose heads
saw the partnership very much between the mentor and the university
tutor, although they said they would happily be called upon if the mentor wished for their advice. The Head of Department expanded on his
authoritative role:

> Quite often, it is they don't want to start teaching in the classroom
> and the reluctance to start planning lessons, going into the class-
> room and taking responsibility for a class. That is what I often mean
> by a bad [student teacher]. My role as being separate from the men-
> tor and being head of department gives quite a lot of authority to
> it and then they realise that we are all talking and we know what is
> happening and we know what the situation is. (Interview with Head
> of Geography – 5 February)

Previous years of working with student teachers influenced how the
head of department worked in the partnership:

> When [ex tutor] was running it we tended to get one good one bad
> [student teacher]. He did misjudge it one year and we got two bad,
> and I was so exhausted at the end of it that I had to say 'we are hav-
> ing a year off'. (Interview with Head of Geography – 5 February)

Such negative experiences may have impacted on how student teachers were viewed in the department's planning:

> The student teacher education work won't be influenced by the fact that we are a training school. Resourcing is all student and pupil based, all the teaching and learning decisions are pupil-based, and the [student teachers] fit into that. (Interview with Head of Geography – 5 February)

In her fourth year of teaching, the school Geography mentor had taken on the role two years previously, and had work shadowed the previous mentor the year before by 'watching, observing and helping in that context' (interview with mentor – 15 January). The ex-mentor was now the university tutor. Having trained at Downtown University the mentor felt that she had an insight into the role:

> The role was kind of pushed my way but I was interested in it. Because I was at [Downtown University] anyway so I really enjoyed and valued the system and thought it was really effective. (Interview with Geography mentor – 15 January)

The tutor also felt it a particular advantage if a mentor had trained at Downtown University as they then had a greater understanding of the student teacher education programme:

> She [the mentor] understands the demands of the course. She particularly knows about the school based assignments and the [university] assignments and I think when it comes to talking about those in the mentor sessions perhaps she has an insight that others may not have, particularly if they haven't had time to read the handbook. I think she is probably coming from the [student teacher's] perspective a lot. (Interview with Geography tutor – 11 May)

The personal experience of the mentor having taken the Downtown student teacher education course is advocated in as far as this implies an awareness of its content. This then appears to make the student teacher education activity in school closely related to that in the university, even if it is only due to a shared familiarity with the subject matter.

The role tended to stay with mentors for two to three years, and was then passed to another teacher if they were considered suitable. Therefore, there was a clear passing down of the responsibility, with the mentor's job modelled for teachers when they were supporting student teachers in their classes, before they then took on the mentoring role. This suggests that the way of working in the position was preset, especially when the current mentor had work shadowed her predecessor before he became the university tutor. The current mentor knew the tutor well and was confident in talking to him as a friend. However, such close-knit systems were perhaps less likely to create new ways of working because of their familiarity:

> Researcher: Did anything arise from the last university mentor meeting?
> Mentor: (Laugh) One person turned up to that meeting and it was me. So it was just me and [tutor] and we sat and chatted for an hour. (Interview with Geography mentor – 27 June)

As with the head of department, the mentor did not express reasons for the department being involved in student teacher education ('I don't know actually. I don't know the ethic behind it' – 15 January). Instead, she concentrated on fulfilling the requirements of the job and commented on the challenges of meeting the expected tasks. A belief that teachers who were ex-student teachers from Downtown University had a greater appreciation of what was required allayed worries about the need to provide detailed training for the teachers in supporting the student teachers in school:

> I haven't felt the need to give [the other Downtown University trained teacher] too much advice, and said that she can come and talk to me, because she went through the system herself. So I think that if someone hadn't gone through [Downtown's course], then a little bit more of a chat might have been useful. (Interview with Geography mentor – 15 January)

Nevertheless, it became clear that the other teacher would have welcomed more detailed explanations of her role when supporting student teachers, and also felt some trepidation in taking on the mentor's role the following year. Student teacher education was not discussed in the department a great deal beyond the logistics of working with student teachers. Some staff commented that the way they were supposed to work with the student teachers in their classes was just taken for granted.

The university Geography tutor was taking on this role for the second year, and although he had taught many sessions at the university, he had not significantly contributed to the design of the course or handbook, and found the student teacher learning process and handbook 'pretty much the same' (interview – 11 May) as when he took on the school mentor role seven years ago at Market Town High School. He acknowledged how the previous tutor had sought mentors' opinions and had group discussions:

> He was really good at writing things down and taking on advice and changing things as a result. So the Geography programme did change as a result of mentors' discussions really. So that was really good. (Interview with Geography tutor – 11 May)

As a part-time tutor (two days a week at the university and three days in school during his first year, and vice versa for the second year), he had more responsibility for the student teacher education course during the research year, as he took on the ex-tutor's lead role when he retired. He felt he had received training from him on fulfilling this role from his first year of working with him: 'I was learning so much from working with him. I would have never been able to do this year if I hadn't done that year with him' (interview with Geography tutor – 11 May). Although having had some preparation for the lead tutor's role, he was aware that being a teacher on the school staff would make a difference for the student teachers when on their school teaching practice. When asked how he would want a student teacher to view his visits:

> As an opportunity to show somebody from the university, their tutor, what they have been doing, and the ideas they have got for their Geography teaching. An opportunity to talk about that, ask questions maybe and an opportunity to talk about the things they are concerned about perhaps not just with teaching but with the course in general, things like assignments and so on. (Interview with Geography tutor – 11 May)

He felt that the idea of talking to an 'outsider' from the university could appear more 'professional' than just talking to a colleague in school, as was the case in Market Town High School, but he also felt that having had some extra contact with the student teacher, and he seeing him as 'part of the department' with friends there, may make the experience more relaxing for him (interview with Geography tutor – 11 May).

## Section 2 Social practices

*Department routines*

The Humanities team rooms were very cramped with desks allocated to staff only, and therefore it was difficult for the student teachers to base themselves in the department working spaces. This meant that with encouragement from some of the teachers, they were expected to vacate the working space for the permanent staff and use the staff rooms for doing their own work. A certain amount of 'angst' was expressed by the head of Geography when considering that the student teachers had to take on a mobile role, but it was felt that 'there's no practical solution to it' (interview with Head of Geography – 5 February). The fact that the staff room was so close to the team room in upper school in particular alleviated some feelings of guilt:

> We are quite lucky because this school is department and faculty based so no one goes to the staff room – they [the student teachers] go to the staff room just because they have got network computers, a place where no one goes in lesson time, they are not very busy at lunch and break times ... the first year when I was here the [student teachers] were always in someone else's space and it was difficult. (Interview with Geography mentor – 15 January)

However, as far as the student teachers were concerned the displacement from the centre of the department's workspace did impact on their feelings of working in the school:

> If they made a little bit of room you'd feel like you had your place as well in the department in general, because right now you do feel like you are an accessory. (Interview with Geography student teacher – 7 June)

The attitude and responsibility of the student teachers themselves was instrumental in the way they worked within the department. A proactive approach from them when working with the staff and utilising the facilities influenced the daily routines of the department, and this could be successful depending upon how adept the student teachers were at working with people and appreciating the effect they had on the working environment. Seeing the student teachers in the second practice work in different ways compared to the student teacher in the first practice indicated this process, and was to do with them coming to the school with a different set of criteria and for a different amount of time (only six weeks as opposed to a period of eight months). This meant that the onus during the first practice was on the structures provided by the student teacher education course (mentor meetings, observation and feedback sessions) to enable student teacher learning, rather than them acting as full and included members of the Humanities faculty. Noticeably, meetings with student teachers took place outside the team rooms, and the Geography student teachers tended to talk to teaching staff after lessons in the classrooms and at agreed times.

*Relationships*

Communication in the department appeared more fragile than in other areas of the school. One department meeting I was due to attend was cancelled as a gesture of gratitude from the head of department for the recent hard work the team had done on moderation. ('It is the only way I can give something back' – field notes, 21st May.) Wanting to see if there was a sharing of teaching and learning as I had witnessed to differing extents in the other department meetings, I was later informed by one of the experienced teachers:

> All the Geography meetings I have been to, have been much less of a debate and much more of a kind of sorting things out type. In terms of how to deliver Geography [student teacher] would have got quite a bit of discussion from certain individuals in the department rather than learning it from group discussions. (Interview with Geography teacher – 11 May)

The Geography mentor also felt that for the student teachers to have any impact on the department was difficult, owing to the team not being very 'close-knit' (interview – 27 June). However, the student teachers were very positive about working in the Geography department. They praised the approachable manner of the teachers, although felt it unfortunate that as student teachers they were not necessarily seen as working alongside the staff by the pupils, because of the team room being less frequented. They praised the progressive lesson planning and enjoyed the relaxed atmosphere. One noted:

> The Head of Department is incredibly relaxed and he views [the second teaching practice] as if you are already qualified by the time you get here. (Interview with Geography student teacher – 7 June)

The Head of Department defended the department staff and aimed to 'protect' them from the stress of having to do focused observations for the student teachers and from providing support:

> There is quite a lot of observation and note-taking, and I think for teachers they find that a bit stressful because they [the student teachers] often come from [Downtown University] with a particular thing they are looking at in a particular lesson and you are not always sure what. (Interview with Head of Geography – 5 February)

He also bemoaned the physical impact and stress of having more practitioners in the department, and explained how he would like to have space just for the Geography department in order to help develop professional working relationships among the staff.

*Resources*

There were fewer examples of staff sharing resources than in other departments, and as in the History department, the lower school schemes of work needed to be accessible for non-specialist Geography teachers. Resources were seen primarily as an integral part of lesson planning, and consequently were viewed in a pragmatic way. If acknowledged as department-wide resources, they lacked the ownership desirable for developing new ideas, and were mainly considered as a necessity for non-specialists to access the curriculum. Occasionally, a teacher commented that certain resources were in need of improvement, but as this was not their job, they were not prepared to work on it. The tutor indicated that lower school resources were seen as a backup for Geography teaching, and that once specialist staff were responsible for examination groups, then creating their own resources was more desirable:

> If you have got the Religious Studies or the History teachers coming up and they are supposed to be teaching lesson 5 on Japan and it's not there or it's rubbish whatever, you are going to get complaints and it's going to be needed to be sorted out, whereas at upper school, because everybody is Geography trained and they are doing [examination classes] it can be much more of a 'get on with it on your own' type of thing. (Interview with Geography tutor – 11 May)

Consequently, resources for upper school were discussed when planning specific lessons during the mentor meetings, and for lower school, they were assessed as far as what was available in the schemes of work. If these were seen to be lacking, then complementing them with newly devised resources was suggested but not essential. One student teacher had considerable difficulty in her second teaching practice when she was asked to follow a lower school scheme of work for a teacher who was not with the class owing to medical leave. When teaching with the resources for the scheme of work, the class had already used them on another module in another humanities subject (holocaust work-sheets had been used in Religious Studies when in the History Scheme of Work). The mentor criticised this, as it went against lower school practice, but the student teacher was then expected to devise another relevant set of lessons for the same scheme of work. She found this challenging, as the purpose of the resources and what they added to the scheme were not discussed. The resources appeared to represent the scheme itself.

## Section 3 Specific student teacher education learning opportunities

*Geography mentor meetings*

There was one mentor and one student teacher in the department for the first school practice and two student teachers for the second. Each mentor meeting took place in the mentor's classroom with the full hour being used. The meetings were focused and kept to an agenda with this being similar each time. All student teachers were very complimentary about the mentor's secure support, and her help seemed to allay any concerns they may have had with some of the other teachers in the department not working so proactively with them.

The meetings were structured in a very similar way, starting with a general checking of how things were going:

Mentor: So how is it going? All ok today?
Student teacher: Period 1, I led it and [teacher] stayed in the team room to give me more credibility
Mentor: Classroom management?
Student teacher: Better
Mentor: Level of noise ok?
Student teacher: Good
Mentor: Any warnings?
Student teacher: One, throwing a pen lid.
Mentor: Question and answer ok?
Student teacher: Fine, and brainstorming.

> Mentor: Were they settled? Hands up? Ground rules? Do get [teacher] in one time a week at the moment – observation form and targets – important they get done – ask him to watch next Tuesday.
> Student teacher: He should have been in yesterday.
> Mentor: No that's all right, how about tomorrow?
> [The student teacher's responses to the mentor's questions are very brief.] (Field notes – 17 January)

This general update was followed by questions about what was needed as far as the student teacher education course was concerned (assignments, school-based tasks, observation lessons and tutor visits), and then the main part of all meetings focused on planning lessons. Occasionally, lessons were planned in a general way with advice on the schemes of work, the school resources and who to contact to organise equipment, but usually planning was in great detail as a joint activity with the student teachers recording ideas ready for their lesson plan. The student teachers particularly valued such practical help and came to the meetings with a list of those lessons they wanted help with. In the first teaching practice with only one student teacher, it was possible to check his timetable and talk through the planning done so far that week, and then help with areas either not covered or where further input was wanted. The mentor felt this to be the most important aspect of mentor meetings and always gave priority to lesson planning rather than to the course requirements:

> The paperwork may be a little bit too much sometimes. And therefore [student teacher] might sit there for 20 minutes when I am going all through this crap – it's not crap – it's relevant, but actually in the end you want to get down to talking about lesson plans. That is what the mentor period should be for. (Interview with Geography mentor – 15 January)

The mentor offered a personal perspective to lesson planning and rarely debated this with the student teacher. For example, in talking about the importance of 'selling' a lesson to pupils:

> Mentor: You have got to sell it [the lesson content] to them and make them want to be in the room. They need you to make it relevant and interesting, even if you look like a real tool. I get enthusiastic about all sorts. Do you know what I mean?
> Student teacher: Yes.

Mentor: I think you do want to do that – the difference of yesterday and your first lesson, and so I want to see that progress again. Is that fair?
Student teacher: Yes.
Mentor: If you get this now you will be able to manage discipline, as all the class will be interested. (Field notes – 24 January)

The student teacher never questioned or challenged the mentor's point of view throughout the teaching practice. The mentor too seemed loath to criticise the student teacher's thinking and would apologise in advance if she gave advice that may be construed in a negative way. When considering that much of the information imparted to the student teachers in mentor meetings was based on the mentor's opinion and her own past experience ('I keep telling stories and am beginning to sound like an old woman' – mentor, 31 January), and not discussed in any great detail, the learning was often viewed as simple transformation of knowledge and was therefore reproductive. It seemed that highlighting the contestation and challenge in educational ideas was seen by the mentor as the responsibility of the university.

The mentor spoke in terms of personalities, which appeared to make the student teacher feel awkward if he wanted to be critical about anything he saw, especially with regard to other teachers. Therefore, any debates about aspects of particular teachers' practice were avoided, and consequently, some opportunities to discuss teaching and learning lost. The 'personality' approach to teaching where skills were seen as highly individualised made criticism seem a personal slight: 'I feel I shouldn't be commenting on that when I talk to people, because I wouldn't like someone to do that to me' (interview with student teacher – 22 February). Had the mentor concentrated on educational ideas rather than how teachers presented their lessons, then debating teachers' lessons may not have been seen in such a personal way.

*Geography tutor school visits*

The Geography tutor emphasised the tutor visits as a supporting mechanism for the student teachers rather than treating them solely as learning opportunities, and spoke in terms of the student teachers' self-esteem:

I think it is quite important to give them a real boost if they're clearly in the face of a lot of criticism from perhaps other members of the Geography department and things like that, which has happened. (Interview with Geography tutor – 11 May)

There was a very supportive feel in that all post-lesson discussions were informal and tended not to interrogate the student teacher. This helped in creating a positive atmosphere and enabled the student teacher to feel that his comments were equally valid. Negotiations on the success of the lessons and the student teacher's learning focused on the consideration of well-designed resources and the planning of effective activities. The agreed successful nature of the student teacher's practice made conversations relatively easy, as agreements in discussions usually meant that the learning was less problematised. There was security in establishing a consensus when commenting on the nature of practice:

> Tutor (to the mentor): We've just talked through the lesson, it was organised with relevant resources – he's come on leaps and bounds in assertiveness. (Field notes – 27 April)

Other aspects of the teaching practice apart from lesson observations were checked with reference to the student teacher's profile:

> Tutor: So just looking at targets on profile – ICT and homework?
> Student teacher: I have possibly been a bit slack with homework.
> Mentor: Yes, your focus has been elsewhere and not on how it was taken in. (Field notes – 27 April)

The fact that the tutor was not an external visitor to the school did mean that his visits were less of an occasion, especially in comparison with those in the MFL department. This helped to alleviate overt pressures of a formal assessment, and unlike the other departments, the team room was never used for discussions or for meetings. Therefore, the visits had a very low profile.

*Lesson observations, support and feedback from Geography department teachers*

An experienced teacher felt that the department's lack of cohesion would make the school experience very different for the student teachers in Geography:

> I think it all boils down to personalities actually, and I think the nature of the Geography department as it is. For example, Science is such a big department but it is kind of run like a well-oiled machine and there is clear leadership and perhaps much more of everyone working towards exactly the same goal type of thing, whereas maybe in

the Geography department, that is not quite the case. (Interview with Geography teacher – 11 May)

This disjointed approach seemed to encourage a 'hands off' attitude, which meant there was little challenge or debate with the student teachers about their teaching from some members of staff. The mentor was conscious of this and made the point that the second teaching practice should not be just about practice but should still be about learning. As in the first teaching practice, the main emphasis for evaluation and planning of lessons was in the mentor meetings.

The student teachers were valued for providing extra time for the regular teaching staff, and one teacher noted this even if the student teachers were struggling, as they were still taking the classes. This member of staff was referred to by another as 'a stand back and go for it yourself kind of guy' (Field notes, 11 May). Another teacher also referred to making the day a bit easier if student teachers were taking your classes, and the Head of Department felt that giving classes to student teachers in the second practice was like giving those class teachers 'the first bite of the cherry' (interview – 5 February). Although these were positive opinions on the benefit of having student teachers in the department, they did suggest a rather passive attitude to student teacher learning. There were fewer examples of teachers actively participating in student teacher lessons and discussing joint work in detail than in other departments.

The first student teacher felt very happy working in the department and talked of how he acted differently with each of the staff, and yet felt comfortable with all of them:

> It's a very easy department just to fit into. I haven't had any difficulties with the actual department so it's been a fairly easy experience. And they try and help me as they don't have to, and it is good that they do. (Interview with Geography student teacher – 22 February)

Feeling fortunate that teachers were willing to help him, the student teacher was appreciative of their efforts. It was alluded to by some of the staff that it might not be easy to express opinions openly with all teachers owing to their perception of how student teacher education should operate. Certain members of the department were hesitant in how best to work in student teacher education and how to work with the student teachers. Having been criticised for going to the photocopier whilst a student teacher was teaching her group the previous year, one teacher felt unsure of her responsibilities:

> I am not sure how present I should be. I didn't ever see [student teacher] with a different lesson plan [from the Scheme of Work] and I wasn't sure if it should be me who was asking him about that or [mentor] and so I just said to [mentor] that I am not sure of how much actual planning [student teacher] is doing. I tried to encourage him though I wasn't really sure that was my place to say. I still don't know. (Interview with Geography teacher – 17 May)

This lack of communication and department overview of how student teacher education should operate appeared to reflect some lack of cohesion felt in the department's social practices with regard to working habits and in matters of teaching and learning.

## Concluding comments

The mentor was the key person in the student teachers' planning work, and the mentor meetings were heavily relied upon for doing this. Contestable aspects of pedagogical issues in research literature, frequently discussed in the History department, were less debated or considered particularly relevant for detailed discussion in the Geography department. As in the MFL department, these ideas were felt to belong more to the student teacher work at the university. Leaving internal reflections to the student teachers' private thoughts, there was less emphasis on the student teacher as an individual and more of a focus on gaining opportunities to learn by working with successful practitioners in a form of learning transfer (Billett, 2003). Defensive in protecting the subculture of Geography (Paechter, 1995) the Head of Geography bemoaned how Science teaching was taking over aspects of the Geography curriculum. Previous difficult experiences in school practice had also made the Head of Geography wary of the demands of working with novices. Consequently, it was made clear that the organisation of department matters meant that student teacher education should not impact on other department work. In the Science department (the final case study in the next chapter), the student teacher education activity also appeared to be separate from the other department's activities. However, in Science, unlike in Geography, it was expected and encouraged that the student teachers would want to work as part of a team and involve themselves in the other areas of the department.

# 8
# The School Science Department: Cultural, Historical and Social Practices in Student Teacher Education

## The school Science department

The Science faculty comprised of departments in Chemistry, Biology and Physics. These departments were situated together on both school sites. There were eleven members of staff working with the student teachers during the research year with two student teachers in the first school practice and three in the second. Science was taught as a compulsory subject in the lower school (11–13 year old pupils) and also as an examination subject in the upper school (14–16 year old pupils). Post 16 students could opt to take science courses in Biology, Chemistry and/or Physics at Advanced level. (For a discussion of the teaching and studying of Science, see Amos and Boohan (2013), Wellington and Ireson (2012), Handelsman *et al.* (2011) and Liversidge *et al.* (2009).)

### Section 1 Cultural history
*Department profile, staffing and links with Downtown University*

With 23 teachers the Science department was one of the largest faculties. A large proportion of these teachers worked with the five student teachers hosted during the school teaching practices in the research year. Described by a teacher in another faculty as a 'well-oiled' machine (11 May), the department worked closely together and was very proud of the detailed schemes of work and the collaborative creation of these:

> That is how we survive a busy year, because everything is so well organised. The schemes of work are written, technicians can service the schemes of work; we don't have to write lists and lists of things we want, and then have to find them. (Interview with Head of Science – 16 January)

The faculty was undergoing considerable physical change with a new building due for completion during the Easter of the research year. The new facilities were seen to be long overdue. In spite of the lack of ICT facilities and inadequate classroom laboratories (leaky in rainy weather and very hot in sunny weather), the faculty had tried to keep abreast of ICT developments and new ideas about teaching. The team rooms on both school sites were extremely small, and therefore proactive ways of keeping staff unity were important with teachers proud of the numerous social events that kept the faculty cohesive and the fortnightly science department bulletins. Many teachers stayed in the department until later in the day than appeared to be the custom elsewhere in the school, and some of the student teachers used this opportunity to contact staff in order to discuss lessons and to have additional time with the mentor.

The Head of Faculty had only been in post for just over a year, although he had worked in the school for some time, as had many of the others ('there's a lot of people who have been here a really, really long time' – interview with Science teacher, 7 June). The ex-head of faculty had been highly regarded ('an inspirational head of science' – interview with tutor, 24 May), and had been promoted within the school to Assistant Head teacher. Teachers were confident and very positive about working in the department ('we are a bunch of very dedicated teachers in Science' – 16 January), and believed it to be an advantageous environment for student teachers:

> I think there is a huge wealth of experience here. I think we are a really, really successful school and a successful team, and there is a huge variety of what's going on and I think people who want to tap into those things can gain a huge amount ... the huge amount you can learn by people telling you things or suggesting things that you might try. (Interview with Science teacher – 7 June)

The faculty had an established programme of internal observations among the staff, and many of the teachers referred to these in interview, considering them as good training and experience for observing student teachers. They were used to evaluating and discussing the teaching in the department with the current team. The head of faculty believed that lesson plans were set, but there was some flexibility in the schemes of work to allow for personal teaching styles:

> The lesson plan is written so within that teachers do vary. People's personalities come through but there are many similarities. Because

we have strong schemes of work, lessons seem to flow in a similar kind of way … yes, we are quite frame-worked by necessity. And the initiatives we bring in we share, and we hope people will integrate those into their lessons. (Interview with Head of Science – 16 January)

He went on to describe the main styles of teaching, which often reflected the level of experience of the science staff:

I think there are predominantly overall two styles of teaching – there's the front teacher who teaches mainly from the front and circulates and then there is the circulating teacher. Overall those two main types and on top of that those that engage an awful lot in Q and A and ones who perhaps go with worksheets and group work. (Interview with Head of Science – 16 January)

Talking about the teaching in a large faculty in terms of set lessons and familiar patterns of delivery suggested a shared understanding of pedagogy among the staff. A shared way of working was evident to enable the smooth running of the faculty with set systems for ordering lesson preparations from the technicians and arranging demonstrations for those outlined in the schemes of work. The student teachers in the first practice often experienced difficulty in organising themselves within this system and were warned about the necessity of ordering equipment and practising demonstrations within the accepted working practices of the department. Tensions were raised whenever they were unable to comply with this.

There were many ex-student teachers from Downtown University in the department, and consequently the student teacher education course was regarded positively:

The number of the people in the department who were trained by [Downtown] is huge so I don't think that any department who is made that way can possibly have negative thoughts about it because every single [student teacher] who comes in could be the next person you are working with next year. (Interview with Science teacher – 25 May)

There were also many ex-mentors in the department, as this was seen as a useful way of gaining professional development ('something people can get their teeth into before they progress on to team leader basis' – interview with Head of Science, 16 January), and therefore the role had been regularly passed on when suitable people were available. The mentor gained a department promotion in the research year and was therefore due to pass the mentor role to another teacher. It was considered too big a role to have alongside another department responsibility. Having ex-mentors in the department did raise the profile of the role and the student teacher education course, and teachers referred to the benefit of working with other teachers that understood the programme.

The advantage that the mentor role was seen as a stepping stone to promotion was one positive aspect for the department of being involved in student teacher education, and another was the possible recruitment of student teachers:

> There have been a number that have come and joined. There are more who would have liked to have come, but went to work elsewhere. Or we didn't have a job at the time. (Interview with Head of Science – 16 January)

The tutor for the second teaching practice had worked in the department previously as a teacher and therefore had many contacts with the school. The teachers felt that the history the department shared with the university was important in enabling them to keep aware of new developments in science teaching, as well as recruiting student teachers when positions arose.

### Working with student teachers, the school science mentor and the university science tutor

The student teachers in the first practice did not naturally fit in to the department's team ethos, and this caused some consternation from the teachers. One science teacher commented that the mentor found it hard to 'mould' the student teachers in the first school practice (Field notes – 13 March). It appeared that their non-conformist way of approaching the practice challenged how the department viewed them as learners. This was unsettling for many of the teachers who expected them to fit into the faculty in a way that was socially compatible:

> We are really welcoming to them [the student teachers] actually. I think we really make the ones who want to fit in feel at home. The majority of them come out on social events with us and behave and act as part of the team, which I think is super. (Interview with Science teacher – 7 June)

Another teacher reflected on the first teaching practice:

> It is the first year I didn't particularly enjoy working with [student teachers]. I didn't feel that my feedback was being taken any notice of; it left a bit of a sour taste in my mouth really. (Interview with Science teacher – 25 May)

The second teaching practice had a tradition of the student teachers working on a project for primary school liaison. This took a significant amount of their timetable and was preset in the way the department wanted the student teachers to work. Because of this project it was requested that three student teachers came from the university during the second practice ('it turned out last year that if they hadn't had three I think they would have really struggled, and we would probably have had to turn some [primary] groups down, so it was a good thing that we did have three this year – interview with mentor, 27 June). One science teacher was responsible for the project and explained its evolution:

> One group of [student teachers] came up with that project and delivered it on just one day to one small cohort of students. Our primary schools were fighting amongst themselves to be next on the list to do it. We then had a series of [student teachers] each year who came in and just reinvented it. I thought that was rather pointless as we ended up with presentations, which are all as equally good as each other, so let's not bother with that but run with what we've got and deliver them. They [the student teachers] are in for six weeks, and it is quite hard to get those 360 year 6 pupils in. (Interview with Science teacher – 24 May)

Working with so many younger pupils was generally considered a very positive experience for student teachers by both the student teachers and the science staff. However, in requiring them to fulfil the arrangements that the school had already made, the head of department acknowledged that the help it provided for the school was more assured than the learning experience it provided for the student teachers:

> They run the project, co ordinate the organisation of the setting up and running with that, so they work with the students. They do have some classes [to teach on the secondary school timetable] but far fewer, so whether or not that is effective for them … that is good for us as we get somebody to run that project. That is great, but whether

or not it is good for them I don't know. (Interview with Head of
Science – 16 January)

Although being helped by a member of staff in the logistics of arranging
the project, it seemed that having the experience itself was considered
the learning opportunity, as no member of the Science team evaluated
or observed the many primary classes the student teachers taught.
By the second teaching practice, the student teachers were generally
treated as fully qualified, and there was a noticeable sense of relief from
some of the science team in that the student teacher education work
now concentrated on enabling student teachers to gain experience with
classes, rather than supporting and evaluating what had been considered weaker teaching in the first school practice.

The school Science mentor had been in role for two years. He had
trained at Downtown University four years previously. He had been
given the job because the mentor from the previous year had been
impressed with his feedback when working with student teachers
in the past. In fieldwork observations, his feedback was always thorough
and extensive, with many targets for student teachers to work on. One
example of a lesson observation sheet gave eleven suggested targets.
Such comprehensive accounts of lesson evaluation and observations
were for the ex-mentor a sign of good mentoring.

The mentor enjoyed working on the student teacher education
course and felt it had prepared him well for his teaching career. He did
not feel that any improvements were necessary with it, and therefore
approached the school and university assignments positively believing
that student teachers needed to comply with all suggested tasks, and
gave advice on completing these in an efficient manner. He also valued
revisiting the university assignment work in order to prompt his own
practice.

The importance of being able to work successfully as part of a team
was highlighted in the mentor's belief of what made a good teacher. He
spoke of the sensitivity of teachers to outside criticism, and believed
in a communal approach to lesson design and development. The
cohesive nature of the Science faculty at the school was important to
him, and working within the department ethos was encouraged and
expected:

It's just the little things like coming in and chatting to people and
asking questions and things that show that you are part of the community. It's a shame that the two [student teachers] we had earlier

in the year, and there were times when they did do those things, but considering how long they were here, I don't think they immersed themselves in it nearly as much as most people would have. (Interview with Science mentor – 27 June)

A negative view of the student teachers in the first teaching practice largely arose from their lack of teamwork, which was highly regarded in the department:

I don't like to be harsh but they [the student teachers] didn't contribute anything to the department, maybe because the view they took was that they were here to learn from us but not to give anything back. (Interview with Science mentor – 27 June)

Ten years before becoming a part-time university Science tutor, the tutor had been a student teacher on Downtown's student teacher education course, although it had changed considerably since then. He had then become a full-time tutor and had worked on the course for seven years. He had helped to completely rewrite the programme with the lead Science tutor, and they had changed its emphasis from that of delivering science to student teachers to seeing student teachers as learners who were learning how to teach science. This change had arisen from their research looking at trainee science teachers learning to teach outside their science subject specialism.

Both tutors (the lead tutor worked at the research school for the second school practice) explained how decision-making on the course design was always done in joint collaboration with mentors in the partnership schools. They felt this important as a way of acknowledging the expertise and status of understanding that was situated in the school departments and gave examples of how school mentors' opinions had impacted on how the course was written.

The university's role in the partnership was described as one that ensured that deep thinking was taking place in the student teachers' learning experiences, and the tutor hoped to challenge preconceptions and attitudes to pedagogy:

I like to think that I can push them to think, which they might not be getting from somewhere else or to take a risk or to think about the theoretical underpinning, which the mentor probably knows but in the busy run of the day hasn't got … the time and space to reflect. (Interview with Science tutor – 24 May)

One aim was to enable student teachers to see the difficulties inherent in teaching, 'helping them to problematise and see the problems of teaching otherwise it can seem oh so simple, you just do a load of activities' (24 May). By appreciating the complexities of the teaching and learning process, this could help student teachers teach science creatively. They should therefore question practices and take risks with many approaches to teaching and learning. The tutor acknowledged that the best school departments did this, but he showed some reserve and sensitivity in how to question practice when in schools:

> I do challenge occasionally, say things like 'if I was in a bottom set I wouldn't work very hard, would you?' I say things like that but not very often, but keep my counsel quite often, as setting kids works for them [the school]. (Interview with Science tutor – 24 May)

One of the principles of the course was to discuss ideas openly and to encourage questioning. Debating issues from a variety of sources with all involved in student teacher education having equal status was seen as the ideal and one that was usually possible to a greater or lesser extent in the partnership school departments.

## Section 2 Social practices

### Department routines

The Science department used a hot desk system mainly because there were not enough work areas for all staff. At the lower school the Science team room was tiny ('like a matchbox' – interview with Science student teacher, 21 February), with only a coffee table and five easy chairs, a small bench with a couple of stools and a computer. This faculty was the most cramped. In the upper school too, the team space was a very awkward L-shaped room (an old preparation room) and had two computers. There were no desks as such but a mid-height bench around the outside of the room with a number of high stools, so it was possible to work there. Neither room was easy to work in, especially in a department with so many staff. Both rooms were some way from the main staff rooms. At break times staff tended to gather in them to make hot drinks, or stayed in their teaching labs.

The university tutor described the team workspace as 'shocking' (interview with Science tutor – 24 May). However, the completion of the new science block after the first student teacher practice changed the facilities considerably with a light and well-appointed team room with four computers, benches and a number of working desks in the middle.

There was still a hot desk system in operation, but space and computers were available should staff want them. The old team room was available as an overspill workspace. The technicians worked in separate preparation areas but used the team rooms for making hot drinks and occasionally for eating during lesson times.

The student teachers in the first practice frequented the team rooms mainly for meetings with the mentor, and spent the occasional period and break time there. The majority of their non-teaching time was spent away from the department in one of the staff rooms. One student teacher explained:

> I use the staff room, as there is computers there I can use, and the team room is a bit small. There is one computer not being used so I could work there, but on the whole I feel more comfortable in the staff room. (Interview with Science student teacher – 17 October)

The Head of Faculty commented on the varied purpose of the team rooms:

> It's a place where you sit down with other people around – hopefully with other people around. We have coffee in there and we natter in there. We bemoan the lesson we've had and catch up on other people's ideas – how do you do this/that? (Interview with Head of Science – 16 January)

The two student teachers in the first teaching practice did not plan or work together. This was a conscious choice, as they appeared to work in very different ways, with one mainly concerned with passing the course and the other anxious to design all his own resources. They were also less integrated into the department than some of the other student teachers, perhaps because of some of the difficulties they experienced during the practice. Their department-based routines were limited when they were not directly involved in observing or teaching classes. Feedback and support was therefore mainly through the established student teacher education structures and not through incidental discussions. They also utilised e-mail and phone calls out of school hours, but recognised that personal contact could have been more beneficial:

> I think that I would probably have benefited by talking to them [staff], but being that my social skills are not the best, I mean that in conversations I am not very bold or eloquent. But in any case I don't

talk to them in general about teaching … I don't feel, it's like where do I sit, where do I stand? It's just very stuffy and I feel that it is an unnecessary stress for me, so I go to the staff room. (Interview with Science student teacher – 21 February)

Had the student teachers discussed their teaching and planning more generally in the department, both may have benefited considerably from incidental conversations with science teachers. A more communal approach to the teaching was seen in the second practice where the three student teachers both integrated more readily with the science team and used the team rooms to meet and discuss their primary school transition project.

*Relationships*

Department meetings, even though large, were discussion based, with a formal structure ensuring that all staff had the chance to express their opinions. Evidence of confidence in the success of the faculty was expressed by many of the teachers:

> I think we are very good at thinking so we have lots of ideas, a lot, and bring those into faculty meetings and we share. And the best place to get good ideas from is the teachers who have tried them. (Interview with Head of Science – 16 January)

Teaching staff showed a lot of confidence in discussing their ideas about science, and there was evidence of sharing across the department supported by the faculty head and the procedures in place for collaborative work. The Science bulletin reported new ideas and informed staff of the peer observations that were taking place. Many staff staying in the department after the school day was also indicative of their interest in the work and of the importance of planning lessons with experiments prepared and tested prior to use. The student teachers were encouraged to prepare all demonstrations. Occasionally, offers of help appeared to pressurise the student teachers. This was also evident when the mentor and the tutor urged the student teachers to get experience of working with teachers in the three different specialist science areas.

Rather than confronting issues as they arose, the student teachers occasionally avoided them by not basing themselves in the department. For some of the staff, this looked as though the student teachers were avoiding responsibilities, and consequently they treated this 'non-committal' and evasive approach with bewilderment. One teacher spoke of the student teacher as 'like having somebody else in your class who is not doing the right things' (interview with Science teacher – 21 May). With both student teachers, relations were strained at various times with a number of staff. This was challenging for the mentor, and he evaluated how he dealt with the difficulties:

> You are shifting between telling somebody off as if you are their teacher or father, mothering somebody as if they are a small child, and looking after them, and then taking the 'mick' out of them as if they are your friend. (Interview with Science mentor – 27 June)

Relationships remained cordial, although there was some consternation on both sides, with the desire to pass the course being the main factor for working in a way that the department would evaluate positively. After the third tutor visit (where the mentor initially signed the form for one of the student teachers to pass and then changed his mind), the tutor felt that he needed to encourage one of the student teachers not to challenge issues so openly, as this had not helped him gain the confidence of the Science department:

> I made him come in after school to see me and I more or less said: 'can you stop bloody questioning?' Something [another tutor] told me, some advice: 'you are not in a position at the moment to question people as much as you are, because they have got to respect you and see you for what you are. You haven't got there yet, so hey, just hold fire'. (Interview with Science tutor – 24 May)

The other student teacher remained very passive and said nothing to upset the science teaching team, but also showed little interest in wanting to gain from their feedback and advice. She had secured a job in a private school early in the teaching practice, and did not always feel that advice given was relevant. Many felt that she did not take advice well, but she would say whatever she felt was political in order to receive a favourable report, and then put in extra effort for the tutor visits: 'I suppose when [tutor] comes in I make sure my lessons are fantastic' (interview with Science student teacher – 23 February).

*Resources*

Sharing of ideas was seen as extremely positive in all situations both informally in the team rooms as well as formally in the bulletin and faculty meetings. A collegiate approach was apparent when discussing lessons, as these were often referred to in terms of the scheme of work they derived from, for example 'Forces 2'. This expected joint understanding of lesson content meant that very quick chats were had in order to comment on specific parts of lesson demonstrations or exercises, with in-depth responses and advice as to the experience of teaching the lessons. This was felt to be very useful for the student teachers:

> For a lot of schools (especially where I trained) [student teachers] were expected to come up entirely with their own lesson. As a faculty we are quite good at talking to each other so if the person whose lesson you are teaching is not around, there will be others who have taught it. (Interview with Science teacher – 24 May)

Discussions about the schemes of work were open to all if they were present. How far student teachers accessed these depended on their working routines in the faculty. Noticeably, in the second teaching practice the student teachers frequently initiated these kinds of conversations.

## Section 3 Specific student teacher education learning opportunities

*Science mentor meetings*

During the mentor meetings, the Science mentor followed the guidelines in the course handbook very closely:

> Mentor: But you need to be in control of where you are at, you need to prove with evidence, need it written down, your sheets and feedback sheets. You haven't always done that. Where do you keep the descriptors? At home? Under the bed? (laugh). This is the purpose of self-review sheets. So we need to decide now.
> (He gets copies of the descriptors with tick box columns and they both fill them in).
> Student teacher: So we are looking at the 'attention needed' column?
> Mentor: Yes, do a quick review and tick where you think you are, and I'll do it too.
> (They do this in silence for 2 minutes.)
> Mentor: Anything with 'attention needed'?
> (The mentor suggests appropriate targets and what the student teacher can ask staff to look for in observations.)
> Mentor: Next week with your feedback and self-evaluation sheets we can see how you have done, OK? (Field notes – Tuesday 16 January)

Regular concern that the student teachers were not participating in a way that was expected, particularly in their personal organisation and taking responsibility for their work made open discussion difficult, as the mentor felt that he needed to tackle these issues. This put the student teachers on the defensive very quickly. Neither student teacher in the first practice enjoyed the meetings and felt that they were constantly being harassed.

The mentor often found the meetings frustrating too and felt he was pressurising the student teachers but had no choice if he was to get to the crux of the problems. Therefore, using the handbook enabled a common ground to be established and one that had been jointly set out by the university and the school. This took the onus off the mentor, and allowed him to use the handbook as a mechanism for setting out their respective roles. In this respect, it often served to close down discussions with its emphasis on standards and codified learning points: 'I found at times that I had to be quite forceful and say "no this is the case, you can't do that, you have to do this"' (interview with Science mentor – 27 June). This went against the idea of opening out differences of opinion, as the handbook appeared to provide all the answers, and the student teachers' practices were viewed in terms of the requirements set out. Tensions in ideas on teaching and learning were rarely brought to the surface, but instead there were tensions in the student teachers not meeting the expectations of the school department staff. The monitoring relaxed somewhat in the second teaching practice when the mentor was more confident with the student teachers' progress. It was also noticeably more relaxed at the end of the first practice when with the pressure off (as both student teachers had just passed their second assessment point) the nature of the discussion was freer with the student teachers contributing as much as the mentor and discussing issues more openly.

*Science tutor school visits*

One of the purposes of the tutor visits appeared to be to monitor progress. To a large extent the visits were characterised by checking how the student teachers were working in the department and what experiences they were getting. Checking what was being done, how it was being done and what needed to be done were regular topics of conversation amongst the tutor and student teachers:

Tutor: Let's start with the profile, then the mentor's report and then my report. Then we will have covered everything. Talk us through [student teacher] and you chip in (to the mentor).

([Student teacher] reads through the profile sheet, which the mentor is hearing for the first time. The tutor quick fires factual questions: Why? Which group? Do they respond? What do you do? Ringing parents? Questions are answered briefly and factually.)
Tutor: Ok good, fine
Student teacher: I helped with the move yesterday.
Tutor: Have you done parents' evenings and meetings? Are you writing weekly profile sheets? Are these used in the mentor periods? Useful? (Field notes – 17 April)

The questions helped to clarify what the student teacher was saying and often required them to go into specifics about what they had written. The profiles were very detailed and consequently it was difficult to have any in-depth discussions. The priority appeared to be about completing the profile sections and checking all the points off. Despite the emphasis on paperwork, the tutor believed that the Downtown student teacher education course was far less 'paper-heavy' than other student teacher education courses. The second school practice student teachers were less participants in an assessment process for their final tutor visit, as there were no observations and just 10- to 15-minute chats with them prior to the form signing. This was seen as an opportunity to celebrate the completion of the course, with the tutor (the lead Science tutor at the university) talking generally with the student teachers about what they had learned in their second teaching practice and what their hopes were for the future.

The tutors acknowledged a concern that student teachers sometimes saw the visits simply as assessments:

It is assessment at one level so you don't want to be too dishonest. On the other hand your visit isn't going to tip the balance between them meeting a descriptor, as that would be ridiculous, but they don't believe that, as you are the tutor from outside. (Interview with Science tutor – 3 July)

Some concerns raised by the mentor in the first practice were noted but not dwelt on in detail, and this led to a number of meetings between the tutor and the mentor without the student teachers present. The tutor sensitively diffused criticism in his school visits:

Mentor: [Teacher] says attention is needed in getting to know names of pupils.

Student teacher: Really?

Tutor: Maybe she ticked the wrong box.

Mentor: Maybe she is saying that you should know them as you have had the class from September. (Field notes – 2 February)

After one of the student teachers left the team room, the tutor was more critical of her: 'Does she believe in what she is saying, or does she just say what she thinks I want to hear? Her lesson plan was scrappy' (Field notes – 29 November).

Concerns about the student teachers continued on and off during the first teaching practice, but without addressing these formally (the mentor was given the opportunity to do this by the tutor) the situation never became a completely open exchange of opinions. Because the science content of the teaching had a prominent place in discussions, there was less opportunity to debate teaching and learning issues. The paperwork (profiles and reports) took priority, and completing these documents appeared to drive many of the meetings. Consequently, discussions on issues that arose from the paperwork were limited. The student teachers felt that the university's check on their progress was the most important aspect of the tutor visits, and this may be a reason why they appeared more concerned with what the university thought than the school. One student teacher acknowledged that the advice from both was often the same or at least similar, but he wanted his progress to be seen as positive and up-to-date by the university:

I know it's probably not this but I feel like I am getting university approval about my progress [during tutor visits] … when they come and see me, it's like they are updating what they think, which feels good because this is where I am. When they say it is satisfactory progress, it means ah yes I am on the right track. (Interview with Science student teacher – 21 February)

This feeling that there was a distinct official opinion, and that any variation from this suggested that progress was less assured, hampered the idea that teaching and learning were complex issues that were best assessed over time and in school.

*Lesson observations, support and feedback from Science*
*department teachers*

Working from very detailed schemes of work meant that teacher feedback was readily available. All members of staff had definite opinions on how best to work with the lesson content, and consequently this led post-lesson discussions with teaching strategies and classroom management issues noted in light of this. Many teachers seemed to treat student teacher observation in a similar way to the science performance management observation cycle, with lessons evaluated with regard to their effectiveness:

> I think because we have such good schemes of work and we team teach, I think people are less sensitive to criticism, whereas some other departments do work much more in a dispersed fashion. (Interview with Science teacher – 21 May)

The time spent on the paperwork (observation and profile sheets, mentor and tutor reports) for the teaching files might perhaps have been more usefully spent in openly discussing important issues that some staff felt were not addressed:

> With [student teacher] in particular there was a mismatch between our judgements and her judgements between good, satisfactory and exceptional. When we were kind of saying satisfactory, and she was saying exceptional. There was a huge gap there and we could have done with more time to talk to her and say we don't actually feel you are as good as all that, and why do you think you are that good? Ultimately, we didn't quite get to the heart of it with her. (Interview with Science teacher – 7 June)

Some of the science staff referred to the importance of student teachers learning how to cope in the classroom, and viewed the teaching practice as an opportunity to experience what a full-time teaching position would be like: 'you can't learn to drive without hours behind the wheel ... the more hours you can get in front of a class, the absolute better' (interview with science teacher – 25 May). Another member of the science team warned against giving too much support and advocated giving student teachers a more autonomous role:

> Next year the support will be far, far less. They won't be being observed or have teacher input on every lesson. They might not have a mentor slot and they have got to learn to take that responsibility for themselves throughout the year. You don't want to support them too much if it means that next year is going to be a struggle. (Interview with Science teacher – 25 May)

Such work in student teacher education prevented a truly collaborative approach, especially when referring to the first school practice. It was generally expected that in the second school practice, the class teacher would take more of a passive and secondary role in the classroom.

## Concluding comments

Opportunities for enhancing student teacher learning in the science department were governed by demands for completing the student teacher education paperwork. This became the main focus of discussions and was time-consuming, and allowed little room for student teacher agency when participating in learning opportunities. General conversations personalising the required codified teaching standards to the viewpoint of the student teachers rarely occurred. The student teachers in the first school practice tended to separate themselves from other science department activities and were therefore not present for general discussions on teaching and learning which in a collaborative culture can lead to effective learning opportunities (Hodkinson and Hodkinson, 2005). Instead, completing the paperwork from the university became the main activity in mentor and tutor meetings.

The four school department case studies have analysed descriptively the concepts that make up a mediational model of activity as described by Engeström (2001): the rules, community and the division of labour of the student teacher education activity systems. Contextualising the student teacher education work in the departments with extended case studies has been preparatory for showing how tools mediate the participants' work on the objects of the student teacher education activity system. The importance of these tools (specific to the student teacher education university course) and other tools (those used in the student teacher education activity more generally) and how their use impact on the learning opportunities for student teachers is further explored in relation to all four school departments in the next chapter.

# 9

# An Analysis of Student Teacher Education Tools: Mediating Student Teacher Education Practice

## Introduction

The case studies in Chapters 5 to 8 give overall impressions of student teacher education practices in the school departments of History, MFL, Geography and Science. This chapter looks specifically at how student teacher education tools were used and why they were appropriated in different ways. More examples are given from the data generated from the fieldwork and these are highlighted to further elaborate the organising concepts outlined in the case studies. The chapter identifies tools as units of analysis and considers how they were selected and appropriated by participants in the student teacher education activity systems in order to mediate the work on the object of activity. As explained in Chapter 3, tools are understood as anything that mediates subjects' actions on objects (Russell, 2004) as in, for example, course handbooks, lesson plans, observation summaries and report forms. This chapter analyses tools in specific relation to student teacher education. The analysis is based on an understanding that the ways in which tools are used says something about the object as well as the culture of the department where the tools have developed (Engeström *et al.*, 1999; Nardi, 2005; Stetsenko, 2005). An indication of how the link between teachers' use of tools and the ways that they think is also revealed, and this helps to appreciate how the relationship between the participants' thinking impacts on and is impacted by the student teacher education activity's object (Engeström, 1999a; Kaptelinin, 2005; Miettinen, 2005; Wertsch, 2007). The use of tools is analysed in order to better understand the relationships in the student teacher education activity systems, and this enables an appreciation of the social situation of development for the student teachers (Vygotsky, 1978).

Other elements in the activity system (rules, community and division of labour) are also considered when analysing the use of tools, and these indicate how the mediation process relates to the social structures within the system and how, for example, aspects of power are developed and demonstrated in practice.

## Tools as rules

If tools are to mediate student teacher learning and not simply act as student teacher education course requirements, they need to enable genuine opportunities for student teachers to act as responsive practitioners. Otherwise, there could be a danger of too much 'emphasis on curriculum delivery at the expense of the experience of responsive pedagogical decision making' (Edwards and Protheroe, 2003, p. 240). Practices may be seen to be responsive if they are developed through questioning and challenging pedagogical decisions with regard to specific contexts. The tools can help this by initiating debate about established pedagogical meanings. If discussions arising from the tools are meaningful to student teachers' pedagogical experiences, these can affect their practices, which may in turn feed back into how future discussions arising from the tools are shaped. Thus, opportunities for mutual and expansive learning can arise when tools are appropriated in this way, with the relationships of the participants using them being open to learning. This is because the tool mediates the work on the object as an evolving problem space, and allows for the process of internalisation and externalisation (Vygotsky, 1978). If tools are appropriated in regulatory ways they work as rules in the activity system, and learning is restricted as new interpretations are not enabled, and meanings are set and do not evolve. As will be seen in this chapter, this is evident in relation to the tasks that are outlined in the MFL course handbook, for example. Rather than being seen primarily as opportunities to work on student teacher learning, the tasks are viewed by the mentor and some of the teachers as a 'dreaded list' (MFL mentor in a mentor meeting – 17 January) that needs to be completed in readiness for the tutor's school visits. Thus, one contradiction in the object of the MFL student teacher education activity system lies in viewing this as managing the relationship with the university tutor in the student teacher education partnership rather than focusing on the student teachers' learning. Consequently, concentrating on student teacher education as a management activity marginalises a focus on learning and reduces the possibilities for new learning.

## Tools specific to student teacher education

The physical tools specific to student teacher education were provided as part of the student teacher education course and therefore derived from the university, although some had been developed with the consultation of the school mentors. Some specific tools were in the course handbooks and these were generic across subjects: mentor informal reports on progress, tutor school visit discussion reports and lesson observation summaries, for example. Other tools were specific to subjects (lesson planning sheets and weekly evaluation sheets) and again these were provided in the course handbooks. Two of the departments (History and MFL) gave examples of how some of these tools could be completed by the student teachers, mentors and teachers. The course handbooks were important tools in the analysis of student teachers' learning opportunities. Their evolution could be more easily analysed than other more generic tools produced by the university. Therefore, for each department I initially analyse the course handbooks as tools in the school student teacher education activity systems and then consider the more generic tools that were contained within the handbooks. These generic tools were used by a greater number of participants in the activity systems, as many of the department teachers working with the student teachers used these tools as part of the student teacher education activity, whereas principally it was only the student teachers, mentors and tutors who used the course handbooks.

## Tools-in-use in the school departments

### The History department

As physical artefacts, the course handbooks produced at the university were designed in very similar ways, with a consistent format across the subject departments using A4 ring binders, identical in colour and font on the covers, and with the university's details and crest. However, each handbook varied in length (from 148 to 238 pages) and was supplemented with other information (for example, separate guidance leaflets for mentors). The handbooks also included course information on assignments, the student teacher education programmes and assessment details. The History handbook was the most detailed with extensive reading lists (both required and optional). Reasons for following the activities were given particular emphasis in History with the intention of developing a high level of critical thinking and a 'critical understanding of teaching through which you can extend your professional development in the future' (History handbook, p. 124).

The university produced the handbooks guided by the ideas of the current or previous tutors and in consultation with the school mentors at their regular meetings in the university. They were reviewed and potentially revised each year. The current tutors had had varying inputs into the handbooks' evolutions. The experienced History tutor could describe how the book had changed since its original inception over 20 years ago:

What we have now is unrecognisable ... it is far more comprehensive; secondly the way in which it is structured changed very significantly when I did my own doctorate. The attempt has been to structure it much more evidently in terms of the nature of experience that [student teachers] get in school. (Interview with History tutor – 14 August)

The History mentor, unlike the other mentors, did not refer to the handbook regularly but was aware of its potential as a pedagogical tool. She was flexible in adapting the tasks and felt that the course was 'a bit full on' (interview – 23 January) during the early weeks. The student teacher valued her flexible reading of the course expectations, and the tutor was happy with this appropriation of the tool as he felt it important that the resource didn't 'distort a reality but work with it' (interview – 14 August). Consequently, the discussions in mentor meetings responded to the social situation of the student teacher's development and did not act upon the expected rules outlined in the course handbook. However, an awareness of the handbook's content initiated dialogue during mentor meetings, as illustrated below with regard to a discussion on historical sources but without necessarily specifically responding to the suggested activities for that week:

[Mentor returns the student teacher's written assignment (required by the handbook) with scribbles on the word-processed work.]
Student teacher: In year 7 I started with sources which [History teacher 1] said were too difficult.
Mentor: Do we need to put other layers in first, raising tension in how we use sources? What are our ideas about students involved in history as a way of thinking about things? Why do students think they do history? Do they view sources as something they get facts from? Their levels of understanding; how do we make the link with practice?

Student teacher: [Pupil] who has got the talk gets level 3 but when written, when he uses the source, he is level 1 [referring to the national curriculum levels which range from 1 to 8].

Mentor: The source is giving perspective on the issue, how do sources lead you into differentiation? … What kind of questions can you use in class? Would you change them on reflection? How are you developing inference skills?

Student teacher: Some could develop that in poster lessons. I see [History teacher 2] and [History teacher 3] in lessons trying to draw out inferences from sources. Would that be worth doing? Scaffolding: pros and cons of frameworks. I presume they [the pupils] ignore me when they don't want to do it.

Mentor: [History tutor] has quite strong views. Upper school exams assume students know strengths and weaknesses of sources and bias. How do we tell higher attainers? What is the evidence base, next step?

Student teacher: I don't know, what is the next step?

Mentor: You don't have to answer now. Should sources be taught explicitly? [Market Town High School] suddenly throws sources in rather than drip-feeding, and that's an issue. (Field notes – 17 January)

Diverse perspectives and opinions on pedagogy were acknowledged, and the student teacher and the mentor debated these. Therefore, the handbook enabled mediation of the student teacher's learning. Even though the student teacher was on the receiving end of many questions here, they were largely rhetorical in function and their purpose appeared to be to demonstrate that there were no easy answers. Three different teachers, the History tutor, the mentor and the school department's schemes of work were mentioned, demonstrating awareness of the diverse perspectives on the topic. Such exploratory talk opened up important distinctions in the conversation, raising questions, which could not be answered immediately, but acted as stimuli for future dialogue about the use and value of sources in History. This recognition of ongoing and dialogic exploration was typical of the discussions in History mentor meetings, and here the handbook could be seen as initiating the dialogue and introducing ideas that might extend it, both at the time and in the future.

The handbook also outlined the expectations and responsibilities of the mentor, how she should work collaboratively with the student teachers in order to work on developing their learning. In response to an interview question about the purpose of the handbook, the History tutor said:

> It is meant to be an integrated programme so we all needed to have the same stuff. But the green sheets, which is the bit addressed to mentors, those were specifically written with mentors in mind given that it is their responsibility to organise the programme in school. We are keen to encourage mentors to take that responsibility and hence those sheets are addressed to them who unpick and elaborate what is intended by those tasks. (Interview with History tutor – 14 August)

This explicitly shared understanding was designed to encourage all parties to fulfil what was clearly presented as a responsibility, and therefore acted as a reminder of what the student teachers should be doing in the school practice. It also reinforced the understanding that the activity was a collaborative one. Therefore, the handbook mediated explicitly (Wertsch, 2007) as a tool to develop student teacher learning but also mediated work on the object implicitly in the way that the dialogue and conversations around it were affected by it.

A key difference in how tools were used in the departments appeared to be whether they were considered as a way of shaping practice or as a way of developing learning. It was noticeable that the mentor and head of department in History had worked closely and extensively with Downtown University on numerous aspects of pedagogy. This work had created a joint intellectual approach to student teacher learning with a similarity of styles in how they worked with student teachers. The mentor included all department staff in her collating the student teachers' reports and did this in a detailed and extensive process of e-mails, recording all teachers' comments. The student teacher in the first teaching practice talked through this in detail and at one point took exception to one teacher's comments. These were subsequently taken out of the report but also discussed with the tutor. Such detailed design and collaborative construction of the tool stood out in how the report was used as a way of engaging all those involved in the student teacher education activity system in the student teacher's learning. The mentor acted as intermediary in gaining teachers' perspectives and worked with them in detail to create an overview of the student teacher's learning. The report was then broached in some detail with the tutor (who had been e-mailed it before the school visit) and this informed the discussions around the student teacher's learning when the tutor visited the school.

Talking with the report content already known and the opinions of staff and the student teacher having taken place openly and with some debate prior to the visit meant that the tool worked in a similar way to the handbook in that implicit mediation of the report was evident in the dialogue that surrounded it. Therefore, operating as a tertiary artefact (one that represents the ideology for understanding the object of the activity) this affected discussions. All were able to play an active role with the tutor working with the student teacher in a very similar way to the mentor, thereby allowing a genuine sharing of ideas and opinions that had arisen as a result of the report. Contestation was not apparent with regard to the way of working on the student teacher's learning but was welcomed as part of the learning process.

Similarly, when the mentor asked the student teacher for explanations with regard to her lesson plans and observation summaries, this helped to open out discussions and frequently extended the debate that ensued beyond the school context. The student teacher's previous experiences and home life influenced her understanding, and these were discussed along with the mentor's own beliefs and background. The relationship was therefore an open and personal one, which was also mirrored by the tutor when he visited the school. The mentor valued the tutor's ability to work in partnership with the student teachers and adopted the same approach:

> I think that [tutor's] visits are always excellent and he has got a great skill in picking up the key issues that there are, and justifying them and combining that expectation that they are students on a course and they are adults and mature learners. (Interview with History mentor – 23 January)

The student teacher, although anxious about the tutor visits and occasionally negative in her feelings on how they went and how her progress was seen, valued the tutor's input. She believed the visits helped her progress and even though pressurised did not override the learning opportunities:

> He [tutor] is able to pick out and tell you why it was good, which maybe I didn't realise why it was good, because that lesson did go particularly well and I was thinking, oh that went well, I wonder why. Whereas he can go through it with you and say you did this, this and this. And I'm thinking, did I? But the fact he has done that means I can apply it to another lesson. So that's really helped me step forward particularly in questioning, which I am obsessed with,

because he pointed out why it worked which was to do with going in at a low level and building up and up and up and asking why constantly. (Interview with History student teacher – 19 February)

By 'going through' the lesson plan and 'pointing out why' it worked, the tutor used the lesson plan as a tool to mediate work on the object of the student teacher's learning, and closely considered her ideas when questioning her thinking. Such mediation of the work on the object was highlighted in the tutor's aspirations for the way he worked with student teachers.

The History teaching staff also appreciated that they were part of a debate and acted as sounding boards encouraging experimentation:

> My philosophy is not to have a set mind of what you want to produce at the end of it. Far from a monopoly of knowing how ... but the main thing is the encouragement to fail in a way. There's a feeling that you've got to know what you are talking about. Obviously, if I saw somebody have a really bad idea I would try and adjust that, but I would want them to keep trying lots of things and if it goes wrong, just to be able to push yourself off and go, 'ok what do I learn from that, and I shall try and not make that mistake next time, but I will keep trying lots of new things'. (Interview with History teacher – 17 May)

This was unusual in comparison with the teaching staff in the other departments, and could be partially as a result of the head of department's influence and lead in giving experimentation and research such a high profile in the department's other activity systems as well as student teacher education. This would illustrate 'the ways in which the practices of a community are structured by their institutional context' (Daniels, 2010, p. 112) and how social mediation impacts on the objects of activity systems as well as on the work being mediated by the kinds of physical tools already mentioned.

Questioning decisions made in student teachers' planning meant that awareness was gained of the variety of options and viewpoints possible with regard to teaching and learning, with no set expectations given of what was the 'right way'. In response to asking how far he felt student teachers' opinions were challenged, the tutor emphasised the importance of listening:

> I aspire to listen to them, and to listen quite hard to them ... I aspire to ask questions rather than just give answers, and to try and make sense of what they are doing and why. (Interview with History tutor – 14 August)

The mentor was in accord with the tutor in wanting the tutor's visits to be learning opportunities, where the tutor was an added resource at the student teachers' disposal during their school teaching practices. Both felt that shared experiences of being in a class together often seemed to enhance the level of discussion, as feedback was then more detailed and paid close attention to what actually happened. This could go on to act as a basis for a more general discussion on teaching and learning. The mentor did not question whether the tutor would challenge the school's perceptions of the student teachers, and the tutor felt that his first priority was in supporting the mentor rather than the student teachers, as he believed that she was probably the key person in the student teachers' learning. This closely tied division of labour in how their roles were perceived further suggested that the object of the activity was shared.

### The Modern Foreign Languages department

There was considerable difference in the ways the handbooks were organised with all except the MFL handbook outlining week-by-week expectations from the student teachers in school. The MFL handbook contained separate lists for fulfilling expected tasks rather than outlining these in a diary format. This gave some flexibility as to when the tasks needed to be completed. The handbook also outlined a large number of optional suggestions for completing activities, which were 'quite demanding in terms of time but very worthwhile' (MFL handbook, p. 41). The theory underpinning the activities and guidance was made explicit:

> We will discuss the different ways by which you might learn to become a language teacher against the backdrop of a theoretical model for the course as a whole. (MFL handbook, p. 17)

The MFL tutor had imported a lot of the ideas into the MFL handbook from her work at another university eight or nine years ago, prior to her Downtown appointment, and had also overseen some changes initiated by other tutors at Downtown. In its emphasis on a specific line of subject-related research, the handbook was in some contrast to the other department handbooks, which had to a greater or lesser extent developed more directly from the original principles of the student teacher education course.

The MFL mentor did not use the handbook as a pedagogical tool. The detailed suggestions for guiding student teachers' learning and for understanding the promoted theoretical model of teaching were rarely seen as relevant to the activities in the school practice, where teaching classes and taking on a timetable were seen as the main concerns. The mentor was keen to promote practical teaching tips and 'survival' techniques:

> I think [Downtown University] is sometimes making incredible demands on the [student teachers'] time; just insane demands to the point of driving people to being on the verge of being ill ... That is when you learn that you teach one lesson from the book [textbook] and one [Downtown] style lesson – you live. (Interview with MFL mentor – 10 January)

The mentor did not adopt the handbook to mediate student teacher learning, as this did not seem relevant to her role as she saw it. Similarly, in the second practice she placed an emphasis on teaching:

> There is academic stuff in the [university] booklet with discussions, but I don't know anyone who does them. The [student teachers] are up to here with it by this stage; they just want to get on. (Field notes – 16 May)

Instead of treating the handbook as a jointly produced document created through the school's collaboration with the student teacher education course, she often used it to represent Downtown University, and hence a somewhat idealistic document with academic intentions that were rarely realistic in the 'real world' of school:

> Student teacher 2: Questionnaire; a year 7 class in the autumn term – not done.
> Mentor: Drat I am going to ignore that feedback and just keep nagging you.
> Student teacher 1: There must be people who just don't do it.
> Mentor: Tick off what you have done. Cobble some kind of survey together. You have to create a questionnaire so do one together.
> [The student teachers are very negative, and the mentor does not attempt to change their minds in the value of the handbook tasks, only in the value of not getting into trouble for not doing them.]
> (Field notes – 31 January)

Her role was to ensure that the practices of the student teachers met with the handbook's requirements. It was stressed in the course handbook that the university tutor visits were not 'assessment visits' but an opportunity for the tutor to work with mentors to develop specific aspects of student teacher competence. However, the visits were frequently referred to as 'assessment visits' by the teachers in the department and the student teachers. Therefore, the handbook explicitly mediated work on meeting the requirements of the course assessment rather than on the student teachers' learning. There was tension between the development of student teacher learning and the managing of the relationship between the university and the school:

> Mentor: We'll sort [student teacher] out for Tuesday. We know [tutor] is signing the thing. If you hadn't been so glaringly honest she would have signed it. Just say thank you and stop talking. Let her find out from trawling through the paperwork, which she won't do. Don't say that some days you are not sure that the classes are learning, show your mark book and say I am pleased, and here is the evidence.
> Student teacher: I have got to stop shooting myself in the foot [a phrase that had been used by the mentor previously]. (Field notes – 28 March)

An instrumental approach was also shown in hastily checking off the completion of set activities, which suggested a lack of priority for working on these, and even though the mentor considered the course a good one (although incredibly demanding on the student teachers), she frequently appeared to play down the learning opportunities that were outlined in the handbook.

Thinking that the handbook activities were 'a waste of time' (interview with MFL student teacher – 22 February) and 'really daunting when you are knackered' (interview with student teacher – 23 February), the student teachers were quick to agree with the mentor's negative stance towards the handbook, and treated it like a set of regulations, which were designed and monitored by the MFL tutor. The tutor was saddened by her perceived assessment role in the teaching practice schools. She still believed in the learning opportunities inherent in the handbook activities but acknowledged a tension in student teachers' feeling that such activities diverted them from gaining experience in fulfilling the demands of being a teacher:

> I keep saying this over and over again, you are not here to simulate a teacher, you are here to learn, and therefore if I ask you to do some marking in a particular way, there's not much point in you saying to me that that is not what teachers do. (Interview with MFL tutor – 3 July)

Student teachers who compared their own school practice experience with the work of established teachers therefore considered specific learning exercises from the handbook as distracting, and did not view such learning opportunities in the way considered beneficial by the tutor.

An important reason for using the tools outlined in the handbook in the MFL department appeared to be for accountability. The university provided the tools and it was expected that they would be used as evidence in the student teacher portfolios to show what they had done in their school practice. The MFL school department did not appropriate certain tools (lesson plans, observation summaries and evaluation sheets) in the same way as the tutor, as they were mainly seen as an administrative part of the department's student teacher education activity system, with their completion necessary for gaining the tutor's approval. Therefore, they could be considered as secondary artefacts (Wartofsky, 1979) in that they were not used in order to initiate discussions but were primarily seen as representations of the student teacher education course and, like the handbook, often viewed as symbolic artefacts of Downtown University.

One student teacher, considered to be very strong because of his classroom presence, had very few targets for improvement on his observation summaries. However, this resulted in one teacher commenting that he ended up 'thinking what have I got to tick' (interview – 7 June) in terms of meeting the requirements of the course handbook:

> He was so strong in all these areas that it had come out naturally that he was tying up loose ends. I don't know necessarily whether the thought process that was probably there in the beginning (with things like good classroom management structure and steps in the planning) was there towards the end of the process. (Interview with MFL teacher – 7 June)

Had pupil learning been considered closely from the start with the student teacher questioned in detail about decisions made in his lesson planning, the student teacher might have been more attuned to the necessary thought processes behind his strong delivery, and might have further developed his understanding of teaching and learning. Subsequent to the fieldwork, the university tutor commented that this student teacher had experienced considerable difficulties during his second teaching practice at another school.

Many teachers preferred the student teachers to take responsibility for the focus of their feedback remarks and others preferred to give general comments, although appreciated that a focus was needed in order to complete the portfolio requirements: 'I like to be able to give general feedback, which you do, but sometimes they want it focused on particular areas' (interview with MFL teacher – 7 June). Specific feedback was felt by some to be contrived, as it meant that lessons were only discussed in terms of what was needed for the portfolio rather than the general outcomes, which the class teacher wanted to emphasise. Other teachers appreciated the structure the university provided as it helped them, and gave the onus to the student teachers:

> We get the long list of all the different criteria you know, the this, that and the other and I have to say I read once five years ago, and I am not going to have the time to learn them all so I have to rely on the [student teacher] to do that. I will comment and say 'tick this box'. We have been given all the descriptors of the criteria, so if I wanted to I could find that and look them up. (Interview with MFL teacher – 7 June)

Considering feedback in terms of how boxes can be ticked points, at least in part, to an instrumental use of evaluation in as far as the way the course requirements needed to be evidenced. This teacher's history of working with student teachers meant that initial understandings of the teacher education course criteria had been filed away and consequently were not used actively when discussing lessons with student teachers. As with the mentor, verbal feedback was used to evaluate the teaching and learning, rather than scrutinising lesson plans and observation summaries, and looking at how the use of these reflected student teachers' thinking. Consequently, student teachers were expected to take the lead with regard to stipulating the lesson objectives in order that they met what was needed for their portfolios, but they were fairly passive when discussing the lessons with teachers, rarely elucidating on their decisions. This meant that they did not openly contribute to their own learning when evaluating pedagogical ideas as intended in the tools' designs.

This contrasted with the work of the MFL tutor who challenged the methods student teachers used:

> Tutor: They didn't produce it [the language] but they repeated it.
> Student teacher: But they did produce it in pairs.
> Tutor: But they did not have the opportunity of a model from you of their production.It does make a lot of the lesson in English, and not the target language. That's what happens with that approach – the

PDP (presentation, demonstration, production) approach allows more of L2 from you as a teacher, so inevitably a lot of what you say is in English.

Student teacher: I accept your points.

Tutor: Try to plan lessons with more of a PDP approach. How much do they speak? Not repeat – they can fudge repeating (tutor mimics pupil not saying words as a repeat). (Field notes – 7 February)

The above conversation led to the student teacher later apologising by e-mail for not appearing receptive to the tutor's advice, with the mentor thinking this a good idea in terms of maintaining a positive relationship with the tutor. Had the mentor and teaching staff made such challenges in school discussions on teaching and learning, one feels the student teacher would not have felt so intimidated when being challenged by the tutor. Instead, implicit mediation of the tools was evident in how teachers talked about and prioritised meeting the course requirements and university expectations above creating learning opportunities for student teachers.

The tutor's authority as far as the student teachers' perceived progress was concerned was indicated by the mentor writing her reports after the tutor visits. They therefore operated as a rubber stamp on progress once this had been agreed with the university tutor. Similarly, the lesson observation summaries used by the teachers in the department when observing the student teachers were given a low status and not looked at by the mentor at all. She valued talking to the other teachers about the student teachers' progress in the team room, and referred to this as 'the word on the street' (interview – 17 January), anticipating that any concerns would naturally arise in discussions. Believing the student teachers were successful this year meant that this was often done openly rather than having to engage in 'whispering in the corridor conversations' (interview – 27 June), which had happened in the past. Such a contrast in her way of working compared to the tutor indicated that they did not share the object of the student teacher education activity system.

### The Geography department

The Geography handbook was less detailed than both History and MFL, and appeared to be designed in a way that mainly recorded the work done during the school practices. The handbook concentrated more on the requirements of the course and less on a theoretical rationale behind the course design. The onus was on thorough planning and appreciating the variety of sources from which the student teachers could glean important information. The Geography tutor had only used the handbook as a tutor since last year, and felt it was similar to when he had worked with it as a school mentor seven years previously.

Tensions in how the handbook was appropriated by the mentor and the tutor were not apparent in the Geography department, as here the handbook appeared to be treated as a rule in both the school and university student teacher education activity systems, rather than a tool mediating work on the object. Set tasks were completed as a matter of course before the rest of the mentor meetings took place. Thereby, the university-initiated activities acted as an adjunct to the meeting. There was a passive compliance on the part of the mentor and student teacher in fulfilling the handbook's requirements ('we kind of get them out of the way at the beginning of mentor meetings' – interview with student teacher – 22 February). The assignments were seen as useful, as the student teacher often initiated discussions on them, which were outlined in the handbook. But these were seen from a practical point of view with advice being given by the mentor on the best ways of getting them done (which classes and lessons to use for certain investigations) rather than debating the educational issues inherent in the tasks. However, it was not clear or brought out into the open how the assignments affected the student teacher's practice. Therefore, the use of the handbook created limited learning opportunities. Without opening up tensions or diversity, or enabling exploratory talks to enable student teacher learning, it did not appear directly relevant to the student teacher's teaching experience.

Set questions on specific worksheets in the handbook (for example, on literacy, sustainability and classroom management) were answered by the mentor with the student teacher keen to complete the sheet rather than to think further about the issue. This was then used for feedback discussions at the university. The topics were not developed in the mentor meetings but tasks involved the mentor dictating:

Mentor: Anything from [university] we have got to discuss and fill in a form for?
(She answers the questions checking that what she says is enough of an answer to fill in the space on the form. If not, she says some more.) (Field notes – 10 October)

There was an increasing lack of priority as far as the tasks were concerned as the teaching timetable increased ('they've become less and less important' – interview with student teacher – 22 February). This appeared to indicate a divide between the university's suggested tasks and those in the teaching situation:

> Maybe some of the school assignments [in the handbook] are not pointless but we don't really need them at this stage. Thinking about planning lessons – the assignments can get in the way. They become the lowest priority and you don't take them as seriously as you should do, just try and get them done. (Interview with Geography student teacher – 17 October)

In spite of the mentor seeing value in the tasks, and the 'good references' (15 January) in the handbook, she did not link practical and research ideas:

> I am not particularly rigorous in terms of following the handbook. I make it as open as possible so that if [student teacher] has got anything that he is worried about then he can advise me. (Interview with Geography mentor – 27 June)

Consequently, the handbook as a tool was sidelined. Implicit mediation of work on the object was evident in the mentor's use of language as a tool to work on the problem space identified by the student teacher.

There was no apparent divide between the mentor and tutor in the Geography department where the mentor was more relaxed in expecting the tutor to be in accord with the school's opinion of the student teachers, as reflected in the mentor's written reports. These were read aloud at all tutor visits by the mentor but were not discussed. Many of the concerns in Geography seemed to be more at an administrative level. The Geography mentor spoke in terms of what needed to be done by her and the student teachers in order to complete the course: 'I have got shed loads for us to do from the mentor meeting [at Downtown University] last night' (Field notes – 24 January). However, tool use rarely involved exploring student teachers' understandings of pedagogy.

In the Geography department, the tools were often used as a way of 'getting what you can' out of the teaching staff (interview with Tutor – 11 May) or in order to fulfil the expectations of the university. Some of the staff showed an ambivalent attitude towards the paperwork generated by the university:

> We have got all the booklets that give all the reference points that we can use, but we usually say to the [student teachers] you fill in the reference points (laugh) because you can be ploughing through them

forever. I do know what they all are but I usually go – oh whichever one. (Interview with Geography teacher – 14 June)

Other staff were also happy to adopt a *laissez faire* approach and particularly liked the freedom that having extra staff in the department gave them. Consequently, they often needed reminders to make the agreed number of observations and work with the relevant tools. Hence, the tools were seen as secondary artefacts representing the requirements of the university and not linked specifically to student teachers' learning opportunities.

The targets outlined in many of the student teacher observations and reports in Geography were to do with issues of general classroom management and the use of resources such as ICT, rather than areas of pedagogical knowledge that could be discussed further. Therefore, tools were mediating work on an object of student teacher learning that appeared more static than one that acknowledged the possibilities of expansive learning (Engeström, 2008). The emphasis in mentor meetings was on planning lessons and not reflecting on work done in previous classes. The main tools appropriated for the meetings were the schemes of work, and the mentor used the key questions in them to suggest the main areas to be discussed for structuring the lesson plans. Therefore, the onus was on future practice rather than gaining an understanding by scrutinising the practice that had already taken place. Filing lesson observation summaries and checking up on how current classes were going was part of 'touching base' at the beginning of mentor meetings in order to get an overview of how the student teachers were feeling. This was not seen as significant in developing the student teacher's learning, as it was believed that this would be best enhanced through practice.

The learning style adopted by the mentor therefore appeared like a traditional apprenticeship model, where skills were outlined, discussed and displayed in anticipation of them being copied and mastered. The mentor frequently made her point by acting out the actual words she would use as if in front of a class, using intonation to highlight the importance of the performance aspect of teaching. The student teachers accepted her advice gratefully, especially as they all worked with the mentor's classes and considered her to be a very successful teacher. The student teacher on the first practice readily acknowledged that he wanted to emulate the mentor's style of teaching, believing it to be exemplary and stronger than any other seen in the department. Noticeably, when planning in the mentor meetings, the student teachers were heavily influenced by the mentor's ideas. The mentor being very enthusiastic about her teaching found it hard to explore the student teachers' ideas as a way of examining their developing understanding of pedagogy. Instead, she gave lesson ideas from her own teaching:

> Mentor: My lesson runs itself over two lessons – gives you a break for next week too.
> [She explains the settlements lesson with the resources and how to divide the group up for the activities.]
> Student teacher: How long for presentations in the second lesson?
> Mentor: Lesson 1, 20 minutes introduction and 40 minutes preparation. Lesson 2, 20 minutes preparation and 40 minutes presentations. (Field notes – 31 January)

The student teacher in the first school practice admitted that being given resources and explicit ways of using them made it more difficult for him to consider lesson ideas afresh. Hence, the mentor was the key person in the student teachers' planning work, and the mentor meetings were greatly relied upon for doing this, giving the student teacher little agency in contributing to his own learning beyond recording the suggestions for his lessons.

The university tutor in the first school practice stressed the general attributes of teaching and overall progress made in the course, rather than concentrating on the detail of lesson structures. This was also evident in his comments on the student teacher's learning after the school practice had been completed:

> Early on when I saw him, he was quite timid and his demeanour had changed at the end from the beginning. He was much more confident and much more assertive and had that skill of professional teachers where you know what to say when. He learnt that, which was probably one of his biggest achievements because he always seemed to be very capable of planning lessons and developing decent resources. (Interview with Geography tutor – 11 May)

The tutor did not actively use tools as a way of opening up student teacher thinking, and appeared to suggest that positive experiences of lesson planning were most beneficial in developing pedagogical understanding.

### The Science department

The Science handbook like that in Geography was less detailed than both History and MFL, and also appeared to be designed in a way that mainly recorded the work done during the school practice. The emphasis was on student teachers collecting information in school assignments and becoming more pupil-centred rather than subject specific in their outlook: 'you may arrive with the expectation of you becoming a biology, chemistry or physics teacher but you will soon start seeing yourself as a science teacher with a particular subject specialism' (Science handbook, p. 3). At Downtown University the tutors worked collaboratively on the handbook design, and the lead tutor commented on a 'big review' of the course after he had joined it full-time nearly ten years ago. He felt that 'every time there has been a national change we have looked again at the course' (interview – 3 July). Consequently, the Science handbook unlike the others seemed to respond to changes in policy rather than primarily as a result of the proactive developments of the kind described in the History and MFL departments, where doctoral research and previous research interests shaped the handbooks' designs.

The mentor in Science shared the MFL mentor's view of seeing the handbook as a symbolic artefact of authority. He was very thorough in how he worked with the student teachers paying close attention to the assignments in the handbook and the suggested topics to cover in meetings. Here the tool tended to be used instrumentally. He used the mentor sheets to write his notes, and these drove the meetings and guided the structure of what was to be talked about:

> Mentor: They have given this year the week-by-week things so you've got the mentor white sheets with suggested things to mention, and to remind you that the assignment is coming up, so mentors haven't got to be wading through the file all the time. That's good so it allows you to look at what the school-based assignment is this week. (Interview with Science mentor – 16 January)

The paperwork helped to structure expectations of what the student teachers should be doing and was used to encourage them to be on task and to think about and reflect on their teaching. The mentor expected commitment to the suggested handbook routines (completing reflection sheets for example), and these dictated the mentor meetings. This affected how the student teachers perceived their learning. For example, they were encouraged to focus on those aspects of their teaching that were deemed by other staff as necessary of attention. This sometimes detracted from their own concerns, which did not get voiced. Instead, the handbook instrumentally directed their thinking into completing task sheets, which were then filled out and filed into their portfolios. This went against the tutor's desires for student teacher learning:

> We don't want them to write for the sake of writing because it's just pointless isn't it? If you give them time to think and talk, they will probably learn more. It doesn't have to be put down on paper. (Interview with Science tutor – 24 May)

Nevertheless, there was an emphasis on written recording in the handbook:

> You should maintain good records of your observations and discussions with your mentor, experienced teachers and your [university] tutor, using the questions and suggestions that **we** [emphasis in the original] provide as guidelines. These records can be kept on the reverse side of the school-based activity sheet in the notes section. (Science Handbook, p. 51)

There was also a weekly profile with open spaces for comments and these were 'formally checked' three times during the year. The design of the handbook suggested that it was seen as part of a monitoring process. The emphasis on following the recommendations of the university department by emboldening the 'we' in the quotation above appeared to come from a wish to heighten the student teachers' awareness of the status of the document, and therefore the expected manner in which it should be used. By constantly trying to evidence that they were meeting the teaching standards required to gain accreditation in both the mentor and tutor meetings, the student teachers were always giving input from an 'unqualified' position, and as such they may have perceived their ideas as being unequal in comparison with the other participants in the activity system. Hence, their feelings of agency were challenged, and the freedom of movement possible in using the handbook as a tool and a way of mediating learning was restricted.

The mentor saw a divide between the work done for the handbook (seen as 'getting the research stuff out of the way', Field notes – 30 October) and the work on teaching and learning in the school. Believing that this work was separate helped to suggest that what was seen as the university's contribution to the activities in school was accepted as preliminary tasks before the main teaching practice began. There was a danger that the handbook assignments were only approached and carried out earnestly when they were desirable for structuring the early part of the school practice. Once teaching responsibilities increased and time was given over to taking classes, the handbook tasks were only tolerated providing they did not interfere with lessons. This reinforced the necessity of being flexible in using the handbook and in understanding the value of the tasks.

There was also an acceptance by the Science tutors that the handbook was not necessarily mediating student teacher learning. Both Science tutors questioned the value of some of the paperwork and wondered how much of an evidence gathering exercise it was purely to satisfy their, and the government's, need for accountability. The standard of the portfolios was often felt to be 'shockingly poor':

> It's just formulaic writing; it's not very good. I would say it's the weakest part of our course. (Interview with Science tutor – 24 May)

> As a useful document, it's useful for what? I think the portfolio was done as an assessment activity for us to monitor different aspects of the meeting of the standards. But is it a document that helps them learn? I couldn't hand on heart say that. We have never had a proper conversation about why we have got this and what should be in it. (Interview with Science tutor – 3 July)

The tutor went on to say that the paperwork and portfolio and self-evaluations in particular were under review in the next university mentor meeting.

Because the school Science department concentrated on helping the student teachers meet the teaching standards for gaining accreditation, the standards were constantly referred to as needing to be evidenced in the student teachers' lessons and planning. The extensive use of the standards terminology in lesson plans and observation summaries encouraged a focus on these in post-lesson discussions. Meeting these descriptors therefore became the priority in lesson feedback. The practice of meeting the standards sometimes appeared to be prioritised before an understanding of why the standards needed to be met, and general conversations personalising the required standard to the viewpoint of the student teachers rarely occurred:

> Science mentor: You are not just teaching from the front now. So select this week what you want staff to look for ... so how about PV2 (planning), P1 pitch and assessment opportunities and teaching ones, time limits and clear transitions? (Field notes – 16 January)

Monitoring of the student teachers' files took place at the university with a tick sheet designed to do this, and thus, this was seen as a university task to do with checking the requirements of the course. This suggested that the value of using these files as part of their working practice with the mentor was less immediate in relation to student teachers' learning. No other department systematically checked the student teachers' portfolios at the university. The other tutors expected the student files to be an integral part of how the mentor worked with the student teachers.

The Science department appropriated the generic tools at a functional level within the work ensuring that forms were completed and progress recorded. Like the handbook, the way many tools were used in Science, with the mentor seeing the observation feedback summaries as evidence for progress, for example, frequently appeared to replace possible discourse on specific contexts of teaching and the student teachers' interpretations of these. This carried over into the tutor visits, where in preparation for the second school practice, the tutor noted down development points for the next mentor:

> Tutor: Let's carry on through your profile then – I'll write that – use information technology more for help. How are we for time [mentor]?
> Mentor: 15 minutes.
> Tutor: Come on then.
> (There are more quick fire questions about the scheme of work and how [student teacher] plans activities.)
> Student teacher: Lesson plans
> Mentor: Much better, only one teacher has given 'attention needed' for pitch. No one has said 'consistent' but you have improved a lot considering the initial concerns.
> Tutor: Ok, I'll make a note of that – pitch improved but still needs working on. (Field notes – 17 April)

As an opportunity to open out the issues of the practice of teaching and learning, it was noticeable that checking forms dominated the visits: Tutor: 'share that now so we can tick more boxes off' (Field notes – 21 November).

The mentor's reports in Science were collated extensively, but the mentor relied heavily on science teachers completing a 'tick box sheet' for their comments on the student teachers' progress. These were not followed up with detailed discussions. Some over-reliance on paperwork as a way of monitoring student teacher progress meant that ambiguity in the reporting process was an issue for some of the Science teachers:

> Having the tick box sheet I found quite difficult because I sort of knew what I wanted to say but wasn't quite sure whether – I can't remember the categories but there was 'further development', but I felt that we all need further development in everything, and whatever the one was below that and then above it, that just felt a little bit ambiguous. (Interview with Science teacher – 24 May)

This way of working also encouraged teachers to simply report back to the mentor expecting him to then deal with their concerns. The Science teachers often did this as a way of trying to get the student teachers in the first practice to work in the manner the department expected. Consequently, their disappointment at how the student teachers sometimes responded to the student teacher education activities (often most great when basic requirements were not being met such as organisation of resources and poor time-keeping) meant that the student teachers constantly felt under scrutiny:

> It is monitoring in addition to maybe feedback because my mentor keeps in touch with all my teachers. For some reason that personally I don't understand, some teachers in the beginning felt more comfortable telling stuff to my mentor than to me. But I have addressed that. I have told all my teachers to tell me everything, and especially those teachers I had from the first term, I think are telling me more. (Interview with Science student teacher – 21 February)

Both the student teachers in the first teaching practice commented on how disconcerting it was to hear of concerns from other staff via the mentor rather than from the teachers themselves. This gave the impression that the mentor was assessing student teacher progress rather than learning, and gave him control of the mentor meetings by possessing 'inside' information from staff on lesson observations. For the student teachers, this meant that some tools occasionally appeared threatening, as they were being used explicitly as monitoring devices. This impersonal approach was also evident when the student teachers produced lesson plans that did not match the required format. Rather than questioning why they had veered from the expected style, and what this said about how the student teachers were approaching issues of teaching and learning, the rules for how the lesson plans should be completed were stressed. The activity system's rules were emphasised and the tools used as a means to enforce them. Consequently, there was very little room for student teacher agency in the system.

## Concluding comments

Considering tutors and part-time teacher tutors in the Geography and MFL departments as assessors did not acknowledge the fact that the mentors and also the teaching staff were crucial and significant in the student teachers' evaluations and in reporting their progress. It also did not acknowledge that the tutors were expected to be treated as further resources for the mentor in developing the competence of the student teachers by using the tools designed to do this. This was readily accepted in the History department and illustrated in the way the tutor visits worked. The History tutor took his lead from the History mentor when visiting the school and responded specifically to the mentor's report, which had been e-mailed and discussed prior to the visit. However, the MFL mentor gave her reports a very low status in relation to the tutor visits, and these were not written until after the tutor visits had taken place, as a way of confirming what had been said. The Geography mentor reports, although read aloud during the tutor visits, were written primarily from the mentor's own perceptions of the student teachers' experience, without the desired detailed dialogue and exchange of ideas with other teachers who had worked with the student teachers over a period of time. Detailed conversations occurred even less in the Science department, where a reliance on monitoring student teachers by disseminating check sheets to the teachers they worked with created a restrictive form of feedback that was open to ambiguity.

Where student teachers were then seen as recipients of feedback, rather than participants acting as learners working jointly on a shared object, the tools were not part of a process of meaning-making at all. Alternatively, in those situations where a mentor and student teacher jointly constructed tools, both were seen to operate as learners, and although novices, the student teachers appreciated that their learning, as well as that of other practitioners, was not pre-determined but evolving:

(The History mentor asks if the student teacher has read 'Learning Without Limits'. The History tutor had also mentioned this book.)
History mentor: The introduction is setting the analysis of the issues and I really like the way it talks about it. It is saying that you have got to think about what students respond to.

(The student teacher mentions Buckaroo and Alfonse the Camel – a lesson done at Downtown University.)

History mentor: Why Alfonse? The kids could choose the name. (She looks at the sheet.) Really good, can I do a copy? I find it's about them engaging with the work and not just about writing stuff down. I sometimes still get it wrong after 11 years. (Field notes – 10 January)

When considering pedagogy from a number of different perspectives with the mentor and student teacher adopting a variety of roles, such as researcher, learner and teacher as indicated in the discourse above, greater exploration of meaning was encouraged. This approach also tended to stimulate considerations of the importance of professional values when conversing on matters of pedagogy, as considering wider perspectives on how work in classrooms was viewed initiated discussions about the point of being there, and the value of education for both pupils and teachers:

Student teacher: Is education the be all and end all? Does it really matter?

History mentor: Just that aspiration to do your best.

Student teacher: To be happy

History mentor: I have a mate who works in a shop, has a girlfriend and kid and loves it. It's about well-being in a system.

Student teacher: Is that wrong or just how it is?

Mentor: Just how it is

Student teacher: But we see education as very important.

Mentor: mmm [Silence]. (Field Notes – 28 March)

As noted in Van Huizen *et al.*'s research (2005) professional values are considered as central to the development of teacher identity. Conversations such as the one above recognise how mentors can 'help student teachers to expand the object of activity … and respond to their expanded interpretations' (Edwards, 2009, p. 159). In this way, school practice as part of a student teacher education course is not just about learning how the school and department works, and then replicating this as a way of becoming a teacher, but about working with others in order to open out the problems of practice so as to develop an ability to interpret teaching and learning situations in order to seek and respond to the complexity within them. This way of working necessitates that student teachers not only work alongside expert teachers, but work alongside expert learners of teaching and learning.

Where there were few opportunities to affect the practice of the student teachers and their ways of thinking, one could view tools as secondary artefacts under Wartofsky's definition, simply acting as a representation of a primary tool in transmitting beliefs and norms, rather than colouring the way one sees the actual world in order to change current practice, which is the quality of a tertiary artefact (Wartofsky, 1979). Considering a tool as a tertiary artefact could be possible with the implicitly mediated way the handbook worked in the History department for example, as discussions in the department opened out ideas that tested thinking and questioned many aspects of pedagogy, which could then lead to changing practice. In the next chapter I analyse in more detail how the objects of student teacher education activity systems were seen in the four different subject departments and also how these were affected by interaction with other activity system objects.

# 10
## The Objects of Student Teacher Education Activity

### Introduction

In the case studies I identified how the four departments worked in student teacher education and described the learning opportunities for the student teachers in relation to this work. Analysing each department's cultural history and social practices in relation to student teacher education created an appreciation of the social situation of development for the student teachers working in them. In Chapter 9 the analysis of tool use further illustrated how the student teachers' learning opportunities varied depending on how the participants in the student teacher education activity systems used tools to mediate the work on the object. For example, student teachers when working with participants who used student teacher education tools to open up their thinking about teaching and learning discussed matters of pedagogy and questioned and debated these openly, interpreting teaching contexts and developing an understanding of their complexity. This was further enhanced where participants jointly experimented with their ideas, and created an ongoing exploration of the variety of approaches possible when doing the work. Where tools were sidelined or treated as rules in the student teacher education activity system, debates tended to centre on lesson ideas in terms of their content and planning potential, with established teachers giving guidance and advice and sharing what worked effectively for them in the teaching context. Student teachers were then encouraged to emulate successful teaching by replicating department practices, or in some cases they were expected to choose and adopt those practices that fitted with their own developing teaching style. Evident in Chapter 9 was the extent of the differences in the learning opportunities for student teachers across the different departments.

This chapter considers the student teacher education activity systems' objects, which were the essence of the activity as they provided direction for the work. The chapter asks three questions of each subject department: what is, how is and why is the object being worked on in the student teacher education activity system? It considers how far the object is affected by tensions in the participants' motives, thereby preventing the object from truly motivating the activity at a systemic level. The intention is to gain further understanding of how the learning opportunities of the student teachers were affected by the student teacher education activity's object, thereby looking specifically at the second research question, which asked why the learning opportunities were constructed differently. In considering how the student teacher education activity systems' objects have been indicated in as far as tool use is concerned in the last chapter, I concentrated on physical tools specifically relating to the student teacher education work. However, the analysis when looking at how the tools mediated work on the object of the activity also identified aspects of the cultural histories and social practices of the departments and how these impacted on the objects too, and how the objects then worked back on the student teacher education activity. The following analysis considers the objects more specifically and builds on previous suggestions of what these may be. It also gives greater insight into the cultural histories and social practices of the departments, and how these further affected the objects.

## The History department

### What is the object being worked on in the student teacher education activity system in the History department?

Both Downtown University and the History department in Market Town High School considered learning and student teacher learning to be a complex process, as illustrated in the similar kind of support given to the student teachers. All considered themselves as learners and viewed ideas as contestable. The mentor's as well as the tutor's object of the student teacher education activity system was student teacher learning, and both saw themselves as working in student teacher education from a broader position than just the school department's student teacher education activity system referring to academic literature and educational research. Department staff appeared to value and promote mutual learning as a way of furthering the work in student teacher education and in the department generally with many staff acknowledging that teaching and learning was a complex area with training new teachers being an 'imprecise' process (interview with the History mentor – 23 January). This shared sense of direction in motivating the student teacher education activity was also apparent in the head of department being involved in addressing all student teachers from the History course at Downtown University, and working in the past on developing the student teacher education course. Such aspects clearly highlighted how the university and the school were united in their approach in negotiating what the object of the student teacher education activity system was.

### How is the object being worked on in the student teacher education activity system in the History department?

As noted in the last chapter, tools were used in a relatively structured way in the History department, and they were used extensively and flexibly in order to give greater relevance to the teaching and learning situation in creating learning opportunities for the student teachers. Student teacher learning was seen as personal to the individual and gained through collaboration with other student teacher education activity system participants. The close working relationships highlighted a joint understanding of student teacher education and reflected a shared history in the development of the activity, and how it interacted with the established social practices of the department. The seamlessness in the work of the school and the university History student teacher education activity systems was evident in the very similar kinds of discussions student teachers had with the mentor and the tutor. There was a shared focus on the student teachers as learners, and where different points of view were discussed, the tutor felt that the contestation illustrated what he felt to be an integral part of the work of history teachers, constructing knowledge 'from a variety of conflicting sources' (August 17). This aligns with Hodkinson and Hodkinson's (2002, p. 9) suggestion made in their research on school subject teachers that the subject of History can be seen as 'an individualistic pursuit, focused upon deeper personal understanding of extensive content'.

Although the cultural history of the History department strongly influenced the learning opportunities for the student teachers in that all staff saw themselves as learners who were involved in constant debate, the student teacher on the first school practice worked alone, and this meant that a proactive approach to her learning was especially necessary, as opportunities for joint work with a second student teacher were not available. The value of pairing student teachers in their teaching practice has been noted by Childs *et al.* (2013, p. 51) as this may help to 'stimulate more discussion with the wider department through the conversations they initiate with each other'. For the first student teacher at Market Town High School, learning opportunities in the History department were affected by the department's social practices in that she worked mainly in the staff room away from the History team, and did not benefit from being involved in *ad hoc* conversations. Although accessing support whenever necessary, she did this mainly through the student teacher education structures and outside the department working space. In contrast, the second shorter teaching practice encouraged the student teachers (greater in number and more confident in their teaching) to work more closely with the History team, albeit with some discomfort from some of the Humanities staff. Everyone valued sharing resources, and this idea was formalised in the department meetings where the student teachers were treated as full participants in the department. However, the department staff were accustomed to working intensely with one another within the department's teaching routines and because of their working habits, the student teachers (and especially the lone student teacher in the first teaching practice) were not often around to experience this work. The department was aware and concerned about this, as was maintained in their open attitude to acknowledging student teacher education shortcomings.

### Why is the object being worked on in the student teacher education activity system in the History department?

The close working relationships that had developed over a considerable period of time between the majority of department staff in the History department and the university tutor in History encouraged the student teacher education work and development to be seen as an ongoing activity with pedagogical issues under constant debate and review. An ethos of collaborative planning and experimentation between History teachers, the tutor, mentor and student teachers meant that this way of working was expected with differences of opinion vital for the development of the work in student teacher education and in the department in general. Accepting that learning to teach is difficult and not straightforward acknowledged that an apprenticeship approach or one that relied upon learning through transfer was not viable. From looking at the approach to student teachers' learning in the department, the advocated identity of a History teacher appeared to be about being a thoughtful and reflective practitioner who worked collaboratively with staff in order to develop aspects of curriculum and pedagogy in a manner that depended upon debate, experimentation and innovation. This appeared to be something that was important for all History staff.

## The Modern Foreign Languages department

### What is the object being worked on in the student teacher education activity system in the Modern Foreign Languages department?

The student teachers' learning opportunities were affected by the way student teacher education worked in the MFL department in that the department staff and the tutor appeared to view the object of the student teacher education activity system differently. The main task for the tutor could be seen as working on the problem space of student teacher learning, and questioning and challenging all aspects of pedagogy opened this up for discussion. The mentor in particular did not appear to value open-ended questioning or consider her own learning as something that was ongoing. She questioned aspects of pedagogy less and concentrated on meeting the requirements of the course as her key objective, and saw the problem space as the relationship between the university and the school, which needed to be carefully managed, especially as the tutor was regarded as the main assessor. The mentor put herself in the role of student teacher representative, protecting them and advising them in how to successfully complete the year. This restrictive object of activity seemed to hamper recognition of the complexity inherent in teaching and learning situations, which was also little discussed in the department's social practices. It was felt to be important that a newly qualified teacher was in the department, as she provided an example of practice that had recently been deemed as appropriate by the university and therefore applicable to the student teachers' learning for this stage of their training. However, many staff differed from this style of teaching and occasionally disagreed with some tenets advocated by the university (not teaching to the test for example). Test results and pupils' academic success were highly valued, and this was seen as an indication of successful teaching and learning. It appeared that an emphasis was on student teachers managing their classrooms carefully with a variety of styles of teaching acceptable provided they gave pupils the opportunity to succeed in the end of unit assessments.

## How is the object being worked on in the student teacher education activity system in the Modern Foreign Languages department?

The learning opportunities for the student teachers were seen as individual to them as far as they were expected to note those styles of teaching that particularly appealed to them and to then adapt these for their own teaching: 'you can only be true to yourself' (interview with MFL mentor – 10 January). Differences of opinion were not highlighted but were still seen as 'valid and worthwhile' (interview with MFL teacher – 19 June) in as much as the people expressing them were experienced staff and therefore had developed their own styles of teaching. Contestation was therefore evident between some practices seen in the school and those promoted by the university, but this was not openly debated within the department either among the staff or when the tutor was present.

Social harmony was apparent and promoted in all department working practices and activity systems. When using the team rooms, the teachers' good intentions in supporting one another were evident, and the student teachers were automatically included in this. Importance was placed on social occasions too, with the department regularly meeting outside of school and also bringing in cakes and wine for personal celebrations within the department and on occasions in department meetings. Instead of debating pedagogical questions, exposure to successful pedagogical practices was promoted, and these were talked about informally with an importance placed on student teachers having opportunities to learn from observing these. Advice and tips were given, and these were particularly valued when they had been gained from extensive experience, which was seen as a major attribute of the department staff. Student teachers were encouraged to take suggestions on board, thereby meeting with staff expectations. Problems with student teachers in the past were often identified as arising from student teachers that did not heed the recommendations of the department staff, and were consequently felt to be a liability in the classroom.

Tensions in the student teacher education activity system were evident when observing the different ways the department and university tutor worked on the object. As a department where the student teacher education tools were less at the forefront of the student teacher education work and were sidelined and treated as rules within the activity system or measures of accountability, a relatively informal monitoring of student teachers meant that specific student teacher education tools were overshadowed by more conceptual tools (the use of language, for example, in teacher advice). This was enabled through close integration of the working habits of the student teachers with the regular staff, spending a lot of time in the MFL team rooms, having their own table to work on and sharing their ideas with whoever else happened to be working beside them. Being used to department teachers giving advice, the student teachers were uncomfortable when the tutor challenged lesson intentions and expected these to be backed up with a thorough understanding of the theoretical model of language learning advocated by the university.

The student teachers did not feel it appropriate to challenge suggestions in school: 'they [student teachers] didn't question us … there was never any problem' (interview with MFL teacher – 7 June). Instead, they were encouraged to take on advice for specific classes, whilst contemplating their own way of working with pupils. It was therefore up to the student teachers to sometimes reconcile conflicting messages from staff and to differentiate between the ways of working advocated by the university and those experienced in the school. With the tutor concentrating on pupil learning rather than student teacher learning, and the mentor focusing on the importance of student teachers developing their own style of teaching, there was little guided help or open acknowledgement of how the student teachers could work within both the school and the university student teacher education activity systems whilst negotiating the tensions between them. The mentor acknowledged that some student teachers and staff saw the tutor's advocated style of language learning as irrelevant to their preferred style of teaching, and consequently student teachers only replicated it for their course 'assessments'. This meant that sometimes it was effectively being demonstrated for the tutor but not necessarily valued as an opportunity to develop personal learning. However, it was up to the student teachers how they then participated in the student teacher education activity system in the university. A history of past student teachers and their ways of coping with this tension was seen as evidence that such training was possible and successful.

### Why is the object being worked on in the student teacher education activity system in the Modern Foreign Languages department?

The MFL team's close working relationships appeared to have developed through a strong social network, which valued harmonious engagement with the work, which meant that contestation in the department community was rare. Experienced staff had already adopted their teaching style and felt this worthy of observation. They believed that seeing this could help the student teachers decide how best to teach their classes. Therefore, their motives for being involved in student teacher education were often expressed in terms of giving something back to the profession and affirming the quality of work going on in the department. By considering the department 'an oasis of success' (21 March), the mentor felt that student teachers would benefit from experiencing their teaching and learning practices which were further affirmed by the department being highly regarded by the university. A respect for academia also enabled staff to personally pursue their own research interests in teaching, but an overall identity of what a successful MFL teacher looked like was not necessarily shared among the staff. It was perhaps felt that this could come in a number of guises.

As far as the student teacher education course requirements were concerned, there was a clear division of labour with staff aware of what was expected from them. They made sure they met the department's criteria for fulfilling their roles, taking their lead from the mentor and ensuring that the student teachers complied with the necessary paperwork, happy to put the onus on them to keep it up to date and filed. The tools specifically designed for student teacher education, although appropriated in a limited way, were seen as necessary in the student teacher education activity, but were not regarded as providing an opportunity for enhancing the learning of all teachers in the department. Student teacher education activity was rarely seen as offering opportunities for experienced staff development, and the way the tools were appropriated suggested that this was not considered part of their function. Instead, they created an opportunity for teachers to record their comments and observations and for the student teachers to take account of these.

## The Geography department

### What is the object being worked on in the student teacher education activity system in the Geography department?

Established subject links between Downtown University and Market Town High School Geography department enabled the development of specific topics for teaching, but here there was less of a focus on learning, and this meant that the mentor was heavily relied upon for guidance in this area. Details of the student teacher learning process or the course 'ethic' (interview with Geography mentor – 15 January) were not considered important by the mentor, head of department or the Geography staff, as noted in the department's cultural history in relation to student teacher education outlined in the case study. Therefore, teaching standards, contestable aspects of pedagogical issues in research literature and concentrating on specific foci for lesson observations were less debated or considered particularly relevant for detailed discussion in the school department. These were felt to belong more to the object motive of the student teacher education activity system in the university. Indeed, the head of department referred to staff being pressurised when aspects of these were commented on when student teachers observed Geography lessons.

The tutor concentrated on the more general aspects of training student teachers (as shown in the case study), and his advice was often to do with the generic skills of teaching. The mentor spoke from her own personal viewpoint and also gave very practical advice that the student teachers valued, as it was felt to help them in their day-to-day work in the classroom. The head of department believed that staff were in agreement on how to teach Geography: 'we don't have anyone that wants to do anything that would be radically opposed. We really do respect the issues based inquiry Geography. I don't have anyone who does the old-fashioned Geography' (interview – 5 February). The student teacher in the first school practice was encouraged to observe lessons that demonstrated how this approach could be made relevant to pupils. Therefore, there were no apparent tensions between the work of the tutor and the department staff. This was seen as particularly important, as the tutor worked part time in the school department.

The student teacher education course requirements were adhered to from the mentor's point of view and staff were encouraged and reminded of their responsibilities in relation to working with the student teachers. However, the benefits voiced in relation to student teacher education activity emphasised the practical implications of having another pedagogue in the department, thereby enabling established staff time to work on other areas. The mentor, rather than emphasising the learning opportunities that were possible through participating in student teacher education practices, spoke of the personal satisfaction she got from hearing how well past student teachers were doing in their career, and enjoyed receiving their messages of gratitude after they had finished the school practice.

### How is the object being worked on in the student teacher education activity system in the Geography department?

The chosen authoritative role of the Head of Geography and the general attitude towards the tutor as an assessor indicated that for the most part the student teacher education activity had been static in terms of experimentation and collaborative learning. Instead, the department relied upon key teachers being familiar with various aspects of the course in order to assist the student teachers. The relative isolation of the student teachers owing to the department's social practices affected their learning opportunities. A passive approach to student teacher education by some of the staff meant that most of the support offered came from just a few Geography teachers. There was little evidence of teamwork with regard to collaborative teaching and learning, and owing to some delicate relationships amongst the staff, gentle reminders to teachers to observe lessons were necessary. Hence, the student teacher education tools were often treated as rules in the system in order to encourage participation from all members of staff. Learning frequently appeared to be a matter of transference from the mentor to the student teachers. A limited approach to debate was also reflected in the lack of opportunities for talking about pedagogy in department meetings and in the department's social practices generally.

Advice given on teaching strategies and classroom management suitable in the department was personal to the teaching staff and not considered in light of the student teachers' own learning perspectives, leaving internal reflections to the student teachers' private thoughts. The mentor reports were read to the university tutor as a way of accounting for student teachers' progress, rather than to further develop student teachers' understanding of their learning needs. For example, comments from the mentor on not setting homework were seen as an indication that this needed to be done in the second school practice, rather than debating how homework was important for pupils' learning. Consequently, ongoing exploration and debate were little encouraged, and the student teacher education activity often remained at the level of rules for participation.

### Why is the object being worked on in the student teacher education activity system in the Geography department?

In Geography, there was less of an emphasis on the student teachers as individuals and more of a focus on them gaining opportunities to learn by working with successful practitioners, by emulating them in a form of learning transfer as in the first student teacher working with the Geography mentor. The department staff did not voice reasons for wanting to be involved in student teacher education beyond the fact that they had always had student teachers and believed there were some benefits to be had from having more staff in the department. However, this was seen as 'a risk' by the Head of Geography (5 February), and previous difficult experiences had made the head of department wary of the demands in working with novices. Consequently, it was made clear that the organisation of department matters meant that student teacher education activity should not impact on other activity systems already in place, and had to work around the department's practices. Therefore, student teacher education was not considered in a way that it could impact on the department's work generally. The desired identity for a teacher of Geography was unclear from the discussions of the department staff, with exemplars of successful idiosyncratic teaching often promoted by the mentor outside the department (recommending the student teachers see other staff so as to help them with issues of classroom management for example). There was less contestation apparent in how to best teach Geography beyond an inquiry approach. This was also linked to the importance of subject content relevance and the engagement of pupils promoted by the mentor.

## The Science department

### What is the object being worked on in the student teacher education activity system in the Science department?

The student teacher education activity system's object in the Science department appeared to be about working on the learning that was available to the student teachers within the established social practices of the department, whether it be teaching classes with their specific schemes of work in the first school practice or extending the activity to working with other primary school classes in the second. Therefore, enabling access to the learning available in established practices and helping the student teachers to learn how to be novices in an established team was felt by many to be the main object motive for the student teacher education activity. The tutors felt this to be important too, but also desired debate and challenge in order to develop student teacher learning opportunities. However, this way of working relied on the compliance of the student teachers with department practices and them meeting with department expectations. When this did not happen there was tension in how the school saw the object of student teacher education activity and then how the university resolved this.

An established way of working in student teacher education fitted into the tightly run faculty, meaning that for the smooth running of the department, the expectations were that student teachers should be 'moulded' (interview with Science teacher – 13 March). Teamwork was highly regarded in the Science department as a way of positively collaborating on their schemes of work, which had been developed over time and with considerable investment. These jointly constructed lessons appeared to act as a way of engendering a cohesive community, which many staff felt to be a special aspect of working within the faculty. Consequently, implicit faculty rules encouraged a collaborative approach to work within school, which spilled into social opportunities outside of school. A confident belief in the value of training in the department was voiced with staff feeling up to date on matters of teaching and learning through the department's own peer observation cycle, the fortnightly bulletins and the sharing ideas slot in the faculty meetings. Therefore, numerous opportunities for student teacher learning could be gained from such central science initiatives rather than from specific student teacher education opportunities, which, although provided, were couched in a rule-bound notion of complying with the course requirements and using tools to evidence the meeting of codified teaching standards.

## How is the object being worked on in the student teacher education activity system in the Science department?

The social practices in the Science department affected the student teachers' learning opportunities in that many of the teachers worked long hours and expected student teachers to pursue such opportunities particularly when getting familiar with demonstrations and scientific equipment. The student teachers in the first school practice kept their distance from the science team feeling that this eased the pressures for them in meeting department expectations and in using the school facilities. However, this put them in a defensive position when challenged, as the team spoke to one another a great deal about student teacher education. Their concerns were aired with regard to expected progress. Confrontation was avoided, but evidence did show a break down in support on occasions with the mentor and staff walking away from the student teacher education situation in order to preserve their own belief that they were doing the right thing. The university tutor sensing the school's bewilderment advised one of the student teachers to challenge less until they started to meet the department's expectations.

Student teachers' thinking was rarely evident or explored as part of the student teacher education activity. There was less of an emphasis on the student teachers as individuals and more of a focus on them gaining opportunities to learn by working with successful practitioners and by participating as novice members in an experienced team. However, even though personal perspectives did not feature in many discussions with the mentor, open discussions were evident in general science staff gatherings, and should the student teachers be present at these, then there were opportunities to informally debate pedagogical and science matters. However, when opinions were challenged by the student teachers in mentor meetings this was in contrast to the established way of working:

> Science mentor: I had a couple of staff come and say that they were concerned about how you [student teacher] were taking advice. I had that in mind when you didn't agree with my problem. I thought I was wasting my time as you didn't want to know, and I thought that other people were also feeling you were not taking advice. That is why I wanted to end the conversation on Friday. (Field notes – 30 January)

General debates on pedagogy were overridden by discussions on the schemes of work and meeting the standards required for gaining qualified teacher status (as illustrated in Chapter 9, where tools were often used instrumentally to evidence the student teacher profiles).

### Why is the object being worked on in the student teacher education activity system in the Science department?

In the Science department many of the current science team had either mentored on the student teacher education course or had completed it themselves as student teachers, and this also impacted on the learning opportunities of the student teachers in that there were established ideas of how the course worked with student teachers in the past. The course was also highly regarded, with many teachers appearing to value staff who had been trained in this way. There were a number of examples of successful teachers within the department who had developed from the training at Downtown University. There was also strong opinion that involvement with Downtown University helped to maintain possible recruitment opportunities for the school and provided professional development for the mentors who had all gone on to take further positions of responsibility within the school after having worked with the student teachers. The experience of student teachers in the second school practice running and teaching the primary school transition project with over 350 primary school children was also a major benefit for the department being involved with the student teacher education course, and this helped to reinforce the value of working with student teachers in a team environment. This appeared to be a strong aspect of how the department perceived the identity of a science teacher, as a team player used to working out of their subject area with support and ancillary staff. The Science department provided such a model of team learning.

## The interaction of school department activity systems

As explained in Chapter 3, participants in activity systems are usually working in more than one activity system (Engeström, 2000). Figure 3.4 (in Chapter 3) illustrates the effect on the object of multiple activity systems, and highlights how tensions may arise from the different perspectives of the participants working in them. How the student teacher education activity systems operated in the departments had an impact on how far they interacted with other activity systems. CHAT encourages researchers to seek complexity in tracing learning and development across multiple and potentially conflicting activity systems (Warmington *et al.*, 2004). All the participants in the student teacher education activity systems in the school departments were also participants in other activity systems and therefore took different positions in and between them. How they worked towards objects in other activity systems (for example, when the tutors worked with the student teachers in the university or when teachers worked in the pastoral and welfare system in school) affected how they saw their work within the school student teacher education activity systems. Each department is considered separately below in order to analyse examples of activity system interaction. This interaction affected the objects of the student teacher education activity systems and therefore impacted on the student teachers' learning opportunities. Activity system interaction helps to indicate further why the student teacher education activity systems' objects differed.

### The History department

The department felt that it greatly benefited from being involved with the work of the university in a number of ways. It therefore actively sought out and celebrated this partnership in many activity systems and not just in relation to student teacher education. This meant that professional development was seen from a broad perspective and often integral to the way the department worked. For example, the head of department's motive for curriculum changes to 'organically develop' (interview – 9 February) through collaborative debate and research on the nature of the schemes of work created a department-wide view of the relevance and importance of the history curriculum, and this was shared with the university. Emphasising joint work in her explanation of how the department approached new developments, it was expected that disagreements would occur. These were evident in department meetings, for example when the team disagreed about teaching British Empire or when they were concerned that lunchtime revision sessions were being encouraged even though staff were not being remunerated for them: 'in principle they should be paid for ... I will feed back to the union if [head of department] mentions it to the Head tomorrow and there is no luck in payment' (History mentor, Field notes – 26 February). Sometimes the university tutor attended these meetings, and disagreements were retold when explaining decisions that had been made in the past. Such contestation was not so openly discussed or apparent in the other departments, but appeared as a prerequisite and a desirable aspect of working within and with other communities in the History department.

The approach to teacher development and learning with all staff opening themselves up to the opportunity of benefiting from being involved in student teacher education activity was apparent in the way the mentor and tutor roles appeared to be seen very similarly. Giving answers to pedagogical questions was not the most helpful way of approaching student teacher learning, with the most beneficial way of working seen as trying new ideas: 'just relax and be prepared to get it wrong lots of times' (interview with History teacher – 17 May). All believed that this was a stated aim in the department teaching and learning situations, and therefore interaction between numerous activity systems was both evident and desirable, with the division of labour in each ideally focussing on the object of the activity systems rather than on the motives specifically related to respective roles. So, in student teacher education this meant that teachers, the mentor and the tutor were all focused on student teacher learning, rather than primarily concentrating on their classes, the course paperwork and the meeting of qualified teaching standards:

### The Modern Foreign Languages department

The student teachers in the first school practice perceived an emphasis in the MFL department on the importance given to pupil achievement: 'I hear lots of talk about grades, I don't want this student in my set upsetting my grades, and stuff like that' (interview with MFL student teacher – 23 February). Schemes of work were seen in terms of the end of unit assessments, and the pupils' success in these suggested the competence of the teachers in the classroom. It was apparent that the possible negative effects on the academic progress of the class by having student teachers take the lessons were raised before the possible developmental learning opportunities gained from having more teachers in the classroom or from the benefits of team teaching. A teacher explained how she referred to student teachers when talking with parents:

> You are sort of building them up the whole time and you never have to play them down and say they are just a student teacher with their L plates on. We never do that. We always have 'visiting teachers'. (Interview with MFL teacher – 7 June)

Parental concerns were mentioned in both the MFL and Science departments with regard to the disconcerting effect of pupils experiencing disruption to their lessons because of student teacher education practices. In her capacity as head of year, one MFL teacher emphasised that she would reassure parents that pupils' progress would not be negatively affected by having student teachers in the classes. This was one example of where student teacher education activity was seen as possibly detrimental to the smooth functioning of the MFL department. Similarly, academic research was not seen to be particularly influential on the working practices within the department. Research interests and opportunities to provide further studies for the teaching staff were regarded as positive in so far as professional development and the interests of staff were concerned, but research was not actively encouraged. There had been no formal sharing of pedagogical ideas up until the research year when a 'good ideas section' had been introduced into faculty meetings. However, the head of department commented:

> I don't think they [student teachers] felt quite brave enough to sort of say ideas themselves, but that could definitely be a forum in the future. We'll have to see. (Interview with Head of MFL – 1 February)

Approaches towards student teacher education activity encouraged a clear differentiation in the division of labour between the roles of the mentor and tutor. The former was there as a support to guide the student teachers in what they were learning by imparting experience and helping them to meet the requirements of the course. The latter was there, from the teacher's perspective, to check that the student teachers were competent in working as teachers and able to model the desired working practices of the university. It was felt in the school that this model was desirable as a preliminary style of teaching and one that stood up to rigorous assessment. However, it could and probably would change once the student teachers gained experience and worked out a teaching style for themselves. Consequently, student teacher education activity was isolated from other department activities and seen as only specific to student teachers, with its object having little impact elsewhere.

### The Geography department

Working with student teachers in the Geography department was also seen more as an adjunct to the work of the department than integral to the professional development of its staff. The negative pressures put on staff by having student teachers in the classroom were balanced with the positive outcomes of gaining some relief of regular staff being in front of a class. Rather than viewing the university partnership as providing access into another activity system that could benefit the work of the department, the head of Geography spoke in terms of 'taking a break' (5 February) from student teachers when the work had been particularly demanding during some years. He also emphasised how working with student teachers needed to fit in with other department activities rather than prioritising student teacher education. With imminent change in staffing in the department in the research year, it was also apparent that a priority for some teachers was being given to other activities, which made the work in student teacher education secondary compared to their motives elsewhere. This was evident in the Geography mentor's reminder to the student teacher: 'You need to catch up with [teacher] tomorrow; she'll just go off on one a little bit. I know talking to her doesn't always work' (Field notes – 21 March).

As in the MFL department, the perceived differing roles of the mentor and tutor emphasised the assessment nature of the student teacher education process, and this was particularly noticeable when the Geography tutor and the MFL second school teaching practice tutor both worked part time as teachers in the respective school departments. Here it seemed as though a divide between the student teacher education activity systems of the school and the university was desirable in order to uphold the differing status of the participants involved in relation to monitoring and assessment. This was also apparent in the different division of labour that grew around the appropriation of tools in the student teacher education activity. This was not apparent in the History department where tools tended to be used in very similar ways. However, unlike MFL, the Geography department mentor and university tutor agreed on all matters of pedagogy, and consequently, teaching and learning appeared less problematised for the student teachers.

## The Science department

The university was clearly seen as having an authoritative role in a number of situations in the Science department, especially when communications between the student teachers and the teaching staff were strained: 'The problems specifically with [student teacher], I got the impression from [mentor] that he was finding it hard to make [Downtown University] realise how frustrated we were about him' (interview with Science teacher – 24 May). The initial desire of the university tutor for student teachers to challenge and ask hard questions of the school working practices was therefore in tension with the student teachers being required to comply with the expectations of the staff. The mentor aired his concerns about the student teachers with the tutor who offered formal procedures for following these up, but perhaps because of the clearly defined boundaries of how the university and the school student teacher education activity systems operated, the mentor felt that such formal procedures could have been detrimental to the student teachers' learning opportunities. The university tutor's involvement in the department was closely related to monitoring progress and collecting evidence for having met the required standards for teaching. Putting formal procedures in place could have enforced this monitoring role further and reduced the perceived student teachers' opportunities for learning. The student teachers saw the university as important in confirming their progress, and prioritised tutor visits and their summative comments throughout the course.

Some major changes in the working of the science department with a new building coming to fruition and new examination courses meant that the focus of staff was strong in these areas. To an extent, the unity in day-to-day activities with the department advocating a strong team work ethic meant that student teacher education activity could have been best enhanced if it interacted closely with the department's other activity systems. In the first school practice the student teachers prevented this from happening in that any incidental opportunities that arose for considering their learning outside the student teacher education practices were not taken, as the student teachers were rarely present in the department team rooms. This meant that student teacher learning opportunities were mainly restricted to specific student teacher education activity, and teachers' motives for enhancing the learning opportunities further were frequently in tension with their motives in other activities, particularly as they perceived the lack of student teacher involvement in department routines as an indication of their questionable commitment to teaching:

> The commitment didn't shine through, and I am not saying he [student teacher] wasn't committed but because of his lack of organisation I found it hard work to have to drive him. He didn't turn up when I expected him to and that came across as somebody who wasn't particularly committed, so I found that frustrating. (Interview with Science teacher – 24 May)

During the second school practice the student teachers were particularly valued when they appeared to work in a separate activity system than that of student teacher education, when they ran the primary school induction project. The learning gained from participating in this may have been considered as a by-product, as the head of department acknowledged in interview. The induction project as an opportunity for student teachers' learning was not prioritised in the department, as lessons were not evaluated or based on the current student teachers' ideas. Instead, the department valued the work for the contribution the student teachers were making to the Science team and to the activity of primary school induction.

## Concluding comments

The different natures of the objects of the student teacher education activity systems reflect a number of factors in relation to the subject departments. Where student teacher learning was seen in similar ways to the learning of all practitioners, as ongoing and specifically in relation to its context, then the object of the student teacher education activity system was more clearly identified and its complexity acknowledged, as seen in the discussions surrounding the student teachers' learning in the History department. A concentration on learning for all staff meant that student teacher learning was seen as just one point on their learning trajectory. This view was different to one that considered the student teacher education activity system's object in a less complex way, with its principal motive being to develop student teachers as able practitioners managing their classrooms, as noted in many of the conversations in the MFL and Geography departments. In the Science department the principal object motive appeared to be about developing student teachers as strong team players, able to adapt to established practices within department communities.

The social practices of the department communities impacted on the student teacher education activity systems' objects. For example, a clear collective team model was demonstrated in Science, as opposed to individual examples of how teachers could work in the other three departments, and the student teachers in Science were encouraged to work within this model. In MFL and History the learning of student teachers was seen in a more individual way. The student teachers' thoughts, perceptions and experiences were recognised as having an impact on their appreciation of pedagogy. In the Geography and Science departments, learning opportunities were viewed more in terms of exposing student teachers to effective practices with them then expected to adopt these once an understanding of their effectiveness was appreciated. In the History and MFL departments, the student teachers' own interpretations of effective practices were expected to affect their learning, with the History staff taking a stronger active role in helping to guide the student teachers' thoughts in this, using student teacher education tools to open these up for analysis. The MFL staff left personal reflection and questioning more to the student teachers themselves who had to reconcile different approaches to pedagogy. Consequently, many of the MFL teachers did not appropriate student teacher education tools in the same way as those in History.

In the MFL department, interaction between the university and the school arose primarily because of the division of labour. The tutor's school visits ensured a different interpretation of knowledge was addressed in relation to student teacher education, but because the differences between the school and university's interpretations of knowledge were not debated, this did not affect other activity systems. Similarly, in Geography the division of labour was clear and was instrumental in the interaction of school and university student teacher education activity systems. And here too, there was less of an open discussion on the nature of the object compared to the debates in the History department. Interaction in activity systems in History (for example, in student teacher education and in the department's development of the curriculum in which the tutor was also involved) arose through the nature of the work itself, which was related to the object (rather than specifically because of the division of labour of the participants), and the open problematising of pedagogy meant that tensions were clearly evident, and discussed as part of this work. Interpretations of knowledge in History both in the school and by the university tutor were similar, making the student teachers and the participants ask difficult questions in order to open up their ways of thinking not only in relation to student teacher education but also in relation to other contexts and activity systems.

In the Geography department, the school and the university tutor also interpreted knowledge similarly. However, the teaching and learning process appeared less problematised, meaning that the participants were comfortable in their general agreements. This lack of contestation seemed to be largely a result of the primary focus being on the rules of the student teacher education activity rather than its object. Hence, the division of labour in the student teacher education activity system in Geography emphasised the separate responsibilities of the participants with regard to the student teacher education course and the student teachers' experience of this, rather than specifically concentrating on their learning. This was also evident in the Science department, where differential interpretations of knowledge from the science staff and the university tutor (the latter initially promoting greater challenge to accepted norms) came together and were submerged in procedural notions of following policy with regard to the rules of the activity. This often closed down the opportunities for debate and for learning within the student teacher education activity system, which because of the way the student teachers in the first school practice worked interacted little with other activity systems in the department.

The differing and sometimes contradictory approaches to student teacher education activity highlighted the importance of the systems' objects acting as the motivating forces in the activities. When the objects were constantly negotiated and renegotiated between the participants, a collaborative development of the activity was possible with the opportunity for new learning. When the student teacher education activity system interacted with others, the clearer and more focused its object, as indicated by a shared understanding of this shown in tool use, the greater possibility that the interaction contributed to the student teacher education activity with less likelihood that participants' actions were guided by object motives of other activity systems. This further indicates why learning opportunities were constructed differently for the student teachers in the four departments.

# 11

# Developing Expert Learners of Teaching and Learning: A Model for Researching and Developing Learning Opportunities in School Settings

## Introduction

Identifying social practices and the cultural history of the school departments' work in the research undertaken in relation to student teacher education indicated why departments have been considered so 'distinctive' as learning environments (Donnelly, 2000). The following discussion of department cultures relates these findings to previous research and questions their impact on student teacher education activity. The chapter considers expansive learning as a possible consequence of the foci on tool use and department culture and introduces a follow-up research study I conducted in student teacher education, which presents a model for researching and developing learning opportunities in school settings.

Learning opportunities for student teachers may have seemed to be similar, as each student teacher and subject department were taking part in the same training course. However, when looking at how learning opportunities were constructed and reconstructed, it was clear that there were considerable differences in the kinds of learning afforded the student teachers, and consequently the potential for these in helping student teachers respond to different classroom contexts. It was therefore important to distinguish the learning opportunities from the way that they were constructed. Innovation was encouraged in the student teacher education activity in the History department. Concentrating on the student teachers' learning and on the learning of all participants allowed for development in the activity through internalisation and externalisation (Vygotsky, 1978), as the teachers, tutor and student teachers interpreted what was happening and then worked in newly informed ways as a result of their interpretations.

Outcomes from discussions were often used in the 'ideas slot' in department meetings in order to present new ideas or to explain how new ideas had worked in the classroom. New ways of working sometimes replaced previous ways, for example:

> (The head of History asks [teacher] to tell everyone about her podcast idea.)
> Head of History: a fantastic idea, it can be put onto the website. They [the pupils] record it themselves and then download one another doing their talks. Better than always writing everything. [Teacher], put together the technical support and let us know. It would be brilliant to download each other's. (Field notes – 26 February)

Feedback from other teachers contributed to discussions and suggestions for ways forward. Action plans designed to further the work were suggested before revisiting the ideas at future meetings.

Such department practices complemented Engeström's (1999b) expansive learning cycle and suggested that new learning was possible and desirable for everyone, with teaching practices not necessarily set in any firmly defined ways. This way of working carried over into the department's student teacher education activity, with the student teachers being encouraged to invest in experimental research in their lessons, which was most easily done when the student teachers worked in pairs. Evident from early on in the year, the head of department acknowledged different ways of teaching History and spurred student teachers on to experiment and 'go for it' even though 'things can go catastrophically wrong' (interview – 9 February).

## Social situations for the development of student teacher learning

In Chapter 4 I considered school subject departments as social situations for the development of student teacher learning where learning emerges from interactions with the social situation of development (Vygotsky, 1978). Learning can be considered in terms of the student teachers' changing relationships with the social situation of development (Edwards, 2010b). Learning is therefore seen as the increasing ability a student teacher has to interpret situations and to act by identifying and using resources effectively. The research findings helped consider how the school departments managed the student teachers' relationships with the social situation of development. How the student teachers in the History department were supported in acting on their interpretations affected their changing relationship with the social situation of development in that their newly considered appreciation of pedagogy became part of the student teacher education learning process and worked on future discussions on contested pedagogical issues. Acknowledged tensions in the department's appreciation of pedagogy meant that further debates accepted the inevitability of contested issues, and there was no single authoritative way of considering these. Consequently, student teachers began to understand this and expressed their own interpretations openly alongside those of the teaching staff.

In the MFL department contestation was also acknowledged, as it was recognised that different staff had different opinions about pedagogy. However, this was accepted as part of individual preferences with regard to personal teaching styles, which were all considered 'valid and worthwhile' (interview with MFL teacher – 19 June). But this was not openly debated, and therefore student teachers were forced into private discussions in order to try and reconcile pedagogical differences for themselves. Their relationship with the department's social situation of development, although close, did not allow for open interaction, and therefore it did not change or develop as a result of further (expansive) negotiations.

With no tensions discussed in the student teacher education activity system with regard to pedagogical issues in the Geography department owing to this not being part of the department's social practices, the student teachers were not encouraged to question aspects of teaching and learning beyond the examples evident when working with the teaching staff. Consequently, favoured teaching styles were emulated and progress seen in how successfully this positive teaching was replicated by the student teachers. This created a relatively static relationship with the social situation of development, as the position of the student teachers remained constant with regard to the department working practices.

The Science department tended to give less opportunities and credence for student teachers to interpret teaching and learning situations and expected them to meet the collective demands of working in a strongly led team. The department was more interventionist in the way it guided student teacher learning opportunities, but had a less individual approach to student teacher learning. When student teachers did not act in ways expected, then their relationship with the social situation of development partially broke down, which was seen when the mentor walked out of a mentor meeting and when teachers occasionally took over lessons. Such tensions, although critical for the student teachers, were regarded as secondary to the importance of meeting the expectations of the university tutor, who eventually recommended the student teachers primarily met department expectations first before questioning practice, although this went against ideal student teacher education partnership principles. Complying with department expectations was felt to be important in order to repair tensions in the social situation of development.

## Department culture

Considering student teachers' relationships with the social situation of their development gives an indication of the kinds of learning available to them. The different department cultures also influenced the nature of the activity and further indicated why the student teacher learning opportunities were constructed differently. Variations in how the departments worked in student teacher education were considered in terms that went beyond previous descriptions of department cultures as individualistic or collegial (Hargreaves, 1994) or as strong or weak departments (Talbert and McLaughlin, 1994). By analysing the cultural history and social practices that influenced student teacher education learning opportunities, greater understanding was gained of how student teacher education practices have evolved in student teacher education activity systems. Strong collective department cultures with cohesive and supportive staff and confident beliefs in the success of the departments' ways of working were seen in both the Science and MFL departments. However, as was illustrated in the MFL department, the focus in the student teacher education activity system was often not on pedagogical matters, which meant that student teachers were not automatically exposed to debates on teaching and learning. An outward display of unity with an apparent strategic compliance by some of the teachers as described by Lacey (1977) appeared to account for accepted but little-discussed different points of views on approaches to pedagogy. Alternatively, department working practices strongly influenced by collective debates on teaching and learning were seen in the Science department, but these were not a priority in the student teacher education activity system and therefore were not readily apparent to student teachers. A weaker department community with a fractured culture and a less confident staff outlook with concerns of 'territorial wrangling' (Paechter, 1995), as noted when a number of staff felt that some aspects of the Geography curriculum were being taken over by new schemes of work in Science, was identified in the Geography department.

Although some vulnerability was felt in exposing personal ideas with more experienced teachers, giving student teachers agency from the outset made them start to answer hard questions and interpret situations automatically without necessarily expecting direct instruction or advice on how to work in given situations. This process was more likely to encourage knowledge *for* practice, useful for working in a variety of situations, as opposed to knowledge *of* practice, which was specific to the department and school context (McLaughlin and Talbert, 2001). The research illustrated how student teacher education practices were not just about disseminating knowledge to novices, as this was only useful for student teachers to a limited degree, but student teacher education should be about new learning, and this could be gained when teachers worked collaboratively. It was particularly noticeable in the History department that a variety of sources were accessed when discussing contestable ideas, for example educational research literature and practices in other schools. This was in contrast to tips and advice that had been gained from experience in working in the research school, which was often forwarded in the other departments.

## The importance of expansive learning for student teachers

Expansive learning opportunities, a concept central to Engeström's research (1999a, 2001, 2008) and described in Chapter 3, took learning forward for participants and acknowledged the importance of context. Such learning opportunities also promoted the possibility of new learning through developing increased abilities to interpret situations. When learning was context bound and therefore not expansive, student teachers appeared less equipped to work out of their training context. As noted in Chapter 3 learning can be viewed in a number of different ways and is more complex than just considering ideas of acquisition and participation. A combination of acquiring specific content knowledge and being involved in non-formal learning processes through participation was viewed as part of a social and cultural process, where knowledge 'connected' with emotion and helped student teachers interpret situations. Where the social situations were managed so that there was a genuine collaboration of ideas and working practices with both student teachers and other participants in the student teacher education activity systems learning together, learning was enhanced. Examples of reproductive or conservative kinds of learning sometimes appeared to be successful within the learning context, but with few alternative viewpoints expressed or choices as to how teaching and learning practices could be varied, the context was not being fully interpreted or its complexity fully acknowledged.

The danger of simply being inducted into established practices is that this could lead to the possibility of student teachers only gaining partial understanding and appreciation of pedagogical concepts (pseudoconcepts) (Vygotsky, 1987; Smagorinsky *et al.*, 2003), as they are simply trying to adapt to a situation. This would likely inhibit future work, especially when student teachers leave the training department context. Expansive learning is only evident if inner contradictions in the work are acknowledged and the object of the student teacher education activity system negotiated and renegotiated. Accepting that the object of an activity system is negotiated, unfolding and often indeterminable means that it is difficult for a researcher to accurately follow a system's object development, its historical formation, and analyse contradictions that emerge. However, it is desirable if a researcher can predict how an activity system may respond, or not, to new forms of practice. Teaching is a continually changing profession where new practices evolve in response to new demands and ways of working (Vescio *et al.*, 2008). A student teacher education activity system should ideally change its practices in order to enable student teachers to manage the social situation of their development and thus allow personal agency, which will then further enable them to respond to new situations in the future and after they have finished at their teaching practice school.

## Other models of student teacher education

Models of student teacher education partnership vary across education systems, and looking to other models of student teacher education that recognise the findings of this research suggests possible forms of development. In England, the student teacher education model prioritises student teachers learning through experience. It values the expertise in schools and relies on the craft knowledge of teachers (Hagger and McIntyre, 2006). Being in school for a large proportion of the student teacher education course reflects the importance of 'working on the job' in order to develop practice. In smaller courses it is possible to collaborate in partnerships on a more personal level with extensive coordination between the higher education institution and the partnership schools in order to work closely on matters of student teacher education, but also on research initiatives that may strengthen student teacher education and the research partnership (see Ellis, 2007; Husbands, 1995). In Scotland, although less market-driven and with greater emphasis on the intellectual and the theoretical, the overall policy thrust is still similar to England (Menter, 2009). However, in Scotland greater onus is given to university tutors in assessing and supervising student teachers rather than relying heavily on joint work with practicing teachers. Nevertheless, both systems tend to separate student teacher learning from the learning in the school department.

Proposals in larger student teacher education systems as in the USA may also share the modernist tendencies as identified in the notion of 'performativity' (Ball, 2003) and accountability noted in England. Cochran-Smith (2009) identifies evaluations of student teacher education programmes in the USA that have been based on pupil outcomes. This has been done by comparing pupils' test scores when taught by experienced teachers with those from pupils taught by new teachers from identified teacher education programmes. The role of the school department in the teachers' learning is not considered at all, and teachers are seen as 'the determining factor in boosting pupils' achievement' (p. 14), ignoring the importance of teachers' professional growth. Change in student teacher education in the USA is seen as possible through changing public policies, which are consistent with a market-driven education system. Teachers' expertise is viewed as the ability to transmit agreed-upon knowledge, with its success demonstrated in pupils obtaining high test scores. Such a limited notion of pedagogy is easily administered centrally. However, this does not replicate the kind of pedagogy described in this study, which highlights the different sorts of learning that different departments facilitated for student teachers, regardless of successful pupil examination outcomes.

A challenge posed by Hogan and Gopinathan (2009) is the solving of a conundrum of how to improve classroom teaching practices in Singapore. These are dependent on improving student teacher education, which, being work-based, is in turn dependent on improving classroom pedagogy. Getting change into a teacher education system that is based on work-based learning by using a top-down approach is evident in Singapore's student teacher education system when developing 'thinking schools' which promote innovation in relation to teaching practice. The aim is to develop teaching expertise that can be 'replicated and vali dated' (p. 113). However, this idea underplays the importance that the central research in this book has revealed in different student teacher education contexts, as seen even in the very local conditions of four subject departments within the same school. The desire to replicate expert teachers also suggests the importance of having a 'one size fits all' understanding of pedagogy, which can be rolled out across different contexts. The problem with the expert/novice approach is that learning can too easily be seen as transferable rather than jointly constructed. If the aim is for teachers to be expert in all contexts, then recognising the differences in these is essential. Therefore, my research suggests it would be preferable to talk in terms of expert learners of teaching and learning rather than expert teachers, as this acknowledges the difference between teaching situations and the changes that take place within them.

My research indicates how change in work-based student teacher education activity systems may be possible. This is seen in how some teachers were better prepared for change in the way they were open to the potential for new learning and innovation. Yet there would still need to be further work in creating other department cultures where the social practices encouraged this way of working too. Perhaps this would be possible, but not in a top-down way, in a student teacher education model that does lend itself to a sociocultural approach to teaching and learning. Professional Development Schools in the USA (Teitel, 2008; Darling-Hammond, 2006; Shroyer *et al.*, 2007) are about research and inquiry into improving practice. Practice is seen as a problem, meaning that an inquiry stance is necessary to address it, and inquiry becomes part of the definition of teaching. It is through this inquiry and implementation process that both teacher and student teacher learning occur and pupils' needs are met. Research thus becomes a tool for improving learning outcomes. University tutors spend most of their time in school settings working with student teachers and supporting staff development, engaging in collaborative research with school faculties and participating in the planning, teaching and problem-solving activities of the school. This creates a bridge between higher education and schools and helps to promote an orientation to problem solving and inquiry. This model appears more closely suited to meeting the conditions for expansive learning as identified in my research.

Considering the school subject departments in this research as prototypes enables prototypical generalisation, and highlights the wider significance of the findings in relation to how school departments work in student teacher education *per se*. As discussed in Chapter 1 the increasing role of schools in student teacher education in England and the growth of importance of the role of schools in professional education of teachers make the conclusions of this research particularly relevant to the current core issues in student teacher education. It is a concern that student teachers' learning depends so much on the individual school department, its social practices and the relationships of teachers involved in student teacher education. Different opportunities for student teacher learning have been apparent in my research, which was based in just one school looking at one student teacher education course. When considering the number of school departments working with student teachers and the number of alternative routes into teaching, it is likely that learning to teach is far from a consistent process. This research has made clear that the process of learning to teach is complex, and it is therefore most important that an understanding of this process and what is involved in helping student teachers learn in numerous contexts in an ever-changing environment is recognised by all those involved in student teacher education.

## An interventionist model

When considering a definition of learning in Chapter 2, I referred to Sfard's (1998) metaphors of learning: the acquisition metaphor typically emphasising the process of learning within individual's minds and the participation metaphor focusing on social practices and activities as bases for learning. A third metaphor of learning has been identified (Paavola *et al.*, 2004, p. 573): the 'knowledge-creation metaphor'. This metaphor includes Engeström's definition of expansive learning to explain a new perspective that 'focuses on anlaysing the processes whereby new knowledge and new mediating objects of activity are collaboratively created, whether in schools or at work'. Such a process is involved in the interventionist research model of Developmental Work Research (DWR) (Engeström, 2006). DWR enables a researcher to work directly with participants in activity systems in order to start testing hypotheses about the conditions for expansive learning and to see how expansive learning may be encouraged in practice. So, for example, opening out participants' thinking by presenting possible tensions and contradictions observed in student teacher education activity systems can encourage negotiations on the objects of these and possibly develop a shared understanding. This then enables participants to look closely at the way they use tools in order to mediate work on the systems' objects. Identifying how far the systems' objects are shared illustrates whether the multi-voiced nature of student teacher education activity is helpful in affording student teacher learning opportunities.

In another student teacher education research study (Douglas, 2012) I considered how the student teacher education activity system's object in a primary school could be negotiated with the school mentors central to the negotiation process. Alongside the researcher, they lead and facilitate a developmental work research intervention by questioning identified contradictions in current practice, negotiating these and then implementing new forms of practice. Therefore, the study aimed to open up new possibilities for learning by giving the school mentors responsibility for negotiating the object of student teacher education activity. Questions on student teacher learning opportunities were addressed over five days of fieldwork comprising participant observation and interviews in the school. This included observations of meetings between student teachers, mentors and university tutors; lesson observations followed by feedback sessions and interviews with all participants involved in student teacher education. The five days of fieldwork were followed by a Developmental Work Research-style workshop with student teacher education school staff and with the university tutor.

Developmental Work Research (DWR) methodology (Engeström, 2007) uses the Change Laboratory method and is a mode of research intervention where researchers and practitioners jointly interrogate the structural tensions in and between different dimensions of activity (in this case student teacher education) as defined by CHAT, such as the rules, tools and divisions of labour that have emerged in student teacher education practices over time. The desired outcome of the DWR meetings is expansive learning at a systemic level. The aim is to encourage participants to explain the focus of their work and so reveal the object motive, and question whether change in practices are necessary in order to work on the object identified. An expansive transformation can be accomplished if 'the object and motive of the activity are reconceptualised to embrace a wider horizon of possibilities than in the previous mode of the activity' (Edwards, 2010a, p. 160).

Using the conceptual tools of activity theory in the change laboratory helps the participants consider how the object of student teacher education activity is constructed and how tools, rules and the division of labour are seen in the activity system. Possibilities are negotiated of how tools could change in order to prevent the tensions noted from the research data. Facilitated by the researcher and the school mentors, the change laboratory uses research data as evidence of current student teacher education practices in the school (known as 'mirror' data, for example, 'everyday understandings of practices collected from individual interviews with staff' (Edwards, 2010a, p. 162)). This data is pre-selected by the researcher for its capacity to highlight tensions in the student teacher education practices. Owing to the research in the study being small scale with only five days of fieldwork undertaken, the mirror data was also supplemented by, and compared to, data from the earlier ethnographic research reported as the central research study in this book (termed 'window' data). Accepting that the secondary high school research data is different, it can help to illuminate points of comparison when considered alongside the primary school data.

There are differences in the implementation of the change laboratory in this research method compared to Engeström's (2007) description of DWR methodology. I did not use video recording and unfortunately, owing to the time of year the research was undertaken, the student teachers had left the school practice and had started teaching as newly qualified teachers. They were therefore unable to attend the change laboratory workshop. The data and findings focus on two identified and closely linked contradictions in the student teacher education activity in the primary school, which were initially analysed after the five days of fieldwork and subsequently discussed in the workshop session with school staff and with the university tutor.

### Contradiction 1: Student teacher critique versus staff support

The first contradiction identified in the primary school student teacher education activity system relates to how critiquing and debating ideas on pedagogy could be seen as negatively impinging on personal support in working relations. The university encouraged and wanted a 'kind of critical enquiry':

> I see it as our responsibility in uni to say 'look there are other ways of doing it' so that they can bring that critical lens to bear on what they see in the classroom. (Interview with university tutor – 18 June)

In interview, the student teachers and the mentors in school emphasised the supportive nature of student teacher education: 'there's this sort of policy of everyone's helping everyone else and everyone's learning from everyone else's experience' (interview with mentor – 14 June). But the notion of challenging one another's viewpoints was seen as possibly problematic:

> I haven't been challenged about that (teaching ethos); I think that would be hard to be challenged by a student, but interesting. (Interview with mentor – 11 June)

Although not dismissing that there could be interest in having to defend one's approach to teaching and learning, it was not an expected way of working that was integral to student teacher education. Similarly, student teachers did not see such challenge as particularly necessary when asked if they would openly challenge teaching strategies:

> I would definitely say 'interesting why did you do that because I never would have thought to do that' or something like that ... But I've seen it more as I'm here to learn, to expand my horizons rather than to shrink someone else's, so if I needed to, I would definitely have that chat, but I've never had that opportunity, or that need. (Interview with student teacher – 16 June)

Commenting in terms of 'shrinking someone's horizons', if questioning their choice of teaching practices, suggests a view of criticism and challenge that is negative and not expansive, in fact quite the opposite. This student teacher feels that communication is important and suggests that commenting on teaching and learning choices is something she would do. However, she focuses on her own learning rather than adopting an expansive learning approach, where the class teacher could learn too. The idea of expected one-way learning is further enhanced by another student teacher's surprise that experienced teachers may also suggest (although not criticise and challenge) pedagogical practices among themselves. This student teacher also did not feel challenged during the school practice:

> No I haven't personally been challenged and I haven't noticed any arguments or disputes; there are always suggestions though and I think I've seen even experienced staff suggesting to each other. (Interview with student teacher – 16 June)

In the change laboratory workshop school staff readily recognised this contradiction and acknowledged that it was desirable to accept the importance of critical enquiry. When negotiating the tension of questioning accepted practices, one mentor commented: 'I am not particularly thinking about their role [as a student teacher] carefully enough' (16 December). She felt that her concern for personally supporting the student teacher sometimes discouraged her from challenging the ideas behind the teaching practice. Another mentor also felt that careful consideration was needed in order to develop genuine debate, and suggested ways forward for encouraging collaboration:

> You have to make an agreement between you if you are observing one another for example, what the purpose of the observation is

and what is going to happen after the observation. (Teacher in the Change Laboratory workshop – 16 December)

Receiving feedback from student teachers 'felt strange' for one of the mentors when she was observed in her classroom. In the change laboratory workshop she accepted that 'maybe it shouldn't' (mentor – 16 December), as it was crucial that everyone was open to learning. This illustrated the value of discussing student teacher education activity for all participants, which was emphasised in the workshop where new ways of appropriating student teacher education tools (such as the example of observation above) were suggested. The opportunity of being able to do this was welcomed: 'it is so lovely to just be able to sit down, share ideas and talk because there's precious little time for doing that' (school mentor – 16 December). The university tutor also acknowledged the thought-provoking nature of negotiating tensions observed during the fieldwork. She commented in the change laboratory workshop: 'I've only just thought about this because you [researcher] are making me think about it' (16 December). Such comments suggest that seeking out tensions in student teacher education practices was not a natural way of working in the school setting.

### Contradiction 2: Student teacher experimentation versus school norms

A second contradiction observed in the student teacher education activity system was evident in how the norms of the school and the classroom were acknowledged as being highly influential on the student teachers' teaching practices and ideas, and also something that needed to be protected: 'From the class teacher's point of view and for the best interests of the children we want to try and maintain what has previously happened by way of routines and consistency and things like that, because we have to pick the children up again when the student leaves' (interview with mentor – 17 June). Yet student teachers were expected not to mimic teachers in the ways they worked: 'I want you [student teacher] to be your own person' (Field notes – 11 June). One school mentor commented:

If they get with a really good teacher who's got a strong personality and you go in and observe, you can almost hear that teacher speaking through the student and you think 'actually I don't want you to do that'. (Interview with mentor – 17 June)

This desire for experimentation also appeared to be in tension with some staff seeing themselves as teachers to be emulated: 'You are aware that you are there as a role model' (interview with mentor – 11 June). Using the term 'role model' suggests that the learning is one way, with the student teachers wanting to aspire to the examples of teaching made available to them. When asked how one mentor felt about the opportunities student teachers get to try out different ways of teaching, she acknowledged the tension:

It's a very good point. In many respects they don't [get the opportunities]. If they have an excellent role model as a class teacher then they're in a very good position. Even if you have a very good role model, that doesn't address the issue of different approaches. I see trainees attempt to model themselves on an outstanding teacher but they don't actually see what underpins the excellence of the teaching. They purely mimic what they're doing without realising what underpins it. (Interview with teacher – 14 June)

One mentor felt that in order to support a student teacher effectively, it was necessary 'to increase the confidence of the class teacher to let go' (interview with mentor – 14 June). This was an issue that was raised in the change laboratory workshop, and both the university tutor and the school mentors felt that this was an essential area for staff development in the support of new teachers:

It's about how to move the students on from safe places. Sometimes we feel we've managed it and other times not. (Mentor in the Change Laboratory workshop – 16 December)

The university tutor acknowledged how the social practices in the school could also pressure student teachers and affect their willingness to try new teaching and learning strategies that may challenge current practices. The university tutor knew the school staff well and her familiarity with them may dissuade student teachers from critiquing school practices:

I go in and I know everybody and everyone, you know hugs and kisses and all the rest of it and I think actually that's quite hard because if they [student teachers] don't get on in that, it's only just occurred to me, they're thinking 'but they're all good friends here'. (Interview with university tutor – 18 June)

Expecting student teachers to be their 'own person' and challenge the status quo of teaching and learning in the school could be considered a demanding undertaking when the student teacher education activity system's rules (norms and conventions) are closely tied in with the social practices of the school. In discussing the above quotation in the change laboratory workshop, the university tutor questioned the social practices in the school:

> It has made me think though that I need to think about how I present myself if I go in like that, so it's been good for me. (University tutor in the Change Laboratory workshop – 16 December)

One mentor questioned the student teacher's opportunity for open discussion: 'she (student teacher) always says that she agrees with what I'm saying but whether or not she does; she could just be being polite' (Mentor in the Change Laboratory workshop – 16 December). The temptation to emulate teachers when working in such a close-knit community and to replicate the social practices evident in the school is understandable: 'watching [teacher] teach has just been amazing and then me trying to do something similar myself' (interview with student teacher – 16 June). However, this way of working does not allow for the possibility of two way learning, but appears like an apprenticeship model, often critically evaluated in student teacher education literature for 'privileging mastery of techniques of management of the classroom and behaviour of pupils [rather than developing] inquiring minds and reflective approaches' (Spendlove *et al.*, 2010, p. 65).

## Concluding comments

Research on student teacher mentoring recommends finding ways to create 'school based activities that give the trainee and the teacher/ mentor opportunities to teach, evaluate and discuss' (Macrory and McLachlan, 2009, p. 268). Another study (Spendlove *et al.*, 2010, p. 76) wishes to ensure that such discussions encourage the exploration of 'different emphases and positions at work ... to nurture a reflexive autonomous and sustainable pedagogical discourse'. Examining differences of opinion on pedagogy and promoting debate and inquiry can be difficult when working in student teacher education partnerships (Cook *et al.*, 2002; Grossman *et al.*, 2000; Smagorinsky *et al.*, 2003; Smagorinsky *et al.*, 2004). But 'in a truly effective collaborative relationship, dissimilarities between partners can in fact fuel the kind of intellectual discourse that interrupts traditional thinking and fosters the development of the teacher as knower' (Schulz and Hall, 2004, p. 267).

This highlights the importance of appreciating the social context of school departments and recognising how these can both afford and constrain learning opportunities (Mutton *et al.*, 2010).

In the change laboratory it was possible for the objects to be negotiated (and in the future renegotiated) between the participants, thereby enabling a collaborative development of the activity. Opening out participants' thinking by presenting possible tensions and contradictions observed in the activity system encourages negotiations on the object of the student teacher education activity, and develops a shared understanding of this. This then enables participants to look closely at the way they use tools in order to mediate work on the systems' objects. For example, discussing expectations of how to use observation can enrich the learning possibilities when using the tool. A better understanding of practice by analysing the discussion in the change laboratory workshop in relation to the mirror and window data was characterised by an awareness of the multi-voiced nature of student teacher education. Opening this up for discussion sought to stimulate new opportunities and enabled 'detachment and possibilities for alternative explanations' (Engeström, 1993, p. 89) in order to negotiate the object of student teacher education activity and to develop student teacher education practices.

The role of the school mentor was seen as one that could potentially work alongside the university tutor in facilitating Developmental Work Research and the change laboratory workshops. In an attempt to counter the possibility that participants 'only comply with and accommodate themselves to [solving contradictions] in order to avoid any conflict' (Langemeyer, 2006, p. 7), it is desirable for negotiations to involve all participants in the activity system. Previous research suggests that student teachers' learning trajectories should ideally be the joint object of student teacher education activity (Jahreie and Ottesen, 2010), and that student teachers need to be able to question and position themselves rather than be positioned within their learning environment: 'This is an important approach because it gives an opportunity to optimize the agency of student teachers' (*ibid.* 233). Working in the way described in the primary school research goes some way to addressing this. Such work would necessitate a paradigmatic shift for participants in the student teacher education process and a deconstruction of established norms in order to set the context for future practice. As noted in the central study in this book, the necessity of negotiating and renegotiating the system's object regularly by all participants is demanding, but this is essential for creating learning opportunities that help to develop critically aware teachers.

The DWR model helps to counter the lack of tension and challenge identified in student teacher research between school teachers and university teacher educators who have been criticised for too readily accommodating different perspectives and therefore restricting discussions to practical rather than pedagogical issues: 'such a process is likely to feel comfortable for the participants but does not fully explore the opportunities offered by dissonant perspectives' (Hutchinson, 2011, p. 189). Also evident in research on partnerships in pedagogy is the 'maintenance of stable relationships through the recognition of the different roles and mutual appreciation' (Spendlove *et al.*, 2010, p. 74). Wanting to minimise possible threats to pedagogical understandings, these are rarely discussed, and instead the focus is on teaching performance. The ability to critically reflect on practice is less considered and impoverishes the learning experience:

> We now need to find ways to make these tensions the subject of discussion and debate within our partnerships, considering the wider context of cultural, institutional and historical situations within which these activities are mediated. (Spendlove *et al.*, 2010, p. 75)

Such research findings indicate the need to promote challenge and debate in student teacher education activity in order to benefit understanding of pedagogical issues for student teachers, teachers and mentors in schools. Adopting an interventionist research methodology is one possible way of doing this. The implications of this for policy and practice are considered in the final chapter.

# 12
# Conclusions, Implications and Recommendations

## Introduction

When I was a school teacher and senior manager, my work in schools was often frenetic, exciting and all consuming. Teaching in classrooms and leading and managing school activities can be exhausting. Undertaking the research reported in this book gave me an opportunity to take a step back and to observe, to listen to and to ask questions of those involved in school-based teacher education. I was already aware that working in different subject departments and with different teachers was likely to afford a variety of learning opportunities for student teachers when on their school teaching practice and I wanted to explore why this was so.

Sometimes as a practitioner in schools I felt as though the school setting was in a constant state of flux, responding to new initiatives, meeting new curricula demands and incorporating new teaching ideas. Yet as a researcher based in one school for one academic year it often seemed as though little had really changed from when I had been training as a student teacher myself, similar classrooms, similar school routines, similar subjects. Of course there were differences but the school structures were easily recognisable. However, as discussed in Chapter 1, currently there are significant changes occurring to the structure of the training process in student teacher education. In England and in other countries too, the onus and responsibility for student teacher learning is shifting from higher education into schools. This is why I believe that a focus on the school setting and how it can afford and constrain learning opportunities for student teachers and teachers is particularly timely.

The research reported in this book is designed to address those areas in the teacher education literature that I feel err on description rather than on an analysis of the reasons behind the actions of the participants described. This book considers the learning opportunities afforded student teachers when participating in school teaching practice and how these are constructed and reconstructed in the school setting. The review of the literature on school subject departments in Chapter 2 and the subsequent discussion on learning suggested that in order to maximise the potential of school practices to support student teacher learning, collaboration with experienced teachers is essential. In guiding student teachers' interpretations of the teaching and learning context and in critically examining teaching practices, experienced teachers can help develop understandings of why particular teaching strategies work in specific classroom situations. Chapter 3 elaborated on the idea of a sociocultural pedagogy and outlined the CHAT framework used to analyse student teacher learning opportunities in school practices. The use of CHAT concepts helps to analyse and reveal what the participants in student teacher education in the schools saw as the object of student teacher education activity, its 'real motive' (Leont'ev, 1981).

Before presenting the four department case studies in the central research study in Chapters 5, 6, 7 and 8, I discussed in Chapter 4 the benefits of working ethnographically and how this helps to contextualise the student teacher education work in the departments by generating rich qualitative data for understanding the social situations of development for the student teachers. The case studies were preparatory for showing how tools mediated the participants' work on the objects of the student teacher education activity system. The use of tools was explored in Chapter 9. Tools appeared to be most effective in engendering learning opportunities when they were used to open out the problems of teaching practice, thereby enabling insightful interpretations of the teaching and learning situation. This necessitated student teachers working alongside and being guided by experienced teachers (and teacher educators) who were also expert learners of teaching and learning and whose interpretations of teaching practices were open to the complexity inherent within the teaching context.

In questioning what the student teacher education activity systems' objects were and how and why they were being worked on by the activity systems' participants in Chapter 10, I analysed the underlying processes behind the student teacher education tools and identified what provided the true direction and motivating forces for the student teacher education work. The sometimes contradictory approaches to the work indicated that when there was regular negotiation of the objects between participants, new learning could occur. This was evidenced when participants worked collaboratively and when they jointly shared an understanding of the object as indicated by their similar use of tools. The clearer the understanding of the student teacher education activity system's object, the more likely other activity systems contributed to it when interacting with student teacher education activity.

In Chapter 11 I considered how other models of student teacher education partnership have developed student teacher learning opportunities. In forwarding my own research study in a London primary school I presented a model for researching and developing learning opportunities in school settings which encourages new and expansive learning (Engeström, 2007). In this, the final chapter, I consider the implications for policy and practice in adopting an interventionist research methodology in school-based student teacher education.

## Implications for practice

Schools and subject departments are key settings for the learning opportunities of student teachers (Childs and McNicholl, 2007; Cook *et al.*, 2002; De Lima, 2003; Ellis, 2008; Grossman, 1990; Grossman *et al.*, 2000; Smagorinsky *et al.*, 2003). My research emphasises that it is not only important that student teachers, school and university departments are aware of this, but teacher education also needs to give better account of school departments as key situations for student teacher learning opportunities, and pay particular attention to the differences in the social situations of development in order to afford the most effective learning opportunities for student teachers.

In England and the USA alternative routes for novice teachers to work in teaching are growing and many of these are school-based (Tang, 2011). The recent government initiatives in teacher education in England support this (DfE, 2010a and 2010b). Nevertheless, just providing student teacher education tools for working on student teacher education activity is not enough, as these are used differently depending upon cultural, historical and social factors. It is important to realise and understand the ways of working in school-based student teacher education activity systems in order to help the participants within them actively make sense of tools for student teacher learning in teacher education courses. Tools in themselves, if used instrumentally as tick boxes or as ways of administering audits for example, may not function in a mediating capacity at all. The research study at the core of this book identified implicit forms of mediation (how the course handbook in History mediated work on the object implicitly in the way that the dialogue and conversations around it were affected by it for example). This implicit form of mediation was less visible and would therefore be less easy to identify in short-term observation looking at and evaluating the work in student teacher education, as in external inspections. Therefore, the kind of learning opportunities that can help create responsive practitioners are often 'messy' and less obvious, because they may be mediating work of an implicit kind, which may only be seen when observing in schools for a lengthy period of time. It was also evident from the research on tool mediation that learning was not necessarily linear or evident as a direct consequence of actions, but it could be complex and 'subterranean' (Engeström, 2007) and could be different in different activity systems as illustrated in the different ways the course handbooks were used in the four subject departments.

How school departments in my ethnographic research saw their role when working with student teachers depended to a large extent on the reasons why they chose to be involved in student teacher education and how they perceived student teachers learn. Numerous motives could influence a department's orientation towards student teacher education: a desire to create better teachers, to enable student teachers to pass their student teacher education course, to recruit new staff, to benefit from closely working with higher education and to enhance current teachers' career development by providing mentoring opportunities in school. All these motives were identified. However, how the school departments viewed student teacher learning was particularly influential on the kinds of learning opportunities and the type of learning afforded. If like Bruner (1999) learning was seen as a 'participatory, proactive, collaborative process', then possibilities for new and expansive learning were forthcoming. Nevertheless, other data suggested that learning was often viewed in terms of imparting hard-gained experience and knowledge or by adopting established practices in an apprenticeship-style process. In such situations opportunities for developing pedagogical practices beyond those already existing in the departments were restricted, as student teacher agency was limited to recognising within-department interpretations of pedagogy. Consequently, new interpretations could not openly impact on department student teacher education practices and further shape them. It was therefore vital that department cultures (and not just department teachers as they may frequently change) were open to the potential to change.

In data from the research studies discussed in this book, there is evidence of the rich fullness of student teacher learning opportunities gained from the benefits of work-based learning, as seen when student teachers worked alongside experienced practitioners questioning and discussing the complexities of classroom practices (as noted in the discussion of the use of historical sources between the History department mentor and the student teacher, for example). However, there are also examples of the downsides evidenced in some conservative and reproductive practices (when student teachers imitating teaching practices in MFL classes found it difficult to reconcile different opinions on effective language teaching). When it was recognised that there was value in student teacher education activity for teaching and learning opportunities generally (by viewing engagement in student teacher education as important to teaching and learning in the classroom rather than just for the learning of student teachers), student teacher education activity contributed to department and school learning. Its benefits were recognised as being relevant to all teachers. Consequently, this further enhanced the learning opportunities for student teachers and encouraged genuine collaborative work and extended mentoring practices. This way of working could be seen as a long-term development opportunity for the whole department and school. Thus, changing the approach to student teacher education activity and viewing it as a long-term strategy may provide opportunities for departments and schools to develop. This may prevent student teachers from being viewed simply as useful for providing new resources, new ideas in information and communication technology and extra help in the classroom for example. This change of emphasis could shift a focus on immediate outcomes when working with student teachers to the development of processes suitable for creating conditions for expansive learning with new forms of collaboration and shared learning. This could therefore enable new forms of practice to emerge from engagement in student teacher education.

One such new form of practice arguably lies in the development of Professional Development Schools (PDS) in the USA. An aim for PDS has been to 'provide serious venues for developing the knowledge base for teaching by becoming places in which practice-based research can be carried out collaboratively by teachers, teacher-educators and researchers' (Darling-Hammond, 1994, p. 102). Criticisms of the model have highlighted the very small-scale alternative position it has within many universities and the lack of effective communication among stakeholders who often share a parochial view of the 'purpose, mission and vision' of PDS partnerships (Ikpeze *et al.*, 2012, p. 281). The success of PDS partnerships has often relied upon a few individual leaders, *ad hoc* financial investment and a lack of policy support (Ross, 1995). Conversely, the Schools Direct initiative (DfE, 2011) in England has the necessary policy support to transform school/university partnerships in student teacher education. Therefore, the relationships of schools working with universities in developing the knowledge base for teaching will change. Adopting a developmental work research (DWR) approach in school settings ideally opens out participants' thinking and develops a shared understanding. This could be further developed with cross-school DWR change laboratory workshops with university tutors taking a lead role in facilitating these. This fits closely with recommendations for preparing student teachers by moving 'toward a collaborative enquiry approach that values all participants' deepening understandings and reflects all parties' vested interest in improving practice' (Anderson and Stillman, 2012, p. 56). However, with less university input into student teacher work-based schemes in England, it is increasingly school teachers that are crucially placed to facilitate expansive learning opportunities in student teacher education.

## Contribution of cultural historical activity theory

Research that looked at teacher learning in school subject departments as reviewed in Chapter 2 tended to offer only partial understanding as to why departments afforded or constrained opportunities for learning. This was because of an emphasis given to the working practices that were currently taking place in the departments, with little exploration of how social practices had developed considering the cultural history of the departments in relation to these. The analysis in the research in this book considers tools as cultural and historical phenomena, and the analytic framework enables a specific drawing on the relevance of the cultural and historical perspectives on teachers' learning and on teacher education. The psychological aspect of analysis is important. Simply concentrating on how learners adapt to social situations tends to separate out the social situations from how the learner thinks. What the participants *did* in the activity systems was not enough to gain insight into the reasons for their actions. I believe that this is where much of the literature referred to in the literature review in Chapter 2 on student teacher education research falls short. The notion of expansive learning in the research is essential if teachers are expected to respond to new situations. Expansive learning recognises that the activity's object is always developing, in that contradictions in an activity system continuously emerge and are then resolved through negotiation. This enables new forms of practice. CHAT helps to value and recognise what the different elements are that go into establishing the conditions for expansive learning by identifying the kinds of mediation and tool use that is taking place in an activity. Where there are tensions or contradictions in the activity system, and these are not being addressed, CHAT analysis considers the cultural and historical reasons behind the tensions in order to help explain why such contradictions exist. Contradictions are necessary for the activity to evolve, but these must be openly acknowledged and welcomed as part of the negotiations.

There are growing numbers of student teachers in work-based learning that are not taking part in school/university partnership courses (Furlong, 2008). Ways of analysing alternative experiences recognising the influence of schools and school departments in affecting the kinds of learning available to these student teachers are needed. This will increase the understanding of the benefits and potential of new and different approaches to student teacher education. Grossman *et al.* (2009) point out that empirical evidence is needed to fully understand how access to various aspects and types of practices both afford and constrain the development of student teachers with regard to their teaching identities and skills. In addition, a critical perspective on practice is essential ensuring that student teachers are not passive receivers of pre-ordained meanings that are taken to be natural and self-evident (Britzman, 2003). Advocating the creation of core practices for structuring student teacher education curricula, Grossman *et al.* (2009) wish to highlight the complexity of teaching. This complexity needs to be acknowledged and worked on in schools too with student teachers working with teachers and mentors to develop their pedagogical understandings. This book increases understanding that student teacher learning is dependent upon a dynamic system that is capable of being worked on, as well as working on its participants, with teaching seen as a collective enterprise and a relational practice embedded in specific social, cultural and historical conditions.

# References

Alvesson, M. and Skoldberg, K. (2009) *Reflexive Methodology: New Vistas for Qualitative Research* (London: Sage).

Amos, S. and Boohan, R. (2013) *Aspects of Teaching Secondary Science* (Abingdon: Routledge).

Anderson, L. and Stillman, J. (2012) 'Student Teaching's Contribution to Preservice Teacher Development: A Review of Research Focused on the Preparation of Teachers for Urban and High-Needs Contexts', *Review of Educational Research*, DOI10.3102/0034654312468619.

Arthur, J., Waring, M., Coe, R. and Hedges, L. (2012) *Research Methods and Methodologies in Education* (London: Sage).

Ashby, P., Hobson, A., Tracey, L., Malderez, A., Tomlinson, P., Roper, T., Chambers, G. and Healy, J. (2008) *Beginner Teachers' Experiences of Initial Teacher Preparation, Induction and Early Professional Development: A Review of Literature* (University of Nottingham: Research Report DCSF-RW076).

Aubrey-Hopkins, J. and James, C. (2002) 'Improving Practice in Subject Departments: The Experience of Secondary School Subject Leaders in Wales', *School Leadership and Management*, 22 (3), 305–20.

Avis, J. (2009) 'Transformation or Transformism: Engeström's Version of Activity Theory?' *Educational Review*, 61 (2), 151–65.

Bakhurst, D. (2009) 'Reflections on Activity Theory', *Educational Review*, 61 (2), 197–210.

Ball, S. (1987) *The Micro-Politics of the School: Towards a Theory of School Organization* (London: Methuen).

Ball, S. (1990) *Education, Inequality and School Reform: Values in Crisis! An Inaugural Lecture in the Centre for Educational Studies* (London: King's College London, University of London).

Ball, S. (1991) 'Power, Conflict, Micropolitics and All That!' in G. Walford (ed.) *Doing Educational Research*, pp. 166–92 (London: Routledge).

Ball, S. (2003) 'The Teacher's Soul and the Terrors of Performativity', *Journal of Education Policy*, 18 (2), 215–28.

Barker, S. (1996) *Initial Teacher Education in Secondary Schools: A Study of the Tangible and Intangible Costs and Benefits of Initial Teacher Education in Secondary Schools*, University of Warwick Institute of Education, Teacher Development Research and Dissemination Unit (London: Association of Teachers and Lecturers).

Beach, D. (2005) 'From Fieldwork to Theory and Representation in Ethnography', in G. Troman, B. Jeffrey and G. Walford (eds) *Methodological Issues and Practices in Ethnography 11*, pp. 1–17 (Amsterdam, Oxford: Elsevier JAI Press).

Billett, S. (2002) 'Workplace Pedagogic Practices: Co-participation and Learning', *British Journal of Educational Studies*, 50 (4), 457–81.

Billett, S. (2003) 'Vocational Curriculum and Pedagogy: An Activity Theory Perspective', *European Educational Research Journal*, 2 (1), 6–21.

Black, J. and MacRaild, D. (2007) *Studying History* (London: Palgrave Macmillan).

Blake, D., Hanley, V., Jennings, M. and Lloyd, M. (1995) *Researching School-Based Teacher Education* (Aldershot: Avebury).

Boag-Munroe, G. (2006) *A Commerce of the Old and New: How Classroom Teacher Mentors Work in Multiple Activities* (unpublished Ph.D. thesis: School of Education, University of Birmingham).

Bonnett, A. (2008) *What Is Geography?* (London: Sage).

Bowen, G. (2009) 'Document Analysis as a Qualitative Research Method', *Qualitative Research Journal*, 9 (2), 27–40.

Breakwell, G., Smith, J. and Wright, D. (2012) *Research Methods in Psychology*, 4th edn (London: Sage).

British Educational Research Association (2011) Ethical Guidelines for Educational Research, http://www.bera.ac.uk/guidelines (home page), date accessed 12 January 2011.

Britzman, D.P. (2003) *Practice Makes Practice: A Critical Study of Learning to Teach* (Albany: State University of New York Press).

Bruner, J. (1999) 'Folk Pedagogies' in J. Leach and B. Moon (eds) *Learners and Pedagogy*, pp. 4–20 (London: P Chapman).

Busher, H. and Blease, D. (2000) 'Growing Collegial Cultures in Subject Departments in Secondary Schools: Working with Science Staff', *School Leadership and Management*, 20 (1), 99–112.

Butcher, J. (2000) 'Subject Culture, Pedagogy and Policy on an Open Learning PGCE: Can the Gap Be Bridged between What Students Need, and What Mentors Provide?' Paper presented at the European Conference on Educational Research, 20–23 September 2000, Edinburgh.

Byram, M. (2013) *Routledge Encyclopedia of Language Teaching and Learning* (Abingdon: Routledge).

Caires, S., Almeida, L. and Vieira, D. (2012) 'Becoming a Teacher: Student teachers' Experiences and Perceptions about Teaching Practice', *European Journal of Teacher Education*, 35 (2), 163–178.

Childs, A. and McNicholl, J. (2007) 'Science Teachers Teaching Outside of Subject Specialism: Challenges, Strategies Adopted and Implications for Initial Teacher Education', *Teacher Development*, 11 (1), 1–20.

Childs, A., Burn, K. and McNicholl, J. (2013) 'What Influences the Learning Cultures of Subject Departments in Secondary Schools? A Study of Four Subject Departments in England', *Teacher Development*, 17 (1), 35–54.

Cochran-Smith, M. (2006) *Policy, Practice and Politics in Teacher Education* (Thousand Oaks, CA: Corwin Press).

Cochran-Smith, M. (2009) 'The New Teacher Education in the United States: Directions Forward' in J. Furlong, M. Cochran-Smith and M. Brennan (eds) *Policy and Politics in Teacher Education, International Perspectives*, pp. 9–20 (London: Routledge).

Cochran Smith, M., Piazza, P. and Power, C. (2013) 'The Politics of Accountability: Assessing Teacher Education in the United States', *The Educational Forum*, 77 (1), 6–27.

Cochran-Smith, M., McQuillan, P., Mitchell, K., Gahlsdorf Terrell, D., Barnatt, J., D'Souza, L., Jong, C., Shakman, K., Lam, K. and Gleeson, A.M. (2012) 'A Longitudinal Study of Teaching Practice and Early Career Decisions: A Cautionary Tale', *American Educational Research Journal*, 49 (5), 844–80.

Cohen, L., Manion, L. and Morris, K. (2011) *Research Methods in Education*, 7th edn (Abingdon: Routledge).

Cole, M. (1996) *Cultural Psychology: The Once and Future Discipline* (Cambridge, MA: The Belknap Press of Harvard University).

Convery, A. (1999) 'Listening to Teachers' Stories: Are We Sitting Too Comfortably?' *Qualitative Studies in Education*, 12 (2), 131–46.

Cook, L., Smagorinsky, P., Konopak, B. and Moore, C. (2002) 'Problems in Developing a Constructivist Approach to Teaching: One Teacher's Transition from Teacher Preparation to Teaching', *The Elementary School Journal*, 102 (5), 389–413.

Cresswell, J. (2012) *Educational Research: Planning, Conducting, and Evaluating Quantitative and Qualitative Research*, 4th edn (Boston: Pearson).

Crossouard, B. (2009) 'A Sociocultural Reflection on Formative Assessment and Collaborative Challenges in the States of Jersey', *Research Papers in Education*, 24 (1), 77–93.

Daniels, H. (2001) *Vygotsky and Pedagogy* (London: Routledge).

Daniels, H. (2010) 'Implicit or Invisible Mediation in the Development of Interagency Work' in H. Daniels, A. Edwards, Y. Engeström, T. Gallagher and S.R. Ludvigsen (eds) *Activity Theory in Practice: Promoting Learning Across Boundaries and Agencies*, pp. 105–25 (Abingdon: Routledge).

Darling-Hammond, L. (1994) *Professional Development Schools: Schools for Developing a Profession* (New York: Teachers College Press).

Darling-Hammond, L. (2006) 'Constructing 21st Century Teacher Education', *Journal of Teacher Education*, 57 (3), 300–14.

Davies, P., Telhaj, S., Hutton, D., Adnett, N. and Coe, R. (2009) 'Competition, Cream Skimming and Department Performance within Secondary Schools', *British Educational Research Journal*, 35 (1), 65–81.

De Lima, J.A. (2003) 'Trained for Isolation: The Impact of Department Cultures on Student Teachers' Views and Practices of Collaboration', *Journal of Education for Teaching*, 29 (3), 197–217.

Department for Education (DfE) (1992) *Initial Teacher Training (Secondary Phase) Circular No. 9/92* (London: HMSO).

Department for Education (DfE) (2010a) *The Importance of Teaching: The Schools White Paper*, Reference: CM 7980 (London: The Stationery Office).

Department for Education (DfE) (2010b) *The Case for Change*, Reference: DFE-00564-2010 (London: The Stationery Office).

Department for Education (DfE) (2011) *Training Our Next Generation of Outstanding Teachers: Implementation Plan*, Reference: DfE-00038-2011 (London: The Stationery Office).

Department of Education and Science (DES) (1989) *The National Curriculum* (London: HMSO).

Donnelly, J. (2000) 'Departmental Characteristics and the Experience of Secondary Science Teaching', *Educational Research*, 42 (3), 261–73.

Douglas, A.S. (2005) *An Exploratory Study of How Oxford University PGCE Curriculum Tutors Articulated Their Understandings of 'Internship' in a Research Interview Situation* (MSc dissertation: University of Oxford).

Douglas, A.S. (2012) 'Creating Expansive Learning Opportunities in Schools: The Role of School Leaders in Initial Teacher Education Partnerships', *European Journal of Teacher Education*, 35 (1), 3–15.

Edwards, A. (2001) 'Researching Pedagogy: A Sociocultural Agenda', *Pedagogy, Culture & Society*, 9 (2), 161–86.

Edwards, A. (2005a) 'Relational Agency: Learning to Be a Resourceful Practitioner', *International Journal of Educational Research*, 43 (3), 168–82.

Edwards, A. (2005b) 'Let's Get Beyond Community and Practice: The Many Meanings of Learning by Participating', *The Curriculum Journal*, 16 (1), 49–65.

Edwards, A. (2009) 'Becoming a Teacher: A Sociocultural Analysis of Initial Teacher Education' in H. Daniels, H. Lauder and J. Porter (eds) *Educational Theories, Cultures and Learning: A Critical Perspective*, pp. 153–64 (London: Routledge).

Edwards, A. (2010a) *Being an Expert Professional Practitioner: The Relational Turn in Expertise* (London: Springer).

Edwards, A. (2010b) 'How Can Vygotsky and His Legacy Help Us to Understand and Develop Teacher Education?' in V. Ellis, A. Edwards and P. Smagorinsky (eds) *Cultural-Historical Perspectives on Teacher Education and Development: Learning Teaching*, pp. 63–77 (Abingdon: Routledge).

Edwards, A. (2011) *Cultural Historical Activity Theory: Educational Research Association online resource*, http://www.bera.ac.uk/files/2011/06/cultural_historical_activity_theory.pdf, date accessed 10 November 2012.

Edwards, A. and Collison, J. (1996) 'Mentoring and School Development' in A. Edwards and J. Collison (eds) *Mentoring and Developing Practice in Primary Schools: Supporting Student Teacher Learning in Schools*, pp. 133–65 (Buckingham: Open University Press).

Edwards, A. and D'Arcy, C. (2004) 'Relational Agency and Disposition in Sociocultural Accounts of Learning to Teach', *Educational Review*, 56 (2), 147–55.

Edwards, A. and Protheroe, L. (2003) 'Learning to See in Classrooms: What Are Student Teachers Learning About Teaching and Learning While Learning to Teach in Schools?' *British Educational Research Journal*, 29 (2), 227–42.

Edwards, A., Gilroy, P. and Hartley, D. (2002) *Rethinking Teacher Education: Collaborative Responses to Uncertainty* (London: Routledge).

Ellis, V. (2007) *Subject Knowledge and Teacher Education: The Development of Beginning Teachers' Thinking* (New York: Continuum).

Ellis, V. (2008) 'Boundary Transformation in a School-University Teacher Education Partnership: The Potential of Developmental Work Research in DETAIL', Paper presented at the Sociocultural Perspectives on Teacher Education and Development: New Directions for Research Conference, April 2008, University of Oxford.

Ellis, V. (2010) 'Impoverishing Experience: The Problem of Teacher Education in England', *Journal of Education for Teaching*, 36 (1), 105–20.

Ellis, V., Edwards, A. and Smagorinsky P. (eds) (2010) *Cultural-Historical Perspectives on Teacher Education and Development: Learning Teaching* (Abingdon: Routledge).

Engeström, Y. (1987) *Learning by Expanding: An Activity-Theoretical Approach to Developmental Research* (Helsinki: Orienta-Konsultit).

Engeström, Y. (1993) 'Developmental Studies of Work as a Test Bench of Activity Theory: The Case of Primary Care Medical Practice' in S. Chaiklin and J. Lave (eds) *Understanding Practice, Perspectives on Activity and Context*, pp. 64–103 (Cambridge: Cambridge University Press).

Engeström, Y. (1995) 'Polycontextuality and Boundary Crossing in Expert Cognition: Learning and Problem Solving in Complex Work Activities', *Learning and Instruction*, 5 (4), 319–36.

Engeström, Y. (1999a) 'Activity Theory and Individual and Social Transformation', in Y. Engeström, R. Miettinen and R.L. Punamaki (eds) *Perspectives on Activity Theory*, pp. 19–38 (Cambridge: Cambridge University Press).

Engeström, Y. (1999b) 'Innovative Learning in Work Teams: Analyzing Cycles of Knowledge Creation in Practice' in Y. Engestrom, R. Miettinen and R.L. Punamaki (eds) *Perspectives on Activity Theory*, pp. 377–406 (Cambridge, Cambridge University Press).

Engeström, Y. (2000) 'Activity Theory as a Framework for Analysing and Redesigning Work', *Ergonomics*, 43 (7), 960–74.

Engeström, Y. (2001) 'Expansive Learning at Work: Toward an Activity Theoretical Reconceptualization', *Journal of Education and Work*, 14 (1), 133–56.

Engeström, Y. (2006) Center for Activity Theory and Developmental Work Research, http://www.edu.helsinki.fi/activity/people/engestro/ (home page), date accessed 26 June 2006.

Engeström, Y. (2007) 'Enriching the Theory of Expansive Learning: Lessons from Journeys towards Coconfiguration', *Mind, Culture, and Activity*, 41 (1), 23–39.

Engeström, Y. (2008) *From Teams to Knots: Activity-Theoretical Studies of Collaboration and Learning at Work* (Cambridge: Cambridge University Press).

Engeström, Y. and Blackler, F. (2005) 'On the Life of the Object', *Organization*, 12 (3), 307–30.

Engeström, Y. and Cole, M. (1997) *Situated Cognition in Search of an Agenda* (Hillsdale, NJ: Lawrence Erlbaum).

Engeström, Y., Miettinen, R. and Punamaki, R. (1999) 'Introduction' in *Perspectives on Activity Theory*, pp. 1–18 (Cambridge: Cambridge University Press).

Eraut, M. (2000) 'Non Formal Learning and Tacit Knowledge in Professional Work', *British Journal of Educational Psychology*, 70 (1), 113–36.

Eraut, M. (2005) 'Early Career Learning at Work (LiNEA) Project', Paper presented at the Early Career Professional Learning Conference, May 2005, University of Oxford.

Eraut, M., Steadman, S. and Furner, J. (2004) 'Learning in the Professional Workplace: Relationships between Learning Factors and Contextual Factors', Paper presented at the American Education Research Association, 12–16 April 2004, San Diego.

Eraut, M., Alderton, J., Cole, G. and Senker, P. (2000) 'The Development of Knowledge and Skills at Work' in F. Coffield (ed.) *Differing Visions of a Learning Society Volume 1*, pp. 231–62 (Bristol: Policy Press).

Eraut, M., Alderton, J., Cole, G. and Senker, P. (2002) 'Learning from Other People at Work' in R. Harrison, F. Reeve, F. Hanson and J. Clarke (eds) *Supporting Lifelong Learning Volume 1, Perspectives on Learning*, pp. 127–45 (London: Routledge).

Esland, G.M. (1971) 'Teaching and Learning As the Organisation of Knowledge' in M.F.D. Young (ed.) *Knowledge and Control: New Directions for the Sociology of Education*, pp. 70–86 (London: Collier and Macmillan).

Evelein, F., Korthagen, F. and Brekelmans, M. (2008) 'Fulfilment of the Basic Psychological Needs of Student Teachers during Their First Teaching Experiences', *Teaching and Teacher Education*, 24 (5), 1137–48.

Fetterman, D. (1998) *Ethnography. Step by Step*, 2nd edn (London: Sage).

Field, K. (2013) *Issues in Modern Foreign Languages Teaching* (Abingdon: Routledge).

Friedman, H. (2011) 'The Myth behind the Subject Leader as a School Key Player', *Teachers and Teaching: Theory and Practice*, 17 (3), 289–302.

Furlong, J. (2000) 'Higher Education and the New Professionalism for Teachers, A Discussion Paper' (London: CVCP/SCOP).

Furlong, J. (2005) 'New Labour and Teacher Education: The End of an Era', *Oxford Review of Education*, 31 (1), 119–34.

Furlong, J. (2008) 'Making Teaching a 21st Century Profession – Tony Blair's Big Prize', *Oxford Review of Education*, 34 (6), 727–39.

Furlong, J. (2013) 'Globalization, Neoliberalism, and the Reform of Teacher Education in England', *The Educational Forum*, 77 (1), 28–50.

Furlong, J. and Smith, R. (1996) *The Role of Higher Education in Initial Teacher Training* (London: Kogan Page).

Geertz, C. (1973) *The Interpretation of Cultures: Selected Essays* (London: Fontana Press).

Gersmehl, P. (2008) *Teaching Geography*, 2nd edn (Guildford: Guildford Press).

Ghamrawi, N. (2010) 'No Teacher Left Behind: Subject Leadership that Promotes Teacher Leadership', *Educational Management Administration & Leadership*, 38 (3), 304–20.

Glaser, B. and Strauss, A. (1967) *The Discovery of Grounded Theory* (Chicago: Aldine).

Goldbart, J. and Hustler, D. (2000) 'Ethnography' in B. Somekh and C. Lewin (eds) *Research Methods in the Social Sciences*, pp. 16–23 (London: Sage).

Goodson, I. and Ball, S.J. (1984) *Defining the Curriculum: Histories and Ethnographies* (London: Falmer Press).

Goodson, I. and Mangan, M. (1995) 'Subject Cultures and the Introduction of Classroom Computers', *British Educational Research Journal*, 21 (5), 613–28.

Griffiths, T. and Guile, D. (2003) 'A Connective Model of Learning: The Implications for Work Process Knowledge', *European Educational Research Journal*, 2 (1), 56–73.

Grossman, P. (1990) *The Making of a Teacher* (New York: Teachers College Press).

Grossman, P. (2008) 'Responding to Our Critics: From Crisis to Opportunity in Research on Teacher Education', *Journal of Teacher Education*, 59 (1), 10–23.

Grossman, P., Hammerness, K. and McDonald, M. (2009) 'Redefining Teaching, Re-Imagining Teacher Education', *Teachers and Teaching: Theory and Practice*, 15 (2), 273–89.

Grossman, P., Smagorinsky, P. and Valencia, S. (1999) 'Appropriating Tools for Teaching English: A Theoretical Framework for Research on Learning to Teach', *American Journal of Education*, 108 (1), 1–29.

Grossman, P., Wineburg, S. and Woolworth, S. (2000) 'What Makes Teacher Community Different from a Gathering of Teachers?' (Washington: Center for the Study of Teaching and Policy).

Hagger, H. and McIntyre, D. (2006) *Learning Teaching from Teachers: Realizing the Potential of School-Based Teacher Education* (Maidenhead: Open University Press).

Hamilton, L. and Corbett-Whittier, C. (2013) *Using Case Study in Education Research* (London: Sage).

Hammersley, M. (1990) *Reading Ethnographic Research: A Critical Guide* (London: Longman).

Hammersley, M. (2003) 'Recent Radical Criticism of Interview Studies: Any Implications for the Sociology of Education?' *British Journal of the Sociology of Education*, 24 (1), 119–26.

Handelsman, J., Miller, S. and Pfund, C. (2011) *Scientific Teaching* (London: W.H. Freeman).

Hargreaves, A. (1987) 'Past, Imperfect, Tense: Reflections on an Ethnographic and Historical Study of Middle Schools' in G. Walford (ed.) *Doing Sociology of Education*, pp. 17–44 (London: Falmer Press).

Hargreaves, A. (1994) *Changing Teachers, Changing Times* (London: Cassell).

Hargreaves, A. and Dawe, R. (1990) 'Paths of Professional Development: Contrived Collegiality, Collaborative Culture, and the Case of Peer Coaching', *Teaching and Teacher Education*, 6 (3), 227–41.

Harris, A. (2001) 'Department Improvement and School Improvement: A Missing Link?' *British Educational Research Journal*, 27 (4), 477–86.

Harris, R. and Haydn, T. (2012) 'What Happens to a Subject in a "Free Market" Curriculum? A Study of Secondary School History in the UK', *Research Papers in Education*, 27 (1), 81–101.

Havnes, A. (2009) 'Talk, Planning and Decision-Making in Interdisciplinary Teacher Teams: A Case Study', *Teachers and Teaching: Theory and Practice*, 15 (1), 155–76.

Hedegaard, M. (1999) 'Activity Theory and History Teaching' in Y. Engeström, K. Miettinen and R. Punamaki (eds) *Perspectives on Activity Theory*, pp. 126–45 (Cambridge: Cambridge University Press).

Helsby, G. (1996) 'Defining and Developing Professionalism in English Secondary Schools', *Journal of Education for Teaching*, 22 (2), 135–48.

Hennessy, S., Ruthven, K. and Brindley, S. (2005) 'Teacher Perspectives on Integrating ICT into Subject Teaching: Commitment, Constraints, Caution, and Change', *Journal of Curriculum Studies*, 37 (2), 155–92.

Hinkel, E. (2013) *Handbook of Research in Second Language Teaching and Learning* (Abingdon: Routledge).

Hodkinson, H. (2009) 'Improving Schoolteachers' Workplace Learning' in S. Gewirtz, P. Mahony, I. Hextall and A. Cribb (eds) *Changing Teacher Professionalism, International Trends, Challenges and Ways Forward*, pp. 157–69 (London: Routledge).

Hodkinson, H. and Hodkinson, P. (1997) 'Micro-Politics in Initial Teacher Education: Luke's Story', *Journal of Education for Teaching*, 23 (2), 119–29.

Hodkinson, H. and Hodkinson, P. (2002) 'Learning in a Workplace Community: Secondary School Teachers in their Subject Departments', Paper presented at the British Educational Research Association Annual Conference, 12–14 September, University of Exeter, UK.

Hodkinson, H. and Hodkinson, P. (2005) 'Improving Schoolteachers' Workplace Learning', *Research Papers in Education*, 20 (2), 109–31.

Hogan, D. and Gopinathan, S. (2009) 'Knowledge Management, Sustainable Innovation and Pre-Service Teacher Education in Singapore' in J. Furlong, M. Cochran-Smith and M. Brennan (eds) *Policy and Politics in Teacher Education, International Perspectives*, pp. 107–22 (London: Routledge).

House of Commons, (2010) 'Training of Teachers', Fourth Report of Session 2009–10, Children, Schools and Families Committee (London: The Stationery Office), http://www.publications.parliament.uk/pa/cm200910/cmselect/cmchilsch/275/275i.pdf, date accessed 12 December 2012.

Hoyle, E. (1982) 'Micropolitics of Educational Organizations', *Educational Management and Administration*, 10 (2), 87–98.

Hunt, M. (2012) *A Practical Guide to Teaching History in the Secondary School* (Abingdon: Routledge).

Husbands, C. (1995) 'Learning Teaching in Schools: Students, Teachers and Higher Education in a School-Based Teacher Education Programme' in V. Griffiths and P. Owen (eds) *Schools in Partnership* (London: Paul Chapman).

Hutchinson, S. (2011) 'Boundaries and Bricolage: Examining the Roles of Universities and Schools in Student Teacher Learning', *European Journal of Teacher Education*, 34 (2), 177–91.

Ikpeze, C.H., Broikou, K.A., Hildenbrand, S. and Gladstone-Brown, W. (2012) 'PDS Collaboration as Third Space: An Analysis of the Quality of Learning Experiences in a PDS Partnership', *Studying Teacher Education*, 8 (3), 275–88.

Jahreie, C.F. and Ottesen, E. (2010) 'Construction of Boundaries in Teacher Education: Analyzing Student Teachers' Accounts', *Mind, Culture, and Activity*, 17 (3), 212–34.

James, C. and Goodhew, C. (2011) 'An Analysis of a Subject Department in an English Secondary School Using the Collaborative Practice Analytical Framework', *Educational Management Administration & Leadership*, 39 (3), 317–32.

Jarvis, A. (2008) 'Leadership Lost: A Case Study of Three Selective Secondary Schools', *Management in Education*, 22 (1), 24–30.

Jarvis, A. (2012) 'The Necessity for Collegiality: Power, Authority and Influence in the Middle', *Educational Management Administration & Leadership*, 40 (4), 480–93.

Jephcote, M. and Davies, B. (2007) 'School Subjects, Subject Communities and Curriculum Change: The Social Construction of Economics in the School Curriculum', *Cambridge Journal of Education*, 37 (2), 207–27.

John, P. (2005) 'The Sacred and the Profane: Subject Sub-Culture, Pedagogical Practice and Teachers' Perceptions of the Classroom Uses of ICT', *Educational Review*, 57 (4), 471–90.

Johnson, K. (2008) *Expertise in Second Language Learning and Teaching* (London: Palgrave Macmillan).

Joke, V. (2004) 'CHAT Is a Tool to Address the Problem of Chemistry's Lack of Relevance in Secondary School Chemical Education', *International Journal of Education*, 26 (13), 1635–51.

Kaptelinin, V. (2005) 'The Object of Activity: Making Sense of the Sense-Maker', *Mind, Culture and Activity*, 12 (1), 4–18.

Kaptelinin, V. and Miettinen, R. (2005) 'Introduction, Perspectives on the Object of Activity', *Mind, Culture and Activity*, 12 (1), 1–3.

Kerry, T. (2005) 'The Evolving Role of the Head of Department', *London Review of Education*, 3 (1), 65–80.

Kozleski, E. (2011) 'Dialectical Practices in Education: Creating Third Spaces in the Education of Teachers', *Teacher Education and Special Education*, 34 (3), 250–59.

Kozulin, A. (1998) *Psychological Tools: A Sociocultural Approach to Education* (Cambridge, MA: Harvard University Press).

Lacey, C. (1977) *The Socialization of Teachers* (London: Methuen).

Lacey, C. and Ball, S.J. (1984) 'Subject Disciplines As the Opportunity for Group Action: A Measured Critique of Subject Sub-Cultures' in A. Hargreaves and P. Woods (eds) *Classrooms and Staffrooms: The Sociology of Teachers and Teaching*, pp. 149–77 (Oxford: Oxford University Press).

Lambert, D. and Balderstone, D. (2012) *Learning to Teach Geography in the Secondary School* (Abingdon: Routledge).

Langemayer, I. (2006) 'Contradictions in Expansive Learning: Towards a Critical Analysis of Self-Dependent Forms of Learning in Relation to Contemporary Socio-Technical Change', *Forum: Qualitative Social Research*, 7 (1), Article 12.

Langemayer, I. and Nissen, M. (2005) 'Activity Theory' in B. Somekh and C. Lewin (eds) *Research Methods in the Social Sciences*, pp. 188–95 (London: Sage).

Lave, J. and Wenger, E. (1991) *Situated Learning: Legitimate Peripheral Participation* (Cambridge: Cambridge University Press).

Leach, J. and Moon, B. (1999) *Learners and Pedagogy* (London: Paul Chapman).

Leont'ev, A.N. (1978) *Activity, Consciousness, and Personality* (Englewood Cliffs, NJ: Prentice-Hall).

Leont'ev, A.N. (1981) 'The Problem of Activity in Psychology' in J. V. Wertsch (ed.) *The Concept of Activity in Soviet Psychology*, pp. 37–71 (New York: Armonk).

Lim, C. and Barnes, S. (2005) 'A Collective Case Study of the Use of ICT in Economics Courses: A Sociocultural Approach', *Journal of the Learning Sciences*, 14 (4), 489–526.

Little, J.W. (2002) 'Professional Community and the Problem of High School Reform', *International Journal of Educational Research*, 37 (8), 693–714.

Liversidge, T., Cochrane, M., Kerfoot, B. and Thomas, J. (2009) *Teaching Science: Developing As a Reflective Secondary Teacher* (London: Sage).

Lunenberg, M. and Korthagen, F (2009) 'Experience, Theory, and Practical Wisdom in Teaching and Teacher Education', *Teachers and Teaching: Theory and Practice*, 15 (2), 225–40.

Macrory, G. and McLachlan, A. (2009) 'Bringing Modern Languages into the Primary Curriculum in England: Investigating Effective Practice in Teacher Education', *European Journal of Teacher Education*, 32 (3), 259–70.

Madden, R. (2010) *Being Ethnographic: A Guide to the Theory and Practice of Ethnography* (London: Sage).

Mauthner, N. and Doucet, A. (2003) 'Reflexive Accounts and Accounts of Reflexivity in Qualitative Data Analysis', *Sociology*, 37 (3), 413–31.

Mawhinney, L. (2010) 'Let's Lunch and Learn Together: Professional Knowledge-Sharing in Teachers' Lounges and Other Congregational Spaces', *Teaching and Teacher Education*, 26 (4), 972–78.

Maynard, T. (2001) 'The Student Teacher and the School Community of Practice: A Consideration of "Learning as Participation"', *Cambridge Journal of Education*, 31 (1), 39–52.

McIntyre, D., Hagger, H. and Burn, K. (1994) *The Management of Student Teachers' Learning: A Guide for Professional Tutors in Secondary Schools* (London: Kogan Page).

McLaughlin, M.W. and Talbert, J.E. (2001) *Professional Communities and the Work of High School Teaching* (Chicago and London: University of Chicago Press).

McNally, J., Cope, P., Inglis, B. and Stronach, I. (1997) 'The Student Teacher in School: Conditions for Development', *Teaching and Teacher Education*, 13 (5), 485–98.

Menter, I. (2009) 'Teachers for the Future, What Have We Got and What Do We Need?' in S. Gewirtz, P. Mahony, I. Hextall and A. Cribb (eds) *Changing Teacher Professionalism, International Trends, Challenges and Ways Forward*, pp. 217–28 (London: Routledge).

Menter, I., Brisard, E. and Smith, I. (2006) *Convergence or Divergence? Initial Teacher Education in Scotland and England* (Edinburgh: Dunedin Academic Press).

Miettinen, R. (2005) 'Object of Activity and Individual Motivation', *Mind, Culture, and Activity*, 12 (1), 52–69.

Miles, M.B. and Huberman, A.M. (1994) *Qualitative Data Analysis: An Expanded Sourcebook* (London: Sage).

Mills, D. and Morton, M. (2013) *Ethnography in Education* (London: Sage).

Mishler, E. (1991) *Research Interviewing, Context and Narrative* (Cambridge, MA: Harvard University Press).

Mutton, T. and Butcher, J. (2008) '"We Will Take Them from Anywhere": Schools Working within Multiple Initial Teacher Training Partnerships', *Journal of Education for Teaching*, 34 (1), 45–62.

Mutton, T., Burn, K. and Hagger, H. (2010) 'Making Sense of Learning to Teach: Learners in Context', *Research Papers in Education*, 25 (1), 73–91.

Nardi, B.A. (2005) 'Objects of Desire: Power and Passion in Collaborative Activity', *Mind, Culture, and Activity*, 12 (1), 37–51.

Newby, P. (2010) *Research Methods for Education* (Harlow, Essex: Pearson).

Nussbaumer, D. (2012) 'An Overview of Cultural Historical Activity Theory (CHAT) Use in Classroom Research 2000 to 2009', *Educational Review*, 64 (1), 37–55.

O'Brien, M., Varga-Atkins, T., Umoquit, M. and Tso, P. (2012) 'Cultural Historical Activity Theory and "The Visual" in Research: Exploring the Ontological Consequences of the Use of Visual Methods', *International Journal of Research and Method in Education*, 35 (3), 251–68.

O'Reilly, K. (2012) *Ethnographic Methods* (Abingdon: Routledge).

Paavola, S., Lipponen, L. and Hakkarainen, K. (2004) 'Models of Innovative Knowledge Communities and Three Metaphors of Learning', *Review of Educational Research*, 74 (4), 557–76.

Paechter, C. (1995) 'Subcultural Retreat: Negotiating the Design and Technology Curriculum', *British Educational Research Journal*, 21 (1), 75–87.

Phillips, I. (2008) *Teaching History: Developing As a Reflective Secondary Teacher* (London: Sage).

Piem, N. (2009) 'Activity Theory and Ontology', *Educational Review*, 61 (2), 167–80.

Pring, R. (1996) 'Just Desert' in J. Furlong and R. Smith (eds) *The Role of Higher Education in Initial Teacher Training*, pp. 8–22 (London: Kogan Page).

Punch, K. (2009) *Introduction to Research Methods in Education* (London: Sage).

Rogoff, B. (1994) 'Developing Understanding of the Idea of Communities of Learners', *Mind, Culture, and Activity*, 1 (4), 209–29.

Ross, J.A. (1995) 'Professional Development Schools: Prospects for Institutionalisation', *Teaching and Teacher Education*, 11 (2), 195–201.

Roth, W.M. (2013) 'Reading Activity, Consciousness, Personality Dialectically: Cultural Historical Activity Theory and the Centrality of Society', *Mind, Culture, and Activity*, DOI:10.1080/10749039.2013.771368.

Roth, W.M. and Lee, Y.J. (2007) 'Vygotsky's Neglected Legacy: Cultural Historical Activity Theory', *Review of Educational Research*, 77 (2), 186–232.

Russell, D.R. (2004) 'Looking Beyond the Interface, Activity Theory and Distributed Learning' in H. Daniels and A. Edwards (eds) *The Routledge Falmer Reader in Psychology of Education*, pp. 307–26 (London: Routledge).

Sayer, J. (2009) 'European Perspectives of Teacher Education and Training' in J. Furlong, M. Cochran-Smith and M. Brennan (eds) *Policy and Politics in Teacher Education: International Perspectives*, pp. 155–68 (Abingdon: Routledge).

Schulz, R. and Hall, C. (2004) 'Difficulties in Promoting Inquiry in Teacher Education Partnerships: English and Canadian Perspectives', *Journal of Education for Teaching*, 30 (3), 255–69.

Sfard, A. (1998) 'On Two Metaphors for Learning and the Dangers of Choosing Just One', *Educational Researcher*, 27 (2), 4–13.

Shaw, R. (1992) *Teacher Training in Secondary Schools* (London: Kogan Page).

Shroyer, G., Yahnke, S., Bennett, A. and Dunn, D. (2007) 'Simultaneous Renewal through Professional Development School Partnerships', *The Journal of Educational Research*, 100 (4), 211–23.

Silverman, D. (2011) *Qualitative Research*, 3rd edn (London: Sage).

Simons, H. (2009) *Case Study Research in Practice* (London: Sage).

Siskin, L. (1991) 'Departments as Different Worlds: Subject Subcultures in Secondary Schools', *Educational Administration Quarterly*, 27 (2), 134–60.

Siskin, L. (1994) *Realms of Knowledge: Academic Departments in Secondary Schools* (London: Falmer).

Siskin, L. (1997) 'The Challenge of Leadership in Comprehensive High Schools: Schools Vision and Departmental Divisions', *Educational Administration Quarterly*, 33 (1 Suppl.), 604–23.

Skinner, N. (2010) 'Developing a Curriculum for Initial Teacher Education Using a Situated Learning Perspective', *Teacher Development*, 14 (3), 279–93.

Smagorinsky, P., Cook, L.S. and Johnson, T. (2003) 'The Twisting Path of Concept Development in Learning to Teach', *Teachers College Record*, 105 (8), 1399–436.

Smagorinsky, P., Cook, L.S., Moore, C., Jackson, A. and Fry, P. (2004) 'Tensions in Learning to Teach: Accommodation and the Development of a Teaching Identity', *Journal of Teacher Education*, 55 (1), 8–24.

Spendlove, D., Howes, A. and Wake, G. (2010) 'Partnerships in Pedagogy: Refocusing of Classroom Lenses', *European Journal of Teacher Education*, 33 (1), 65–77.

Stake, R. (1995) *The Art of Case Study Research* (Thousand Oaks: Sage).

Stake, R. (2000) 'Case Studies' in N. Denzin and Y. Lincoln (eds) *Handbook of Qualitative Research*, pp. 435–54 (London: Sage).

Stanulis, R. (1995) 'Classroom Teachers as Mentors: Possibilities for Participation in a Professional Development School Context', *Teaching and Teacher Education*, 11 (4), 331–44.

Stark, S. and Torrance, H. (2005) 'Case Study' in B. Somekh and C. Lewin (eds) *Research Methods for the Social Sciences*, pp. 33–40 (London and Thousand Oaks, CA: Sage).

Stetsenko, A. (2005) 'Activity as Object-Related: Resolving the Dichotomy of Individual and Collective Planes of Activity', *Mind, Culture, and Activity*, 12 (1), 70–88.

Stodolsky, S. and Grossman, P. (1995) 'The Impact of Subject Matter on Curricular Activity: An Analysis of Five Academic Subjects', *American Education Research Journal*, 32 (1), 227–49.

Strauss, A. (1987) *Qualitative Analysis for Social Scientists* (New York: Cambridge University Press).

Talbert, J.E. and McLaughlin, M.W. (1994) 'Teacher Professionalism in Local School Contexts', *American Journal of Education*, 102 (2), 123–53.

Tang, S.Y.F. (2011) 'Asian Perspectives on Teacher Education', *Asia Pacific Journal of Education*, 31 (1), 110–14.

Taylor, C. (1985) *'Human Agency and Language Philosophical Papers 1* (Cambridge: Cambridge University Press).

Taylor, A. (2008) 'Developing Understanding About Learning to Teach in a University-Schools Partnership in England', *British Educational Research Journal*, 34 (1), 63–90.

Teaching Agency (2012) 'Initial Teacher Training (ITT) Criteria', http://media. education.gov.uk (home page), date accessed 5 April 2012.

Teitel, L. (2008) 'School/University Collaboration: The Power of Transformative Partnerships', *Childhood Education*, 85 (2), 75–80.

Thomas, G. (2011) *How to Do Your Case Study: A Guide for Students and Researchers* (London: Sage).

Troman, G. (2002) 'Method in the Messiness: Experiencing the Ethnographic PhD Process' in G. Walford (ed.) *Doing a Doctorate in Educational Ethnography*, pp. 99–118 (Oxford: JAI Press).

Ure, C. (2010) 'Reforming Teacher Education through a Professionally Applied Study of Teaching', *Journal of Education for Teaching*, 36 (4), 461–75.

Van Huizen, P., Van Oers, B. and Wubbels T. (2005) 'A Vygotskian Perspective on Teacher Education', *Journal of Curriculum Studies*, 37 (3), 267–90.

Vescio, V., Ross, D. and Adams, A. (2008) 'A Review of Research on the Impact of Professional Learning Communities on Teaching Practice and Student Learning', *Teaching and Teacher Education*, 24 (1), 80–91.

Visscher, A. and Witziers, B. (2004) 'Subject Departments as Professional Communities?' *British Educational Research Journal*, 30 (6), 785–99.

Vygotsky, L.S. (1960) 'The History of the Development of the Higher Mental Functions' (pp. 197–8) in A.N. Leont'ev 'On Vygotsky's Creative Development [1]' in R. Rieber and J. Wollock (eds) 1987 *The Collected Works of L. S. Vygotsky Volume 3: Problems of the Theory and History of Psychology* (New York: Plenum Press).

Vygotsky, L.S. (1978) *Mind in Society* (Cambridge, MA: Harvard University Press).

Vygotsky, L.S. (1986) *Thought and Language* (Cambridge, MA: MIT Press).

Vygotsky, L.S. (1987) 'Thinking and Speech' in R. Rieber and A. Carton (eds) and N. Minick (trans.) *Collected Works Volume 1*, pp. 39–285 (New York: Plenum).

Walford, G. (2009) 'For Ethnography', *Ethnography and Education*, 4 (3), 271–82.

Walford, G. and Massey, A. (1998) *Children Learning in Context* (London: JAI Press).

Warmington, P. (2011) 'Divisions of Labour: Activity Theory, Multi-Professional Working and Intervention Research', *Journal of Vocational Education and Training*, 63 (2), 143–57.

Warmington, P., Daniels, H., Edwards, A., Leadbetter, J., Martin, D., Brown, S. and Middleton, D. (2004) 'Conceptualising Professional Learning for Multi-Agency Working and User Engagement', Paper presented at the British Educational Research Association Annual Conference, September 2004, Manchester: UK.

Wartofsky, M. (1979) *Models, Representation, and the Scientific Understanding* (Boston: Reidel).

Wellington, J. and Ireson, G. (2012) *Science Learning, Science Teaching*, 2nd edn (Abingdon: Routledge).

Wenger, E. (1998) *Communities of Practice, Learning, Meaning and Identity* (Cambridge: Cambridge University Press).

Wenger, E., McDermott, R. and Snyder, W. (2002) *Cultivating Communities of Practice: A Guide to Managing Knowledge* (Boston, MA: Harvard Business School Press).

Wertsch, J. (1998) *Mind as Action* (Oxford: Oxford University Press).

Wertsch, J. (2007) 'Mediation' in H. Daniels, M. Cole and J. Wertsch (eds) *The Cambridge Companion to Vygotsky*, pp. 178–92 (Cambridge: Cambridge University Press).

Wertsch, J., Tulviste, P. and Hagstrom, F. (1993) 'A Sociocultural Approach to Agency' in E.A. Forman, N. Minick and C.A. Stone (eds) *Contexts for Learning: Sociocultural Dynamics in Children's Development*, pp. 336–56 (Oxford: Oxford University Press).

Whitty, G. (2002) *Making Sense of Education Policy* (London: Paul Chapman).

Wildy, H. and Wallace, J. (2004) 'Science as Content, Science as Context: Working in the Science Department', *Educational Studies*, 30 (2), 99–112.

Williams, A. (1994) 'The Mentor' in A. Edwards (ed.) *Perspectives on Partnerships: Secondary Initial Teacher Training*, pp. 134–50 (London: Falmer).

Yin, R. (2003) *Case Study Research, Design and Methods*, 3rd edn (London: Sage).

Zeichner, K. (2010) 'Rethinking the Connections between Campus Courses and Field Experiences in College- and University-Based Teacher Education', *Journal of Teacher Education*, 61 (1–2), 89–99.

# Index

Lightning Source UK Ltd.
Milton Keynes UK
UKOW06f1152210515

251995UK00007B/39/P